The History of Early English

The History of Early English provides an accessible and student-friendly introduction to the history of the English language from its beginnings until the end of the Early Modern English period. Taking an activity-based approach, this text ensures that students learn by engaging with the fascinating evolution of this language rather than simply reading about it.

The History of Early English:

- Provides a comprehensive introduction to early, middle and early modern English;
- Introduces each language period with a text, from writers such as Chaucer and Shakespeare, accompanied by a series of guiding questions and commentaries that will engage readers and give them a flavour of the language of the time;
- Features a range of activities that include discussion points, questions, online tasks and preparatory activities that seamlessly take the reader from one chapter to the next;
- Is supported by a companion website featuring audio files, further activities and links to online material.

Written by an experienced teacher and author, this book is the essential course textbook for any module on the history of English.

Keith Johnson is Emeritus Professor of Linguistics and Language Education in the Department of Linguistics and English Language, University of Lancaster.

LEARNING ABOUT LANGUAGE

Series Editors:
Mick Short and the late Geoffrey Leech, Lancaster University

The History of Early English

An activity-based approach

KEITH JOHNSON

Routledge
Taylor & Francis Group

LONDON AND NEW YORK

First published 2016
by Routledge
2 Park Square, Milton Park, Abingdon, Oxon OX14 4RN

and by Routledge
711 Third Avenue, New York, NY 10017

Routledge is an imprint of the Taylor & Francis Group, an informa business

© 2016 Keith Johnson

British Library Cataloguing in Publication Data
A catalogue record for this book is available from the British Library

Library of Congress Cataloguing in Publication Data
A catalog record has been requested for this book.

ISBN: 978-1-138-79546-4 (hbk)
ISBN: 978-1-138-79545-7 (pbk)
ISBN: 978-1-315-75840-4 (ebk)

Typeset in Sabon
by Out of House Publishing

Printed and bound in Great Britain by
TJ International Ltd, Padstow, Cornwall

For H and H

Contents

Acknowledgements

In the early days, when this book was being mooted, I was much encouraged by Geoffrey Leech, Mick Short and Nadia Seemungal. Mick has continued to be a guiding force throughout, providing his usual large amount of detailed, perceptive and constructive comments, with a commitment that much exceeds what any author has a right to expect from an editor. His influence is there everywhere in the book. Nadia has also been helpful throughout, opening doors, making things possible that might not otherwise have been so.

A big thank you also to my wife Helen, who has looked in detail at what was being written, commenting on the general and the particular with an eye that manages to both penetrate and twinkle at the same time. Also to son Hugh, who sportingly and valiantly agreed to turn his hand to understanding Chapter 3's 'dead reeve passage', providing useful insights into what people today will find easy and difficult about confronting Old English.

Now that the book is ready, I am grateful to all at Routledge – Helen Tredget and the rest of the team – for their help; also to Sue Browning for her excellent editing. I hope that the resulting book, which has been such fun to write, will be as much fun to read.

The author and the publishers are grateful to the copyright holders for permission to reproduce the following material:

Extracts from Nevalainen, T. and Raumolin-Brunberg, H. 2003 *Historical Sociolinguistics: Language Change in Tudor and Stuart England*. London: Pearson Education Ltd. and from Culpeper, J. 2015 *History of English, 3rd edition*. Abingdon: Routledge, reproduced with kind permission of Taylor & Francis.

Extract from Barber, C. 1997 *Early Modern English (revised edition)*. Edinburgh: Edinburgh University Press, reproduced with kind permission of Edinburgh University Press.

About this book, and how to use it

This book is not just for native speakers of English, and certainly not just for speakers of my version of English, which is southern British English. Nor is it written just for non-native-English speakers. It is for *all* these people. You will quickly become aware of this because in the text you are often asked to think about some aspect of 'a version of English that you know well', or of your native language. Questions like these should be answerable by all readers, whatever their language background.

The book is 'activity-based', and activities really are an integral part of it. Every chapter has an *Activity section* towards its end, and when an activity is mentioned in the text, you will find it in that section. The idea is that you do activities as you go along. You are not expected to do every one, and the assumption is that you will want to pick and choose. A very common procedure is to ask you to stop and do an activity (or simply to think about an issue) *before continuing to read the text*. This is usually because the text's next paragraph discusses the issue, and hence provides the 'answers' to the activity. This procedure gives you the option to avoid an activity if you so wish – you just continue reading the text.

Sometimes there may be not just activities, but actual sections of the text that you wish to leave out, because they deal with linguistic concepts you are already familiar with. Incidentally, when new pieces of linguistic terminology are first introduced, they are in **bold face**.

Nearly every chapter has an *Answer section* which gives solutions to questions raised in the chapter and its activities. An (AS) in the text signals that solutions appear in this *Answer section*. Where, as often happens, solutions are given in the text itself, they are not repeated in the *Answer section*.

As well as regular activities, there are also suggestions at the start of chapters for points to explore before reading. Sometimes these include finding out about aspects of language or linguistics mentioned in the chapter. These usually involve searching for information on the internet or elsewhere. You will be invited to use the internet a lot.

This book has a companion website (CW). Like activities, the CW resources are integral to the book. They are more than 'add-on extras'. You are always directed to these resources by a specific mention in the text and the CW logo in the margin. Among the resources these entries contain are:

- short descriptions of aspects of English today (grammar points, for example) which need to be understood to follow the text;
- example passages to supplement those given in the text itself;
- additional activities and information.

The letters CW in the text direct you to a website entry. For example, in Chapter 2, West and North Germanic languages are discussed. The companion website looks at some differences between them, and includes a small related activity. The entry is indicated in the text by CW2.2 (*Germanic language differences*). 2.2 means it is the second entry for Chapter 2. As with activities, you may decide not to look at some of the CW entries.

I hope you enjoy the book's 'activity-based approach'. I believe that making some effort to work things out for yourself helps learning and makes it more memorable.

KJ

Phonetic symbols used

Sounds found in RP

'Received Pronunciation' is discussed in Chapter 10, Section 3.

p	pet
b	boy
t	tell
d	dad
k	key, car
g	go
tʃ	child, nature
dʒ	jail, age
f	father
v	vote
θ	think, Athens
ð	this, rather
s	sit
z	zip, rise
ʃ	sheep, ratio
ʒ	pleasure
h	hope
m	music
n	now
ŋ	ring, anger
l	love
r	right
j	yet
w	war, square
ɪ	hit, rabbit
e	bet, many
æ	cat, attack
ɒ	hot, what
ʌ	shut, love
ʊ	good, should
i:	sea, me
u:	do, spoon

ɑː	car, heart
ɔː	saw, shore
ɜː	bird, earn
ə	about, teacher
eɪ	lay, face
aɪ	cry, lie
ɔɪ	boy, choice
əʊ	throw, no
aʊ	how, foul
ɪə	dear, here
eə	fair, wear
ʊə	sure, poor

Non-RP sounds

hw	Also written [ʍ]. As in Scottish and American *when*. The sound is used in the transcription in 14.3, and is discussed in 14.4.1.
ɤ	Used in EModE where RP has [ʌ]. See 14.3 for mention of this sound. There are audio examples of it in CW14.5.
ɛː	As in the French word *même*. The vowel is discussed in 12.1.
eː	As in German word *sehen*. The vowel is discussed in 12.1.
oː	As in the German word *Sohn*, and the French *chose*. The vowel is discussed in 12.1.
aː	As in the Australian pronunciation of *bath* and *palm*. The vowel is discussed in 12.1.
əɪ	As a West Country British speaker would say the word *line*. The vowel is discussed in 12.1.

Part I
Preliminaries and Ancestries

1 History, and historical change

1.1 History: is it bunk?

This is a history book. It is not the history of a country or a people, but of a language – English. So here, right at the very beginning, it is worth asking whether there is really any value in studying the history of a language. After all, knowing the history of English will probably not help you speak it better, and familiarity with Chaucer's or Shakespeare's versions of the language is unlikely to help your own written English very much. Why bother, then? Is it worth studying the history of English? What value do you expect that study to have? If you wish, think beyond language, about the value of history in general. Do all your thinking before you read on.

In 1916, the American car industrialist Henry Ford is supposed to have said 'History is bunk' ('bunk' is a word not much in use today, meaning 'nonsense'). 'We want to live in the present', he continued – there is no point in living in the past. Others have given history an equally bad press. The British politician Augustine Birrell talks about 'the great dust-heap called history', and the Spanish philosopher George Santayana says history 'is a pack of lies about events that never happened told by people who weren't there'.

But plenty of people disagree, and there are generally two sorts of argument in defence of the study of history. One is to do with understanding the here and now. 'The past is the key to understanding the present' is how the historian Edward Carr put it. It is certainly true that looking into the history of English will throw light on its present. For example, people say that English has a particularly large vocabulary. How did that come about? As we shall see, it happened partly through invasions, like the Norman one in 1066, which brought French vocabulary with it. Interest in classical cultures also had its effect, particularly at the time of the Renaissance, which brought Latin and Greek words flooding into the language. Then there was British colonial expansion abroad, where part of the bounty carried home was new words. History will also throw light on small details. For example, why do some British English speakers today say *adult* with the stress on the first syllable, while others stress the second? It is in fact the remnants of a conflict between English's Germanic roots, where the stress generally falls on the first syllable, and the influence of French which came in with the Norman conquest, where the stress is often on later syllables in words. You see the same conflict in the word *garage* in British English today. Again, some speakers stress the first syllable, others the second (as in the French). There is also the consonant at the end of the word. Some use the consonant found in the French *garage* (the same as in the middle of the word *leisure*), and others prefer to say it as if it were written 'dg' (also changing the preceding vowel – 'garidge'). These few examples suggest that the past can indeed throw light on features of the present, big and small.

The second sort of argument is rather more grand, and to do with culture more generally. Tolstoy said in *War and Peace* that the aim of history is 'to enable nations and humanity to know themselves'. Even more grandly, here is what Henry, Archdeacon of Huntingdon in the twelfth century, claims: 'The knowledge of past events … distinguishes rational creatures from brutes'. This type of argument suggests that learning about the history of English will tell you something about yourself (if you come from an English-speaking culture), or about the culture (literature, art) that you are studying.

How convincing do you find these arguments? After exploring your own thoughts, you might wish to find out what others have written. Try using an internet search engine to look up 'what's the point of history?', or 'the value of history', or even 'history is a waste of time'. You will also find that many books on the teaching of history include a chapter on 'why teach history'. Sites that you may wish to go straight to are mentioned under *Further reading*.

Before embarking on this study of English, another question worth asking is how much you know about the history of your own language, whether it be English or some other language. Activity 1A (*About your L1*) invites you to think about this. The term **L1** (for 'first language') is used to refer to someone's native or mother tongue.

1.2 How English has changed

The novelist L. P. Hartley famously begins his book *The Go-Between* with the words: 'The past is a foreign country: they do things differently there.' Being prepared to find the past different from the present is a healthy starting-point for anyone studying history, including the history of a language. 'Past English' is, in many ways, a foreign language; they spoke and wrote differently there.

Languages change over time. This may seem a statement so obvious that it is not worth making. But many people, institutions and indeed whole countries have tried to stop language change from happening. France has its Academy to regulate the French language (the 'Académie française' will be discussed in 19.2.1 – Chapter 19, section 2.1 – but why not take a look now at https://en.wikipedia.org/wiki/Académie_française). The Academy makes 'rulings' on linguistic matters, stating what words can and cannot be used, and frowning severely on foreign words entering the language. Britain does not have anything equivalent, but the history of English does show attempts to stabilize and fix the language against change. Individuals also resist change. The letter columns of newspapers, as well as many an internet blog site, are full of complaints against people misusing words by deviating from their original meanings (what the words 'really mean'). Warburg (1962) tells of a lawyer who upbraided a witness for calling an accused man 'hysterical'. The word, the lawyer points out, comes from the Greek word meaning 'womb', and men do not have wombs (incidentally, you can still see the womb connection in the word *hysterectomy*). The lawyer is trying, for his own ends, to suggest that the meanings of words do not change over time.[1] Change is happening as much now as it did in the past, of course, and people continue to complain about it. The words *fewer* and *less* are examples. The 'old' rule, which many still follow today, is that *fewer* is used with plural nouns, and *less* with singular ones. So you say *fewer hours* but *less time*. But this is changing, perhaps because of the influence of *more*, which can be used with both singular and plural nouns (*more hours* and *more time*). Nowadays many people use *less* only, and *fewer* is slowly disappearing. Conservative speakers will complain in letters and blogs, but ultimately it makes no difference. As Anthony Burgess (1992) put it: 'No man, however learned or powerful, can exert control over a language.' Trying to prevent languages from changing is like trying to stop the tide from coming in.

To begin exploring some of the ways in which English has changed, here are three versions of a short passage from a book that has made an appearance at all stages in the history of English and has played an important role in that history: the Christian Bible. The passage is taken from the opening of The Gospel According to John, and describes the beginnings of the universe. Read through these three versions and attempt to put them into chronological sequence. Think about, and perhaps write down, the reasons for your conclusions.

Version 1

1. In the begynnyng was the worde, & the worde was with God: and that worde was God.
2. The fame was in the begynnyng with God.
3. All thynges were made by it: and without it, was made nothing that was made.
4. In it was lyfe, and the lyfe was the lyght of men.
5. And the lyght fhyneth in darkeneffe: and the darkneffe comprehended it not.
6. There was a man sent from God, whofe name was John.
7. The fame came for a witneffe, to beare witneffe of the lyght, that all men through hym might beleve.
8. He was not that lyght: but was fent to beare witneffe of the lyght.
9. That lyght was the true lyght, which lyghteth euery man that commeth into the worlde.

Version 2

1 On frymðe wæs Word, and þæt Word wæs mid Gode, and God wæs þæt Word.
2. Þæt wæs on fruman mid Gode.
3. Ealle þing wæron geworhte ðurh hyne; and nan þing næs geworht butan him.
4. Þæt wæs lif þe on him geworht wæs; and þæt lif wæs manna leoht.
5. And þæt leoht lyht on ðystrum; and þystro þæt ne genamon.
6 Mann wæs fram Gode asend, þæs nama wæs Iohannes.
7. Ðes com to gewitnesse, þæt he gewitnesse cyðde be ðam leohte, þæt ealle menn þurh hyne gelyfdon.
8. Næs he leoht, ac þæt he gewitnesse forð bære be þam leohte.
9. Soð leoht wæs þæt onlyht ælcne cumendne man on þisne middaneard.

Version 3

1. In the bigynnyng was the word, and the word was at God, and God was the word.
2. This was in the bigynnyng at God.
3. Alle thingis weren maad bi hym, and withouten hym was maad no thing, that thing that was maad.
4. In hym was lijf, and the lijf was the liyt of men.
5. and the liyt schyneth in derknessis, and derknessis comprehendiden not it.
6. A man was sent fro God, to whom the name was Joon.
7. This man cam in to witnessyng, that he schulde bere witnessing of the liyt, that alle men schulden bileue bi hym.
8. He was not the liyt, but that he schulde bere witnessing of the liyt.
9. There was a very liyt, which liytneth ech man that cometh in to this world.

The chronology of the versions corresponds to how much like today's English they are. Version 2 (V2) is the oldest one, written in approximately AD 990. Version 3 (V3) comes next, dated towards the end of the fourteenth century. Apart from some odd spellings, Version 1 (V1) is quite comprehensible to modern readers. It was written in 1568.[2] The different versions show just some of the ways in which English has changed. To consider these in some detail, do Activity 1B (*Bible changes*). This needs to be done before you read on (the 'answers' are in the next paragraph).

Graphology is the name given to the study of writing systems and the symbols they use. In V2 you find a number of symbols we do not have today. They are: 'ð', its capital form 'Ð', and 'þ' – all versions of today's 'th'. There is also 'æ', a vowel rather like the 'a' in today's British English *hat*. In the sixteenth century's V1, there is just one letter not in use today – the 's' form written 'ſ' (and pronounced as an 's'). All these letters (and indeed other linguistic points mentioned in this section) will be discussed in detail in later chapters; the purpose here is just to draw attention to the fact that graphology changes over time.

On the level of **orthography** too (the spelling system of the language) there are many forms not found in today's English. Concentrating just on V3, we have (among others), a 'y' where we would today have an 'i' – in *bigynnying* and *hym*, for example. We also find words ending with an 'e', not present today (*shulde* and *bere*) – though there is also *cam* where today we would have a final 'e'. There are also other vowel differences like *maad* and *ech*. There are punctuation differences too. In V1 a colon (:) is used. Today we use this mark to introduce lists or explanations, but here it seems to be acting more like a comma, or perhaps a semicolon (;).

As far as grammar is concerned, V1 (and V3) have *-eth* on the end of some verb forms – *commeth* and *schyneth*. You may well have come across this form in literature, but in today's English we would use an *-s* (*comes* and *shines*). In addition, V3 has a curious verb ending on *comprehendiden* (*comprehended*). Notice also the way of forming negative sentences shown in *comprehendiden not it*. Again, you may have come across something similar (in Shakespeare plays, for example), but today we use a completely different structure – we would here say 'did not comprehend'). There are also some odd preposition uses in V3. There is *the word was at God* in verse 2, while both V1 and V3 have *of* following *witnesse* (*witnessing*). Today we would probably use *to*.

V1 and V3 contain an interesting example of a word-meaning change. 'The light shineth in the darkness', V1 says, 'and the darkness comprehended it not'. This use of the word *comprehend* may well mystify modern readers. Today the word means 'understand', and although it might be possible to interpret the Bible's usage metaphorically to mean this, the interpretation seems a little unnatural. In fact, one of the meanings of the word, which has disappeared today, is 'to overcome' or 'control' (and the verb *genamon* in V2 has roughly the same sense).

Word-meaning change is an area where it is particularly easy – and fascinating – to see how languages vary over time. Changes can lead to 'historical false friends', and these are discussed in 9.2.1 – Chapter 9, section 2.1. These are words which existed in the past and still do today, so you think you understand the old uses already; they seem like 'friends'. But the friends are 'false', because their meanings have changed. *Comprehend* is like this, and here is another example. In 1608 John Chamberlain, a celebrated letter writer, wrote to a friend saying 'I am sorry to hear Sir Rowland Lytton is so crazy'. To us today, *crazy* means 'mad', but the older meaning was 'damaged' or 'frail', and it could refer to health, both physical and mental. The same use of the word is found in Shakespeare's *Henry VI, Part I*, where a character talks about 'crazy age'.[3] Shakespeare is full of such examples. For more opportunities to identify historical false friends, look at Activity 1C (*False friends in Shakespeare and elsewhere*).

We have here considered just a few linguistic levels, but historical changes occur at every level. One which is not so thoroughly studied, yet which may contain many surprises for us today, is the level of 'language use' or **pragmatics**.

This is about how we use language to undertake **speech acts** (to greet, to invite, to make plans and so on). We follow 'rules' when we do these things; they are not grammatical rules, but **rules of use**. Take a look now at CW1.1 (*Saying hello in Old, Middle and Early Modern English*). It gives an example of pragmatic change in relation to the speech act of greeting. Incidentally, the companion website (CW) contains important information, examples and activities relevant to specific points mentioned in the text. To benefit from it, you need to refer to it as you are reading.

Another important level is to do with sounds and pronunciation. It is likely that in your own experience – whatever your L1 is – you can detect pronunciation differences between old and young L1 speakers. It is easy, then, to imagine that considerable changes occur over centuries. Pronunciation will not be dealt with here, but out of interest you may wish to listen to a YouTube clip which has the Old English Bible passage (Version 2) being read aloud.[4]

If languages did not change, the history of English would be very short and rather uneventful. But change they do, and the aim of this book is to plot those changes in the period we shall call 'Early English', from the language's beginnings until the end of the seventeenth century.

1.3   In a nutshell

This section is the book in a nutshell. It gives the barest outline of the history of Early English. The aim is to provide a very broad overview from the start, a firm orientation to keep in mind as, in subsequent chapters, details come thick and fast.

From about AD 449, Germanic tribes started to cross over to Britain from the European mainland, bringing their languages with them. These became the basis of English at its first stage, which we now call **Old English** (OE), or Anglo-Saxon. English was then, and still remains, a Germanic tongue. But it was not long before other influences impinged. Thus in 597, St Augustine did much to introduce Christianity to England, and since the language of the Church was Latin, the religion brought with it the influence of a new tongue.

Next to arrive were the Vikings, whose raids on Britain from Scandinavia started in around 787. Their influence is still evidenced in English today. In addition to place names, there are between 400 and 900 Scandinavian words still used in modern English. King Alfred came to power in the west of England in 871, and he did a great deal to establish his West-Saxon dialect as England's standard language. But another major invasion was soon to follow, this time from the south. William the Conqueror and the Norman French invaded England in 1066. It was natural that, following this event, French should become a predominant language in England. The French influence on English was great, particularly in the vocabulary, with many Norman French words entering the language. But gradually, over centuries, the use of French waned and English became the main language again. The stage of English from 1066 until about 1509 (when Henry VIII became king) is known as **Middle English** (ME).

The time of the Tudor monarchs, especially Elizabeth I, was one of expansion and development for England. Foreign exploration brought with it vocabulary from various foreign languages. But the greatest influence of all was from a dead language – Latin. This is because the age looked back to classical times. It was the Renaissance, or 'rebirth' of classical values and learning. The English language underwent huge, sprawling growth at this time, with large quantities of vocabulary being borrowed from Latin (and Greek). This stage is called **Early Modern English** (EModE).

The dates when the stages of English started and finished are of course rather arbitrary. People did not stop talking ME on the 20th April 1509, and start talking EModE on the 21st, when Henry VIII became king. The date given for the end of the EModE stage is particularly open to differing views. 1660 is a popular choice – the date of the Restoration, when Charles II came to the throne. We shall here use a slightly later date, 1700 – the beginning of the eighteenth century – by which time the language had settled down.

This book does not go beyond EModE. But to complete the picture (still in a nutshell), the language developed into **Late Modern English**, a period containing the eighteenth-century attempts to standardize the language (following the sprawling growth of the Renaissance), and also the spread of English into other parts of the world with the establishment of the British Empire, the increasing growth of American influence, and the recent development of English as a global language. Alongside OE, ME and EModE, another abbreviation we shall use in this book is for the language we speak today – PDE stands for **Present Day English**. There are, of course, many versions of it; unless specified otherwise, the one referred to in this book is the British English variety.

It is always more than a little dangerous to attempt short characterizations of a language. But here is one for English. It is basically a Germanic language, with characteristics of Germanic languages that we shall consider in future chapters. But it also has a huge overlay of other influences, and, particularly, an extremely cosmopolitan vocabulary. It is Germanic, but has developed eclectically, taking on a wide variety of foreign influences. The rest of the book will add flesh to this skeleton.

Activity section

1A About your L1

How much do you know about the history of your L1 (whether it be English or some other language)? Your first thought might be 'not very much', but perhaps it is more than you think. Here are some specific issues to consider, whatever your L1 is (including, of course, English):

- Are there specific developmental stages that your L1 has gone through? Perhaps they have specific names?
- Identify some aspects of past versions of the language which are no longer found today. These may be particular words which have different forms, or different grammar structures.
- What famous authors are associated with early stages of your L1?
- What do you know about your L1's 'family tree'? What other languages is it related to? What languages are its close relations?

1B   Bible changes

The purpose of this activity is to draw attention to a few of the ways in which English has changed.

(a) Concentrate on Versions 2 and 1 (V2 and 1), and focus on the letters of the alphabet. V2 contains several letters that we no longer use in English today, and V1 contains one. Identify these.
(b) Concentrate first on V3, and identify words which still exist today but are spelled differently. Then look at the punctuation of V1, which is sometimes different from how we would punctuate the passage today.
(c) Turning now to grammatical differences, look at the verb endings in V1. There is one form which is not in common use today. What is it? Find also the odd verb ending in Verse 5 of V3. Then look at the negative sentence contained in both V1 and V3. It has a form which we do not use today. Identify that. Finally, concentrate on V3's use of prepositions. There are some which would be different today. Which prepositions would we use?
(d) Think now about changes in word meaning. V1 and V3 contain the word *comprehend* used in a way which is strange for us. Any ideas about what this might mean?

Incidentally, the last word of V2, *middaneard* is interesting. Looking at the last words in Vs 1 and 3 will suggest what it means. What might its literal meaning be? Using an internet search engine might help (and if you cannot find the exact form, try for *middangeard*).

All the activities above involve comparing the passage versions with English today. As an additional activity, you might compare V3 with V1. This will suggest some of the ways in which the language changed between the fourteenth and sixteenth centuries.

1C   False friends in Shakespeare and elsewhere   AS

(a) Here are five examples of historical false friends, all taken from the works of Shakespeare. Think first about the modern meaning of the **boldface** word. Then try to work out what it means in the passage. This will not always be easy. Sometimes trying to think of similar, related words in today's English may help. If all fails, there is always the *Answer section* (the initials AS above indicate that the *Answer section* gives answers to this activity).

(i)   Hamlet hears that his father's ghost has been seen:

My father's spirit! In arms! All is not well.
*I **doubt** some foul play. Would the night were come!*

(ii) In *Richard III*, Buckingham is flattering the future king:

As well we know your tenderness of heart
*And gentle, kind, **effeminate** remorse*

(iii) These lines from *Cymbeline* describe what sometimes happens when you visit a tavern:

*you come in faint for **want** of meat, depart reeling*
with too much drink.

(iv) There are two passages to clarify this example and the next.
      Here is how the young (and probably very slim) Romeo is described in *Romeo and Juliet*:

*[He] bears him like a **portly** gentleman.*
And, to say truth, Verona brags of him
To be a virtuous and well-governed youth.

And in *Pericles*, a fleet is seen approaching:

We have descried, upon our neighbouring shore,
*A **portly** sail of ships make hitherward.*

(v)   Portia (in *The Merchant of Venice*) assures the court that Shylock will receive justice:

He hath refused it in the open court.
*He shall have **merely** justice and his bond.*

And in *Antony and Cleopatra*, Enobarbus advises Antony that chance and nothing else is what will assist him:

*Give up yourself **merely** to chance and hazard*
From firm security.

(b) Here are ten more words that have changed their meanings over the centuries. Use a dictionary which gives word origins (**etymologies**) to track how the meanings have changed. If you can, note when the modern meanings first came into use. Incidentally, you will certainly find that at some points in history there will be more than one meaning in use.

| silly | nice | bully | shroud | abandon |
| buxom | hospital | girl | gay | walk |

Answer section

Activity 1C   False friends in Shakespeare

(i) *doubt* = suspect (a sense that you find in the Modern French *se douter de*); (ii) *effeminate* = tender, gentle (it could also carry the pejorative sense which it has today, meaning unmanly); (iii) *want* = lack; (iv) *portly* = dignified or stately; (v) *merely* = absolutely, completely.

Further reading

On 'what is the value of history?', the historian Penelope Corfield discusses the issue at www.history.ac.uk/makinghistory/resources/articles/why_history_matters.html.

Neil Munro discusses the three viewpoints mentioned in the text, at www.philosophypathways.com/essays/munro3.html.   www.historians.org/pubs/free/WhyStudyHistory.htm has a discussion by the American historian Peter Stearns.

For an interesting, if rather controversial, viewpoint on how the study of Shakespeare can help today's students of English as a foreign language, take a look at David Crystal's article 'Shakespeare and ELT' available on his homepage (www.davidcrystal.com/).

There is a section (1.8) discussing the reasons for historical language changes in Denison and Hogg (2006). That whole chapter provides an excellent overview of the history of English.

Notes

1 Warburg takes the 'hysterical' example from Wellman (1903).
2 V1 is from the so-called Bishop's Bible, dated 1568. V2 is dated *c*.990, and is taken from Bright (1904). V3 is from the Wycliffe Bible (dated 1382 to 1395). Taken from www.bibledbdata.org/onlinebibles/wycliffe_nt/43_001.htm.
3 The example from Chamberlain's letter is taken from Nevalainen (1999).
4 At www.youtube.com/watch?v=Mu2AKjMMAXM.

2 Languages and their daughters

This chapter looks at language 'family trees', and how similarities between languages reveal family backgrounds. We will consider one family in particular, called the Indo-European, and will see how nineteenth-century linguists studied its origin and growth. One group within that family – the Germanic languages – will be of particular interest to us, because it includes English. Here are some issues to think about before you read:

- Find out something about the Indo-European group of languages and its members; also something about what languages are *not* members of this group.
- If your native language is not English, what are its family connections?
- The chapter discusses nineteenth-century 'comparative linguistics'. Find out something about this movement.
- Two topics briefly mentioned in this chapter are the language Sanskrit, and the linguist Jacob Grimm. Find out something about each of these.

2.1 Trees

It is through the sorts of language change discussed in Chapter 1 that new languages emerge. Barber *et al.* (2009) characterize the process like this. Imagine, they say, a language spoken just by the populations of two adjacent villages. With time, differences will appear between the two versions of this language. The less the villages have to do with each other, the quicker the changes will take place. But slowly or quickly, changes will certainly occur and at some point we would speak about there being two dialects. Imagine that the inhabitants of one village then migrate en masse to some distant place. Distance and lack of contact would make the dialects diverge even further, and soon we could be speaking of two separate languages. Because the languages have common origins, they remain related, and will have many elements in common. But there will be differences, possibly becoming substantial ones over time, so that the two groups of inhabitants may no longer easily understand one another.

There are some respects in which languages are like people. One is that they have relations, families and, as a consequence, family trees. Here is how Barber *et al.* characterize the language situation we have just described:

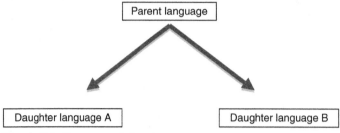

Figure 2.1 Parents and daughters

To take this comparison between people and languages a little further: people belong to families; they have siblings, sisters, parents, grandparents, ancestors. They share characteristics with their family members, but they also have personal traits which make them distinct. So too with languages; they also have family relations going back into the past. In some ways these are like language relations, in other ways not. These similarities and differences often reveal themselves in words. You will quite possibly have come across languages which have vocabularies so similar that you suspect they are related. Table 2.1 explores this by looking at the English word *good* in various languages.

Table 2.1 Different words for the English *good*

English	*good*
Danish	*god*
Swedish	*god, gott*
Croatian	*dobro*
Dutch	*goed*
German	*gut*
Icelandic	*goður*
Frisian	*goed*
Turkish	*iyi*

Before reading on, work out what the table suggests about which languages are in the same family. The table contains words suggesting that two of the languages are from quite different families. Identify these.

Of course, looking at just one word (or even a few words) will not give you anything like sure information about family membership. As an example of how not, consider the English word *robot*. It comes from Slavic languages: *robota* is, for example, a Polish word for 'work'. But you would be foolish to conclude from this that English is in the Slavic language family. It is just that we happen to have taken that particular word from a Slavic source. Family membership will only truly reveal itself by looking at large quantities of words, and even then you have to be aware that (as mentioned in Chapter 1) English has borrowed huge numbers of words from languages with very different family backgrounds. But based on just the one word 'good', the suggestion is that English, Danish, Swedish, Dutch, German, Icelandic and Frisian are members of the same language family, known as Germanic. The Croatian and Turkish words are quite different from the others, correctly suggesting different family membership. You might like to find out what families Croatian and Turkish come from; you can also use online dictionaries to explore other word similarities and differences in these nine languages. Activity 2A (*Family words*) encourages you to do this, and also to explore word similarities in another language family.

2.2   The Indo-European tree

Anyone who has been involved in constructing their own family tree will know that both the fun and the challenge is in going back far in time. It is the same with language trees, and behind it all is the tantalizing question: was there originally just one language which was spoken by our species and which in time evolved into a series of daughter languages? These daughters then had daughters of their own, ending up in the situation today where there are some 7,000 languages, all different from each other to a greater or lesser extent. Some religions speak of there being one original language. The Christian Babel story has mankind speaking one tongue until the Tower of Babel was built, as a result of which God introduced a 'confusion of tongues'.[1]

The search for 'ancestral origins' was a preoccupation of nineteenth-century scholars in many areas of enquiry. In the study of the natural world, Darwin and others were concerned with identifying species of living things, seeking connections between them, grouping them together, developing evolutionary 'family trees', and identifying ancestors and origins. There was also much interest in attempting to identify 'fixed laws' which could account for evolutionary change. These preoccupations were part of the spirit of the age, and hence it is not surprising that they should be reflected in linguistics, particularly because many saw language as a living organism much like the organisms that Darwin was studying. William Jones, a British judge with a strong interest in linguistics, made an early contribution in this area. In 1786 he was working in India and learning the ancient Indian language, Sanskrit. He was only four months into his study when he became aware of similarities between Sanskrit and two languages apparently unrelated to it – Greek and Latin. The similarities were so strong that he was led to conclude that these languages came from a common source. They were, in other words, daughter languages ultimately related to one parent language. Here is how Jones put it his 1786 paper:[2]

> The Sanskrit language, whatever be its antiquity, is of a wonderful structure;
> more perfect than the Greek, more copious than the Latin, and more exquisitely

refined than either, yet bearing to both of them a stronger affinity, both in the roots of verbs and the forms of grammar, than could possibly have been produced by accident; so strong indeed, that no philologer could examine them all three, without believing them to have sprung from some common source, which, perhaps, no longer exists; there is a similar reason, though not quite so forcible, for supposing that both the Gothic and the Celtic ... had the same origin with the Sanskrit; and the old Persian might be added to the same family.

Jones was not in fact the first to notice these language connections, but his work certainly acted as a stimulus to linguists to search for other links between languages, and he is therefore sometimes regarded as the initiator of the field of **comparative linguistics**. The 'common source' he mentions became known as Proto-Indo-European (PIE). Another influential figure working in the same tradition was the German August Schleicher. CW2.1 (*Schleicher's fable*) is about him, and gives you the chance to take a look at an example of PIE.

The result of work done by Schleicher and many others was to identify a group of languages spoken in Europe and Asia, making up a 'family' and having their own 'family tree'. These are the Indo-European (IE) languages. Their tree has a number of major branches, and has similarities with the branching trees that a person's family would show. There are various versions of the IE tree available, differing in the terminology used and the amount of detail given. Figure 2.2 shows one version.

Notice that some of the languages mentioned are marked by an asterisk, meaning that they are 'hypothetical' languages. If you want to look further into language similarities in the Indo-European families, do Activity 2B (*IE words*). And if you would like to spend more time familiarizing yourself with the IE tree, take a look at Activity 2C (*Family membership*).

2.3 The Germanic languages

The version of the IE tree in Figure 2.2 has six major language families, shown in the top line under PIE. The one that we are most interested in, because it includes English, is Germanic. One of our sources of knowledge about the early Germanic peoples is the Roman historian Tacitus. His book, commonly referred to as the *Germania*, was written in about AD 98. The Germanic peoples, as Tacitus describes them, had blue eyes, reddish hair and were well-built. They were of a warlike disposition, liked their food and drink, and although they could tolerate the cold, were unable to support the heat. They also had many virtues which, Tacitus pointedly suggests, Romans citizens would do well to copy. They were egalitarian, monogamous, and treated their women fairly. They lived in the north of Europe, but perhaps because of their requirement for more living space, moved outwards in all directions. Indeed, in Tacitus' time they were already a force in Europe to be reckoned with – particularly by the Romans, because their

16

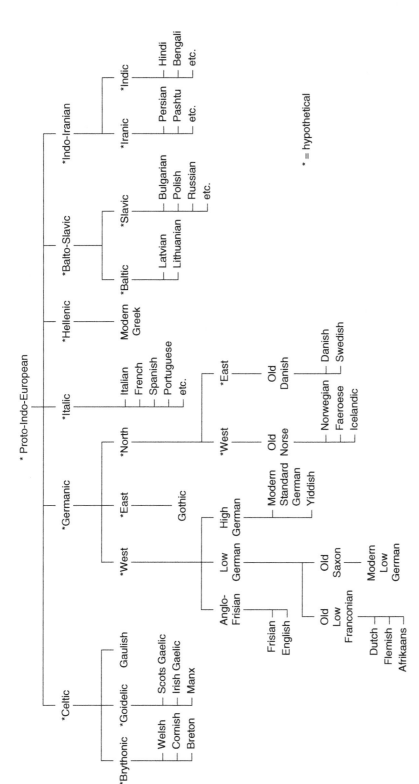

Figure 2.2 The Indo-European family tree (from J. Culpeper, *History of English*, 3rd edn (Routledge, 2015), p. 116)

southward expansion took them to the edges of the Roman empire. They also moved north into Scandinavia, east into Baltic regions, and west into Netherlands.

Their original language is known as *Proto-Germanic (PG), with that asterisk indicating that the language is a reconstruction. As we saw at the beginning of this chapter, when people separate, their languages begin to diverge, and this is exactly what happened to the Germanic tribes on the move. As the IE family tree shows, one of the daughter language groups was East Germanic, spoken in the Baltic regions. Gothic was one of these languages. But this language group fared badly. The Goths moved into France, Italy and Spain, and their language was submerged by the 'Italic', or Romance languages spoken in those places. Notice this use of the word 'Romance'. It is used to describe languages of the Italic family, descended from Latin. Gothic and the other members of the East Germanic branch have long since died out. The North Germanic branch fared better. In Scandinavia, it eventually subdivided into Eastern and Western variants. The Eastern branch gave us Swedish and Danish, and the Western led through Old Norse to Norwegian and Icelandic (among others). West Germanic languages include Low and High German – geographically separated versions of German, with the 'low' variety being used in the northern plain lands. It also gave us Dutch. CW2.2 (*Germanic language differences*) contains some information (and a short activity) about differences between the West and North Germanic language families.

2.4 A Germanic law

Nineteenth-century linguists, as we have seen, were interested in assigning languages to families and in providing ancestral family trees. But they were also, like the Darwinian scientists looking at the natural world, preoccupied with uncovering the laws underlying the changes from one part of a tree to another. One example revealing this preoccupation relates to characteristics which the Germanic languages share, and which separate them from others in the IE family. The law describing these characteristics was formulated by the German scholar Jacob Grimm, also known for the collection of German fairy tales that he compiled with his brother, Wilhelm. **Grimm's Law** was concerned with consonants, and is sometimes called the **First Germanic Consonant Shift**. Grimm noted that some consonants found in Indo-European languages changed in the Germanic languages, and that these changes followed regular patterns. You can see some of them in Table 2.2, which you can use to work out the law's basic principles for yourself. The columns on the left of the table show some words in PIE, Latin, and Greek. On the right are columns showing related words in the Germanic languages, OE, German, and PDE. Concentrate on the first consonant in each word and note the consonant shifts that occurred. Use statements like 'x becomes y' to express these changes. You will recall from 1.2 (Chapter 1, section 2) that OE 'þ' was a version of our present-day 'th', and that 'æ' was a vowel like the one in PDE 'hat'.

Table 2.2 Some Germanic consonant shifts

	PIE	Latin	Greek	Old English	German	English
1		piscis		fisc	Fisch	fish
2		pedem	pous	fōt	Fuss	foot
3	pur			fyr	Feuer	fire
4	pulo	pullus		fola	Fohlen	foal
5			treis	þreo		three
6		tenuis		þynne		thin
7		tu		þu		thou
8	tum (swelling)			þuma		thumb
9		genus		cynn		kin
10	genu			cneo	Knie	knee
11			gune	cwēn	Königin	queen
12		granum		corn	Korn	corn
13			kardia	heorte	Herz	heart
14		centum		hundred	hundert	hundred
15			kannabis	hænep	Hanf	hemp
16	krn			horn	Horn	horn
17	ed	edo		etan		eat
18		decem		tīen		ten
19	demə			tam		tame
20	drew			trēow		tree
21			kannabis (look at boldface consonant)	hænep		hemp
22	abel			æppel	Apfel	apple

Table 2.3 shows these six consonant changes (and in fact Grimm's Law covers a few more besides):

Table 2.3 Grimm's consonant changes

Examples	Changes
1–4	p → f
5–8	t → th
9–12	g → k
13–16	k → h
17–20	d → t
21–22	b → p

If you know any French, Italian, Spanish (or any other non-Germanic IE language), you may be able to think of some more examples in some of the categories. You might, for example, be able to think of words in those languages which begin with a /p/, and have English equivalents beginning with /f/ (like the French word *plume*, which can mean 'feather'), and so on.

'But wait a minute', you might say. 'I can think of some English words that do *not* show this consonant shift.' You would be right. Take the Latin *pedem*, for example. There are plenty of 'ped-' words in English that have a 'foot' connection, but retain the initial 'p' rather than 'f'. *Pedestrian* and *pedicure* are examples. Why did Grimm's Law not apply to them, giving us **fedestrian* and **fedicure* (there is that asterisk again, used to show that a form does not exist)? The answer is that words like these came into English after the time of Grimm's consonant shifts. *Pedestrian* comes from Latin, and the first example (**citation**) given in the *Oxford English Dictionary* (the *OED*) is 1716, while *pedicure* entered the language though French and has a first *OED* citation in 1784. Examples like these show that even though linguists can formulate laws, languages can show almost as many exceptions as there are rules. Activity 2D (*Non-Grimm consonants*) invites you to explore more of these.

The *OED* is mentioned above – the first of very many mentions in this book. Now would be a good time to look at CW2.3 (*The OED*). It talks about the dictionary, about its citations, and also describes how to use it online.

Grimm's Law is only part of the picture, and the comparative linguists' search for fixed laws had other results. Verner's Law (after the Danish linguist Karl Verner) explained some of the exceptions to Grimm's Law.

2.5   And so to English

There is one branch of the West Germanic tree called Anglo-Frisian, and it has just two family members. One is Frisian, a little-known language, but doubtless one of English's closest relatives. You may like to use the internet to check where Frisia (Friesland) is, and perhaps also to find an example of the language being spoken (there is one at https://www.youtube.com/watch?v=MRXoCixqyk8, for example). The other language is of course English. We have arrived at what might be regarded as the beginning of our story.

Activity section

2A   Family words   AS

There are plenty of foreign language dictionaries available online. Some, like Google Translate (http://translate.google.com/), allow you to deal with different languages extremely quickly.

(a) Use one of these dictionaries to find words in the mentioned languages for the English words in the top row:

English	good	hat	man	rain (n)	hand
Danish	god				
Swedish	god, gott				
Dutch	goed				
German	gut				
Icelandic	goður				
Frisian	goed				
Croatian	dobro				
Turkish	iyi				

(b) Now do the same for these four languages:

French
Italian
Spanish
Portuguese

Part (a) will give you further evidence that Danish, Swedish, Dutch, German, Icelandic and Frisian belong to the same language group, while Croatian and Turkish do not. Part (b) will reveal similarities between four members of the *Italic* or *Romance* language family. Notice, though, that sometimes you will need to be prepared to 'cheat' a little: languages invariably have more than one word to express the same idea. When the dictionary gives you a choice, choose the word which most reveals family connection. As the 'AS' at the beginning of this activity indicates, the *Answer section* gives you answers.

2B IE words AS

The table below gives you the words for *water*, *house*, *dog* and *animal* in ten languages. The languages come from three different Indo-European families – three per family – plus one other language which is not Indo-European. Put the languages into their families according to the similarities in the words.

	water	house	dog	animal
1	jal	ghar	kutta	pasu
2	voda	dom	pas	zivotnja
3	agua	casa	perro	animal
4	kútvíz	lakóház	kutya	allat
5	apa	casa	caine	animal
6	jl	ghi	kutraa	pshu
7	вода (voda)	дом (dom)	nec (pes)	zivotnoye
8	woda	dom	pies	zwierze
9	acqua	casa	cane	animale
10	jala	ghara	kukura	pasu

To repeat a word of caution already mentioned: identifying the family in which a language belongs cannot be done on the basis of so little data. For one thing, the words chosen above have been selected to make similarities clear. You need to realise that Language 1 (for example) has many more words for *water* than the one given. If another had been chosen, similarities would have become less clear.

2C Family membership

(a) As a way of familiarizing yourself with the IE tree, you may like to character-ize a few of the languages on it. For example, you might describe Bulgarian as: 'an Indo-European language on the Slavic branch of the Balto-Slavic fam-ily'. Use Figure 2.2 to produce similar descriptions for Portuguese, Gothic, Hindi and Cornish.

(b) Use the internet to find out the same information about these languages, not mentioned in the figure:

Lycian   Catalan   Marathi   Turkish   Farsi
Where are (or were) these languages spoken?

(c) The answers to Activity 2B mentioned three modern European languages which are not in the Indo-European family. Remind yourself what these are, and find more non-Indo-European languages used elsewhere in the world.

2D Non-Grimm consonants   AS

Look at Table 2.2. There are quite a few words in the PIE, Latin and Greek columns which have made their way into PDE without showing the Germanic consonant shifts. The example discussed in the text is *pedem*, which gives us PDE *pedestrian* and *pedicure*. Think of at least one PDE word associated with each of these:

kardia   pur   tenuis   tum   genus   genu   granum   centum   kannabis.

If you can, use an etymological dictionary (the online *OED* would be perfect, if you have access) to find out when the associated words came into English, and from where. It is likely that all of them will have come after the OE period, a good number perhaps in the sixteenth century, when borrowing from Greek and Latin was common.

Answer section

Activity 2A

(a) Danish: *god, hat, mond, regn, hand.* Swedish: *god/gutt, hatt, människa, regn, hand.* Dutch: *goed, hoed, mens, regenen, hand.* German: *gut, Hut, Mann,*

Regen, Hand. Icelandic: goður, hattur, maður, regn, hönd. Frisian: goed, hoed, man, rein, hân. Croatian: *dobro, kapa, čovek, kiša, ruka.* Turkish: *iyi, şapka, adam, yagmur, el.*

(b) French: *bon, chapeau, homme, pluie, mann.* Italian: *buono, cappello, uomo, pioggia, mano.* Spanish: *bueno, sombrero, hombre, lluvia, mano.* Portuguese: *bom, chapeu, homem, chuva, mão.*

Activity 2B

The languages are: 1 = Hindi; 2 = Croatian; 3 = Spanish; 4 = Hungarian; 5 = Romanian; 6 = Marathi (an Indian language); 7 = Russian; 8 = Polish; 9 = Italian; 10 = Bengali.

1, 6 and 10 are members of the Indo-Iranian family. 2, 7 and 8 are Balto-Slavic languages. 3, 5 and 9 are Italic languages. Hungarian (4) is not an Indo-European language. It is a member of the Uralic family, a group which also includes Finnish and Estonian.

Activity 2D

Some associated PDE words are: *cardiology, pyre, tenuous, tumour, genus, genuflect, grain, century, cannabis.*

Further reading

Sampson (1980), a book about the various schools of linguistics, has a chapter on nineteenth-century historical linguistics. Sampson's website (www.grsampson. net/Q_PIE.html) also has interesting information on PIE.

König and Van der Auwera (2002) is a useful edited collection of papers about the Germanic languages. It is in Routledge's 'Language Family' series, and other books in that series (about other language groups) may also interest you.

There is an entertaining and informative video on YouTube about Grimm's law (which also covers other issues mentioned in this chapter). It can be found at https://www.youtube.com/watch?v=VnjfHu9eJLM.

Notes

1 One of the artists that produced pictures of the Tower of Babel was Pieter Bruegel the Elder. You can find more information about these at https://en.wikipedia.org/wiki/The_Tower_of_Babel_(Bruegel).

2 Jones' paper was called 'The Third Anniversary Discourse'. It was delivered to the Asiatic Society of Bengal. There is a copy online at www.eliohs.unifi.it/testi/700/jones/Jones_Discourse_3.html.

Part II
Old English

3 Old English

A first look

Language developments must, of course, be considered within their historical context. So we begin our look at Old English with some historical background. A short passage of Old English follows. It introduces you to a language which, although it is English, is not so easy for a reader today to understand.

If you are English, a useful starting-point before reading may be to think what you already know about English history from about 55 BC till AD 1066. If you are not English, what do you know about historical events taking place in your country during this period?

Here are some more things you can also use the internet or other sources to find out about:

- A large number of places are mentioned in the chapter. Two of these, Kent and the River Thames, you will need to know to do one of the activities. Find these on a map. Some other places to find are: Angeln, Jutland, Hordaland (Horthaland), Lindisfarne, Iona, Wessex (more difficult, this one – you will not find it on a present-day map).
- As for people, find out about: Bede, Alfred the Great; Pope Gregory the Great, Augustine (the one who came to England), Boudica.
- Our introductory Old English passage is from the *Anglo-Saxon Chronicle*. Find out about this book.
- The passage contains some OE letters no longer used in PDE: 'æ' (known as 'ash'), 'ð' and its capital form 'Ð' ('eth'), and 'þ' ('thorn'). Find out something about these.

3.1 Four events

The third-century Roman writer Eumenius had some nice things to say about the British Isles. 'O fortunate Britain...', he wrote, 'justly hath nature enriched thee with all the blessings of the heavenly climate and of the soil'. We do not often today think of the climate as 'heavenly', but what he meant was that it was never too hot or too cold. It was a land, he goes on, abundant in corn, with plenty of cattle and sheep ... and no fierce animals.[1] But there is one way in which apparently 'fortunate' countries are not fortunate at all. Another Roman historian,

Tacitus, describes them as *pretium victoriae* – 'worth conquering'. They attract invaders. The early history of Britain is full of conquests: people trying to enjoy the climate, making use of the soil, raising cattle and sheep, avoiding fierce animals. In this section we will take history up to one of the most major invasions – the Norman conquest of 1066, which marks the end of the OE period. Our historical background will centre around four important events.

Long before Eumenius wrote about 'fortunate Britain', it was inhabited by Celtic folk – from about 600 BC perhaps. This group of tribes had settled in many parts of Europe, including France (Gaul), Spain, Italy and central Europe. They were imposing people. Yet another Roman historian, Diodorus, said of them: 'their aspect is terrifying... they were very tall in stature... they look like wood-demons, their hair thick and shaggy'. But they were also sophisticated people, with trade links with many parts of Europe. They did much to develop agriculture and industry in Britain.

The first of our four events was the arrival of Romans. Julius Caesar landed in 55 BC. *Veni, vidi, vici* he is said to have announced on arrival: 'I came, I saw, I conquered'. He did come, he did see, but he did not in fact conquer. He was repulsed, and the same happened in the following year when he returned with a larger force. The successful invasion had to wait almost another hundred years – until AD 43, when Emperor Claudius arrived. This time the *vici* part really was achieved, though not without robust challenges, particularly from Queen Boudica (also called Boadicea). In AD 60 or 61, her forces massacred over 70,000 Romans and Celts sympathetic to the Romans, also destroying the Roman settlement of Colchester in the process. But the Romans won through, and England was subjugated. The invaders created towns, roads, infrastructures, and a wall to keep out the marauding Scots (Hadrian's Wall). By no means all the 'locals' objected to Roman rule as Boudica had done. There is a Roman palace at Fishbourne in West Sussex, built some thirty years after the invasion, and lived in by locals. It shows just what luxury could be enjoyed by those who were sympathetic to the invaders. Doubtless there were many well-off, influential families who were quite happy to have their children grow up learning Latin.

England remained a part of the Roman Empire from about AD 45 till AD 409 – over three hundred and fifty years. That is a very long time. To drive home the time scale: the Europeans first landed in Australia in 1606, Shakespeare died in 1616, and the Pilgrim Fathers landed in America in 1620. English membership of the Roman Empire was just a little shorter than the time span between these events and today. But the Roman Empire began to decline at the beginning of the fifth century (its end is sometimes dated as 476). Invasions of their continental territory by a succession of Visigoths, Vandals and Huns led to a Roman departure from England by 410. They needed the troops elsewhere.

When the Romans left, tribes of Picts from the north of Britain, and Scots from the west, attacked the Celts. What happened next – our second event – is recounted by another historian who provides a valuable chronicle of the period – the Northumbrian monk known as The Venerable Bede. His

Ecclesiastical History of the English People (written in Latin and appearing in around 730) earned him the title of 'the father of English history'. The title of its Chapter 15 describes how, in 449, 'the Angles [under the chieftains Hengest and Horsa], being invited into Britain, at first drove off the enemy; but not long after, making a league with them, turned their weapons against their allies'. These so-called 'Angles' were in fact, Bede explains in the chapter, 'the three most powerful nations of Germania' – the Jutes, Saxons and Angles. The Jutes probably came from Jutland, partly modern-day Denmark. They settled in Kent. The Saxons were from the German region of Schleswig-Holstein and they put down roots in the area south of the Thames. The Angles were from the area called Angeln, today partly German and partly Danish. They established themselves north of the Thames. Whether or not they were 'invited', as Bede says, a glance at a map of the area shows that the sea journey west from their homelands leads them quite directly to Britain. It was a natural migratory route. Put arrows on this map to show the movements just described:

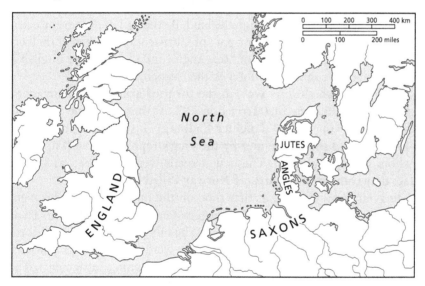

Map 3.1 Migratory routes westwards

At first the new arrivals came in uncoordinated groups, and their arrival is marked by many a place name. Essex had the east Saxons, Wessex the west Saxons, with southern folk in Suffolk and northern folk in Norfolk. But gradually they became more organized, and by 700 occupied most of England. They set up seven kingdoms, called the Heptarchy (*hepta* is from the Greek word meaning 'seven'): Northumbria, Mercia, East Anglia, Kent, Essex, Sussex, Wessex. Different parts of the Heptarchy were powerful at different times. In the seventh century it was Northumbria, in the eighth, Mercia, and in the ninth, Wessex. The name 'Angle' to describe all these groups stuck, and the country became called 'Englaland' – the land of the Angles. The Celts were driven to the fringes of the island – to Scotland, Cornwall, Wales, and overseas to Brittany. To add insult to injury, the word the invaders used to describe the Celts (who were there first!) was *wealas*: 'foreigners'. The word gives us the name Wales. The language of the new arrivals formed the basis of English. It is known as 'Anglo-Saxon', though today most prefer to use the name Old English, abbreviated to OE.

There is a story about Pope Gregory the Great which describes the beginning of our third event. He was one day walking in the Roman market place when he saw a group of fair-haired slave boys. They were, he was told, 'Angles' from Britain. The name was appropriate, he said, 'because they have an angelic face, and it is fitting that such should be co-heirs with the angels in heaven'. In 597 he sent his friend Augustine as a missionary to bring Christianity to the island.[2] In fact, Christianity had already arrived in Britain, brought by the Irish abbot Saint Columba, who had founded a monastery at Iona in 563. To this Celtic version of the religion, Augustine added a Catholic one. His task of converting the English was made much easier by the fact that the Jutish king of Kent, Æthelbert, was married to a Frankish Christian, named Bertha. Æthelbert agreed to be baptized, and Christianity began its spread through the land. By the end of the seventh century, England had become an important part of Christendom. When Æthelbert was converted, Pope Gregory styled him 'Rex Anglorum' ('king of the English'). England had become a recognized country with a recognized king.

But the fourth event was on its way, in the form of a new set of invaders. According to one account, they first arrived in 787. At that time, one Breohtric was king (married to King Offa's daughter Eadburg). Just three ships arrived in the first instance, and they were met by the king's representative (known as a 'reeve'), whom they slaughtered. The new arrivals were described as Danes, though in fact they came from an area of Norway called Horthaland.

The Scandinavian nations were at that time on the move. The Swedes went east to Russia. The Danes (with some Norwegians) came west to Britain. Their language was Old Norse (ON), and perhaps it is the ON word for 'bay' or 'fjord' which gave their name. The word was *vik*, and they were called Vikings (another possible derivation was the Anglo-Frisian word *wik*, meaning settlement). The Vikings followed various routes. Some went to Shetland and Orkney, then on to Ireland – the city of Dublin started life as a Viking settlement. Then they travelled to the Isle of Man, and on to north-west England. The *Anglo-Saxon Chronicle* (mentioned at various times in this book; see 7.2 particularly) for the year 793 records the first major raid against the north-east, in which an important centre for Celtic Christianity – the Lindisfarne priory – was ravaged. In 851, Canterbury and London were captured. Then in 865 came what is sometimes called the 'Great Heathen Army'. It was led by Ivar the Boneless and his brother Halfdan, both sons of Ragnar Lothbrok (Lothbrok was apparently the Old Norse for 'hairy breeches'). In 866 East Anglia was plundered, and in 867 York fell.

All these places were towards the east of England. The most westerly of the Heptarchy kingdoms was Wessex, and indeed the name means 'west Saxons'.

Unlike Essex and Sussex, it no longer exists as a county today, though the writer Thomas Hardy used it as a fictitious setting for his novels. Precisely because of its westerly position, Wessex was initially spared from the attention of the Vikings. But in 870, the invaders began to look in that direction. The Wessex king Ethelred died in 871 and was replaced by his son, Alfred, who became known as Alfred the Great. He fought long and hard against the Vikings, and eventually prevailed. Indeed, the Viking chieftain Guthrum was so impressed with his enemy that he converted to Christianity in 878. In that year the Vikings and Anglo-Saxons signed the Treaty of Wedmore (a village in the county of Somerset). A line was drawn from Chester in the north to London in the south. The area east of the line became known as the Danelaw, and was ruled by the Vikings. Alfred held the Anglo-Saxon lands in the west.

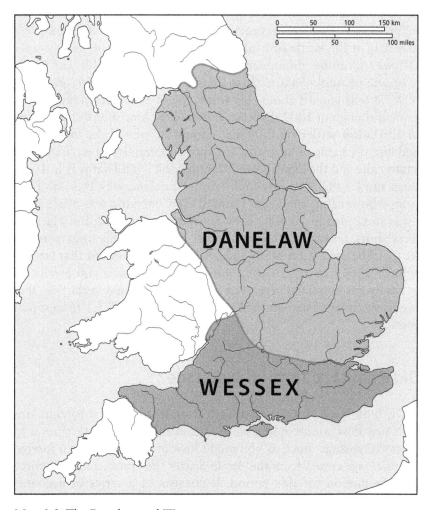

Map 3.2 The Danelaw and Wessex

Over time, the Danes and the Saxons learned to co-exist. Although the former were invaders, there was a feeling of racial kinship between the two groups – much more than had been felt between the Anglo-Saxons and the Celts.

Alfred's Wessex became a powerful and flourishing culture, possibly the most advanced in western Europe at the time. The king did much to further education, and particularly to support the development of English. He himself translated various important works from Latin, including Pope Gregory's *Pastoral Care*, a treatise about the responsibilities of the clergy. Alfred also encouraged others to write works in English, particularly the *Anglo-Saxon Chronicle*, mentioned earlier. The English language was in a much better state when Alfred died in 899 than it had been at his birth. In the years after Alfred's death, Wessex made inroads into the Danelaw, and by 924, when Alfred's grandson Athelstan became king, it was of both Saxon and Danish lands.

But the Vikings were not done. What is sometimes called the 'Second Viking Conquest' took place in the tenth century, led by, among others, the Norwegian king, Olaf Tryggvason ('son of Tryggvi'). The Anglo-Saxons suffered great losses, particularly at the battle of Maldon, a town in Essex (the name comes from the OE *mæl* meaning 'monument', and *dun* meaning 'hill'). The battle is the topic of one of Anglo-Saxon's best-known poems, called *The Battle of Maldon* – CW7.4 tells you all about this work. Anglo-Saxon resistance to the raids was poor, although in 1002 the king, Ethelred the Unready, did order the massacre of all Danish settlers in England – doubtless one of the foolish acts which earned him the name of 'unready' (or, more accurately, 'ill-advised'). He was driven into exile and the Danish King Canute took over. That was in 1013, and from then until 1042 – twenty-nine years – England was Danish. Then Ethelred's son, who became known as Edward the Confessor, was made king. He in turn was succeeded in 1066 by King Harold (Godwinson). But Harold's reign was very short, terminated by yet another invasion – this time from the south rather than the east: from Normandy. Much, much more of that later.

So much for history. Activity 3A (*In a nutshell*) suggests that you produce a summary of the events described here. And if you are interested in the way that English place names reflect language history, take a look at CW3.1 (*Linguistics in place names*).

3.2 Old English: a foreign language?

What does OE look like? At first encounter, it may seem like a foreign language. That is just how we are going to treat it in this section, asking you to look at a short OE passage much as you might look at one written in a foreign language. Our passage comes from the *Anglo-Saxon Chronicle*, a major source of historical information for this period. It consists of a series of accounts of English history from the time of the Roman invasion until at least 1154. There were four major versions kept by monks in various English towns: the

Peterborough Chronicle, the *Winchester* or *Parker Chronicle*, the *Abingdon Chronicle* and the *Worcester Chronicle*. The passage comes from the first of these. It has been 'doctored' a little here, to help with comprehension; proper nouns, for example, have been given the capital letters they would have today. You will be asked to go through the passage several times, and you should certainly not expect to understand much of it on first reading. Indeed, even by the end of the section, your comprehension will be only partial. The value of the procedure is that it will encourage you to engage with the language in a way that should help you come to terms with it. Here is the passage; read through it quickly. Are there any words you can guess the meaning of? Can you glean any sense of what it is about?

> Her nam Breohtric cining Offan dohter Eadburge & on his dagum comon ærest iii scipu Norðmanna of Hereðalande & þa se ge refa þær to rad he wolde drifan to ðes ciniges tune þy he nyste hwæt hi wæron & hine man ofsloh þa Ðæt wæron þa erestan scipu Deniscra manna þe Angel cynnes land gesohton

Now here it is again, this time in a table with spaces given below each word for you to write in what you think words mean as you go through the procedure over the next few pages – it might be prudent to write in pencil, so that you can make changes as you proceed. A few spaces are filled in to start you on your way.

Table 3.1 The 'Peterborough Chronicle Passage'

Her Here	*nam*	*Breohtric*	*cining*	*Offan*	*dohter*
Eadburge	*&*	*on*	*his*	*dagum*	*comon*
ærest	*iii*	*scipu*	*Norðmanna*	*of*	*Hereðalande*
&	*þa* then	*se* the	*ge* also	*refa*	*þær*
to	*rad*	*he*	*wolde*	*drifan*	*to*
ðes	*ciniges*	*tune*	*þy* because	*he*	*nyste* did not know
hwæt	*hi* they	*wæron*	*&*	*hine*	*man*
ofsloh	*þa* then	*Ðæt* that (these)	*wæron*	*þa* at that time	*erestan*
scipu	*Deniscra*	*manna*	*þe* that	*Angel*	*cynnes*
land	*gesohton*				

Add words to the table as you go through the stages below.

(a) The passage describes an event mentioned earlier in this chapter. Read through the passage quickly and identify the event. You may have to search section 3.1 a little, but the proper nouns will soon give the game away. Once you have identified the event, say who or what some of the proper nouns refer to (at this stage you will probably not be able to work them all out). You may also be able to guess the meaning of one common noun, *refa* – he is a character in the story. Do all this before you read on.

The event which the passage describes is of course the arrival of the Danes. The names you will certainly recognize are: *Breohtric*, *Offan*, and *Eadburg*. The *refa* is the king's reeve who ends up dead (and in fact we will call the passage the 'dead reeve passage'). You may possibly also have suspicions about who or what some of the other proper nouns refer to: *Norðmanna*, *Hereðalande*, and possibly *Deniscra*. And *Angel*? It does not mean 'angels'; however, as we saw in 3.1, Pope Gregory thought that some of them looked like angels (this is a broad hint!). Knowing the events that the passage describes may well help you with the meanings of some other verbs. Only move to stage (b) below when you have worked out as much as you can, given what you have been told.

(b) There are some words whose meanings may become easier to work out if you know how they are pronounced. So here are just a few points about OE pronunciation – the topic is covered in more detail later in the next chapter (4.2):

- You will have noticed that the passage contains some unfamiliar letters not used in PDE. Three of these – 'ð', its capital form 'Ð', and 'þ' – are all pronounced as if written 'th' (either as in PDE 'thin' or 'this').
- The vowel 'æ' is pronounced as in the PDE word 'hat'.
- The sequence 'sc' was sometimes pronounced [ʃ], as if it were written 'sh'.
- A written 'g' was sometimes pronounced [j], like the 'y' in 'yet'.

This is a good point at which to say that this book uses phonetic symbols quite a lot. There is a list of these, including sample words containing them, on pages xv–xvi.

Find the words in the passage containing the letters mentioned in this paragraph, and try pronouncing them. In a moment you will be asked to make guesses as to what the words might mean. An important point to bear in mind here is that OE uses many suffixes to carry grammatical information – again a topic that will be covered in depth in Chapter 6. For this reason, when trying to work out OE word meanings it is sometimes worth focusing on the main part of the word, ignoring suffixes. Consider also that context often helps reveal the meaning of a word.

Bearing these things in mind, now go through the passage making guesses about possible meanings of the words you pronounced. You will almost certainly not be able to guess every word, but with luck, just a little bit more of the passage will become meaningful.

Here are a few examples of the kind of help that pronunciation plus 'suffix ignoring' might have given. *Norðmanna* would be pronounced as if written 'Northmanna'. Take off the *-a* suffix, and you are left with a good idea about the identity of the people being referred to – or at least where they come from. Then there's *scipu*, pronounced as if written 'shipu', and *dagum*, pronounced as if 'dayum'. Again, taking off the suffixes *-u* and *-um* gives away the meanings of the words. Add the words you have now worked out to Table 3.1.

(c) Because OE is a version of English, you would expect many OE words to have come into PDE. Looking through the passage for words resembling PDE is therefore likely to be useful. Similarly, if you happen to know modern German, this might help you too, since OE is a Germanic language. Read the passage again, looking specifically for words resembling modern English and (if you can) German too. Remember the 'ignoring suffixes' advice as you do this. Do any resemblances lead you to understand more of the passage's content?

This strategy might enable you to work out what the word *dohter* means. With *hwæt*, try reversing the 'h' and the 'w'. Using the 'ignoring suffix' principle, drop the *-on* suffix from *comon*, and *wæron* and this will help work out what these verb forms mean. There are other words which are less easy to work out, but which may be worth a guess, bearing in mind the context. These include the nouns *cining* (considering what you know about Breohtric may solve that one), and *tune*, together with the verb forms *rad*, *drifan*, *ofsloh*, and *gesohton*. In the case of this last word, take off not just the suffix *-on*, but the prefix *ge-* too. Then there's *cynnes*. Minus the *-es* ending, this is *cynn*. Think of the PDE *kin*; the OE word means 'people'. As for German words, *nam* may remind you of that language's verb *nehmen* – 'to take'. The OE version was *niman*, and *nam* here means 'took'. Modern German would also help you with *ærest* and *erestan*, which both mean 'first' (German *erst*).

(d) At the end of these efforts, you can still expect there to be many words you have not worked out. In a moment, you will be given a word-for-word translation. But do not look at it until you have exhausted every last ounce of effort to work meanings out. Look at those parts of the table you have filled in, and try to guess what might fill the remaining blanks. Where this is not possible, at the very least try to guess what kind of words the missing ones are – verbs, nouns, adjectives, or what?

Here now is the word-for-word translation. Use it to fill in any gaps remaining in Table 3.1.

The dead reeve passage

Her nam Breohtric cining Offan dohter Eadburge & on his dagum comon ærest
Here took Breohtric king Offa's daughter Eadburg and in his days came first

iii scipu Norðmanna of Hereðalande & þa se ge refa þær to rad
3 ships of Northmen from Horthaland and then the reeve thereto rode and

he wolde drifan to ðes ciniges tune þy he nyste hwæt hi wæron
he wished to drive to the king's manor because he knew not what they were

& hine man ofsloh þa Ðæt wæron þa erestan scipu Deniscra manna þe Angel
and him one slew then. That were the first ships of Danish men that the Angle

cynnes land gesohton
people's land sought.

If you want to spend a little more time on the passage, Activity 3B (*More about the dead reeve*) gives you the chance to glean a little more linguistic information from it.

3.3 Suffix-rich, English, Germanic

In the course of this discussion about the 'dead reeve passage', two basic points have emerged:

(i) *Old English is … English*. It looks like a foreign language, with its unfamiliar letters and odd-looking words. But your efforts to work out the passage's meaning may have revealed that the language really is a version of English – surprisingly similar to PDE, you may think, especially when you realize that well over 1,000 years have passed since the *Chronicle*'s description was written.

(ii) *Old English is suffix-rich*. The passage gives some suggestion that, unlike in PDE, suffixes abound in OE, and that they serve grammatical purposes. The next chapter starts our more detailed look at the language, and suffixes will be explored in depth.

A number of other Germanic languages are also suffix-rich. We have also seen evidence of 'Germanicness' in the vocabulary of the 'dead reeve passage', with words like *nam* and *ærest* having equivalents in modern German. Our two basic points therefore take us back to a third, made at the end of 1.3, about English in general. It is that despite all the foreign influences it has absorbed, English remains basically a Germanic language. Its family relations, branch and tree, are unequivocal.

Activity section

3A   In a nutshell

You may be one of those people who find that creating a summary of historical events a useful way of retaining facts. If so, produce a table of the events described in 3.1. Record these in chronological order, giving dates and brief descriptions of what happened.

3B   More about the dead reeve   AS

(a) Now that you have seen a word-for-word translation of the 'dead reeve passage', you are in a position to explore other points about OE that the passage exemplifies:
   (i) Notice just how many words resemble PDE words.
   (ii) Mention is made in the text of suffixes. King Offa appears in the passage. What might the 'n' on the end of *Offa* signify?
   (iii) There is one noun that appears twice, but with a rather different form. What is it? Any ideas about why the form should be different?
   (iv) Does *wolde* remind you of a PDE verb? Which one?
   (v) Does the passage contain any information about what form the infinitive of verbs might take?
   (vi) OE word order is often different from PDE. Identify examples in the passage. Look particularly at the position of verbs in sentences.

(b) The translation given in the text is word-for-word, and hence very literal. Write a 'freer' translation which captures what the passage says in more idiomatic PDE.

Answer section

Activity 3B

  (i) There are very many words resembling PDE words. In the first ten words alone: *her* ('here'), *cining* ('king'), *dohter* ('daughter'), *his* ('his'), *dagum* ('day').
  (ii) The *-n* suffix can be like PDE *-s*; it is 'King Offa's daughter'.
  (iii) *cining* appears also as *ciniges*, the latter meaning 'king's'.
  (iv) *wolde* may remind you of PDE 'would'. The OE form means 'wanted' or 'wished to'.
  (v) There is one infinitive *drifan*, 'to drive', correctly suggesting that the *-an* suffix can be an OE infinitive form.

(vi) The verb sometimes comes before the subject, in *Her nam Breohtric*, for example, and *comon … iii scipu*. Sometimes it comes at or towards the end of the sentence, as in *hine man ofsloh* and *manna þe Angel cynnes land gesohton*.

Further reading

A short, engaging account of Anglo-Saxon history is contained in Chapter 1 of Schama (2000).

A much more detailed look at the period is presented in Higham and Ryan (2013).

You can find a copy of the *Anglo-Saxon Chronicle* at http://archive.org/stream/Anglo-saxonChronicles/anglo_saxon_chronicle_djvu.txt. As well as locating the dead reeve events (AD 787), you might also use it to find reference to Julius Caesar's arrival, and to St Augustine's.

Notes

1 Eumenius wrote this in his *Panegyric to Constantine*. Part of the reason why Britain was fortunate was, he argued, that Constantine spent time there.
2 This Augustine is not to be confused with the fourth-century Augustine of Hippo, who wrote the *City of God*.

4 OE writing, pronunciation, and a devil of a mouthful

This chapter takes a short look at some more OE letters, as well as at how the language was pronounced. One topic touched on briefly is word stress, an issue which will play an important role in how the language develops. Then you are given a longer passage of OE. This will serve as a basis for our look at the details of OE vocabulary and grammar in the next two chapters. The passage is about a nun who bites – yes, bites – the devil: hence the chapter's title.

Section 4.2.4 asks how we know about the way OE was pronounced. Think about this issue before reading on. How can we find out about the pronunciation of a language no longer in use?

You may also like to use the internet or other sources to find out in advance about some other things mentioned in the chapter:

- The poem *Bēowulf*. It is touched on in passing here, and makes a longer appearance in Chapter 7.
- Pope Gregory's *Dialogues* (from which the passage about the nun and the devil is taken); Bishop Werferth, who translated Gregory's book into English; King Alfred's attempts to promote English – which involved asking his friend Werferth to translate Gregory.

One possible beginning date for the OE period is 449, when the Germanic tribes first landed. A possible end date is the Norman conquest of 1066. If we use these dates, then the OE period lasted 617 years – a very long time, during which any language would change a lot. OE also existed in various dialect forms which were quite different from each other. For these reasons, all questions about what OE was like can only be answered in terms of one specific time span and one specific place. Like most books on the subject, we will here deal mostly with the West-Saxon version of the language, spoken in Wessex during Alfred's time.

4.1 A few more OE letters

In the early days of writing, the Latin alphabet (on which today's writing system is based) was not in use. Signs called runes were used instead. The runic alphabet is thought to be an adaptation of the Etruscan alphabet, and versions of it were found among the Germanic people of northern Europe. Figure 4.1 shows an OE version. Use it to do Activity 4A (*Working with runes*). The Latin alphabet started to replace runic script in OE by the seventh century.

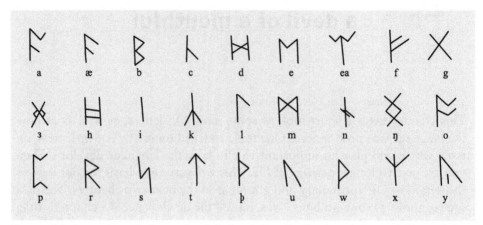

Figure 4.1 A version of the runic alphabet (after D. Freeborn, *From Old English to Standard English* (Palgrave Macmillan, 2006), p. 26)

As we saw in the 'dead reeve passage', there are some symbols in OE that we no longer use today. These were mentioned in the shaded area at the beginning of Chapter 3: 'eth' (ð and Ð), 'thorn' (þ), and 'ash' (æ and Æ). You will also have gathered from the passage that the 'ampersand' (&) – was commonly used. There are a few more symbols you are likely to come across in your travels through Old English. One is 'ȝ'. This is 'yogh', and in modern editions is usually written 'g'. 'Wynn' is another, written 'ƿ' and today mostly shown as a 'w'. So *maniȝ* is now written *manig*, and *ƿyn* written *wyn*. You are also likely to find lines, called 'macrons', written above vowels to indicate that they are long. So alongside *þæt* you find *tǣk*. In fact, the macron is a modern addition, and Old English texts themselves do not show them. We did not use these in the 'dead reeve passage', but will do so from now on

4.2 Pronouncing OE

4.2.1 Consonants

Here are some OE words; their PDE meanings are not always immediately clear:

wicce	cēosan	secg	ecg	biddan
hoppian	hræfn	lifde	scearp	fisc
scufan				

In nearly all these cases, knowing something about how OE consonants were pronounced will help clarify meanings. As we saw in the 'dead reeve passage', OE 'sc' was pronounced [ʃ] like our 'sh'; so *scip* in the passage was said like 'ship'. This rule will help you with some of the words above. Here are more rules that will help in the same way. Together, they will enable you to make probably quite accurate guesses as to what the words above mean. When you have made your guesses, check the meanings in the *Answer section* (**AS**):

- written 'c' was often pronounced like a 'k', but could also be [tʃ]. The word *sprǣc* was pronounced as if written 'spræch';
- 'cg' could be pronounced [dʒ], as if written 'dg'. You find it in the word *bricg*, and once you know this, the word's meaning ('bridge') becomes clear;
- 'yogh' ('ʒ' – usually written, as we have seen, as a 'g') was pronounced [j]. So again the pronunciation suggests the PDE meaning in a word like *maniʒ* – 'many';
- double consonants were usually pronounced separately. So *fyllan* was pronounced with the 'l's as in 'all-loving', and *sunnum* with 'n's like in 'pen-knife';
- there was a letter 'f', but no letter 'v'. Written 'f' was sometimes pronounced [f] and sometimes [v]. Knowing that 'f' could be [v] helps clarify the meanings of words like *giefan seofon cnafa hæfde* – 'give', 'seven', 'boy' (think 'knave') and 'had' (think 'haved'). In our example words, the letter 'f' is always pronounced 'v' when it occurs inside the word (what is called **medially**).

4.2.2 Vowels

How were OE vowels pronounced? We saw from the 'dead reeve passage' that the [æ] in *þæt* was pronounced like the vowel in PDE 'hat'. Here are some more OE words. Use the information in Table 4.1 to help pronounce them.

siþþan	tīd	fugel	clypian
fūl	lȳfan	lagu	sendan
brȳd	tōþ	sōþ	hē
wann	wolcen	āscian	næfre
þū	hālig	hider	bysig
folgian	fæder	guma	bæc
wīs	Lēden	benc	lǣne
		(remember how 'c'	
		can be pronounced)	

Some of the words on the list were chosen because we will be meeting them in later chapters; others because they are 'guessable'. You might like to try and guess what some of the words mean (**AS**).

The last word on the list – *lǣne* – is an interesting one. It means 'transitory' or 'temporary' and is connected to our PDE word 'loan' (loans being temporary arrangements). It occurs in the sentence: *līf is laǣne: eal scæceth lēoht and līf somod* ('life is transitory: all men leave this world and life together'). J. R. R. Tolkien, an Anglo-Saxon scholar as well as the writer of books like *The Hobbit* and *The Lord of the Rings*, used the phrase in 1936 to describe the attitude towards life expressed in the most famous of all Anglo-Saxon poems, *Bēowulf*, an epic written largely in West-Saxon dialect during the tenth or eleventh century.

Table 4.1 Old English vowels

Letter	Phonetic symbol	Rough modern resemblances (Southern English unless otherwise stated)
a	[ɑ]	close to *man* but a bit shorter
æ	[æ]	*hat*
e	[e]	*bet*
i	[i]	*hit*
o	[o]	*hot*
u	[u]	*pull*
y	[y]	French *vu*
ā	[ɑː]	*car*
ǣ	[æː]	*bad*
ē	[eː]	German *sehen*
ī	[iː]	*see*
ō	[oː]	German *so*
ū	[uː]	*fool*
ȳ	[yː]	French *ruse*

4.2.3 Stress

In OE, as in other Germanic languages, the stress generally came on the first syllable of a word. Some of the names in the 'dead reeve passage' illustrate this. It is *Breohtric*, not *Breohtric*, *Eadburge*, *Norðmanna*, *Hereðalande*. There were some exceptions. For example, when a verb started with a prefix, the stress came on the root element, not the prefix: it is *gesōhton*, not *gesōhton*. Putting the stress on the first syllable has some very important implications for the development of English, which will be mentioned at various points during the book (in 7.3 for example).

4.2.4 OE pronunciation: how do we know?

A question which may well have occurred to you as you have been reading this section is: how can we possibly know how a 'dead' language was pronounced? With a living language we can find out by listening to the speech of native speakers. But there are no native speakers of OE alive today. Where does our information come from?

It is not easy to find out about historical pronunciation. As Hogg (1992: 70) puts it: 'in reconstructing an older language we are, as it were, trying to complete a jigsaw without a picture … and we may not even know how many pieces there are'. In some historical circumstances we might find a linguistically minded writer who will conveniently describe the sounds of a language on paper. But this did not happen for OE.

How words are written can give some information about pronunciation. It is true that written forms rarely reflect pronunciation accurately, but the way people write *is* associated with the way they pronounce. Hogg's example is the OE word *bedd* (= 'bed'). We may not know exactly how each letter – 'b', 'e' and 'd' – was pronounced in OE, but the use of these three letters does give some rough general information as to the kind of sounds involved. This information is reinforced by our pronunciation in PDE which is, after all, a later version of the same language.

Plausibility is an important consideration when we are attempting to reconstruct historical pronunciations. Any theory about how a particular sound is pronounced must fit in with what we know about how a language has changed, and indeed with what we know about language change in general. Hogg's example here is the OE *hit* (PDE 'it'). To account for the change from OE to PDE here, we must hypothesize a process whereby the initial 'h' stopped being pronounced and eventually got dropped in the spelling. Is this plausible? Very much so. Indeed, 'h dropping' happens all the time, not just in English (with Cockney dropped haitches) but also in some circumstances in other languages.

As another example of plausibility: in 4.2.1 we saw that the OE consonant 'c' could be pronounced as either PDE [k] or [tʃ]. How likely is it that one spelling should represent these two sounds? It is very likely, because the change from [k] to [tʃ] involves a process which occurs in many languages, and there are many other examples in English. It is called **palatalization**. Sometimes a consonant comes to be pronounced with the tongue nearer to the hard palate, and this is partly responsible for a sound like [k] becoming a palatalized form: [tʃ]. This happened in OE. By the end of the OE period, the two sounds had become distinct, though the 'c' spelling remained the same. You sometimes find the [tʃ] version distinguished by a dot above the 'c' – ċ.

It really is a jigsaw without a picture. But looking at spellings and developing hypotheses that make linguistic sense, can get us somewhere. In 14.5 we will revisit the 'how do we know' pronunciation question, but in relation to an age when more types of evidence were available.

4.3   The nun, the devil, and a lettuce

The 'dead reeve passage' gave us a short introduction to OE. To provide some more exposure to the language, as well as a starting-point for looking at OE in detail, here is a longer passage. It comes from the pen of one Werferth. He was the bishop of Worcester during King Alfred's reign, and the two were friends. As part of Alfred's campaign to increase knowledge of Latin writings, while at the same time promoting English, Alfred asked Bishop Werferth to translate Pope Gregory's *Dialogues* from Latin into English. Written in 593, these provide a picture of Italian ecclesiastical life. Here is a delightful story, in which Gregory describes what happened one day to a nun who was, just for one terrible moment, negligent. The moral of the story is that you really must be ever on your guard. You might read the 'lettuce story' (as we shall call it) to yourself as 'pronunciation practice'. Then try to make as much sense of it as you can without looking at the word-for-word translation provided; you may at least be able to identify a few words because of their similarity with PDE.

The lettuce story

Sōðlīce, sumum dæge hit gelamp þæt an nunne of þæm ilcan
Truly, on a certain day it happened that a nun from the same

mynstre eōde inn on hyra wyrttūn. þā geseah heō ænne leāhtric, and
nunnery went in to her garden. There saw she a lettuce, and

hire gelyste þæs. Heō þā hine genam, and forgeat þæt heō hine mid
to her pleased it. She then it took, and forgot that she it with

Cristes rōdetācne gebledsode, ac heō hine freclīce bāt. þa wearð heō
Christ's sign of the cross should bless, but she it greedily bit. Then was she

sōna fram deōfle gegrīpen, and hrædlīce nyðer afeōll. Þā þā heō swȳðe
immediately by the devil attacked, and quickly down fell. When she severely

wæs gedreht, þā wearð hit hraðe gecȳðed þæm faeder Equitio, and hē
was tormented, then was it quickly called Father Equitius, and he

wæs gebeden þæt hē ofstlīce come, and mid his gebedum hire gehulpe.
was asked that he quickly come, and with his prayers to her helped.

Sōna swā se hālga fæder wæs inn āgān on þone wyrttūn, þa ongann
As soon as the holy father was in gone to the garden, then began

se deōfol, þe þa nunnan gegrāp, of hire mūðe clypian, swylce hē dædbōte
the devil, that the nun attacked, from her mouth to call out, as if he amends

dōn wolde, and þus cwæð: 'Hwæt dyde Ic hire? Hwæt dyde Ic hire? Ic
make would, and thus spoke: What did I to her? What did I to her? I

sæt mē on ānum leāhtrice, þā com heō and bāt mē!' Hē þā, se Godes
sat me on a lettuce, then came she and bit me'. He then, the of God

wer, mid mycelre yrsunge him bebeād þæt hē fram hire gewite, and þæt
man, with great anger him commanded that he from her come out, and that

hē nāne wunungstōw e næfde on þæs ælmihtīgan Godes þeōwene. Hē
he no dwelling place never have in the handmaiden of Almighty God. He

þærryhte aweg gewāt, and nā leng syððan hire æthrīnan ne dorste.
immediately away went and no longer thereafter her to touch dared.

The translation is very word-for-word. Perhaps you might like to turn it into a more idiomatic one.

4.4   Five words that may ring bells

The next chapter is about OE words. As an introduction to the topic, here are five words from the passage that might remind you of more recent English words, or ring other bells for you. They are: *sōðlīce*, *cwæð*, *wer*, *mycelre* and *stōwe* (on the end of *wunungstōwe*). Do they ring any bells for you? Give some thought to this before reading the information below.

(a) *sōðlīce*. You came across *sōð* in section 4.2.2's pronunciation practice. It means 'truth' or 'true'. The suffix *-līce* is equivalent to today's *-ly*, used to make adverbs out of adjectives. Thus *sōðlīce* means 'truly'. You may have come across – in Shakespeare for example – the related word *forsooth*. Find other examples of the *-līce* suffix in the 'lettuce story'.

(b) *cwæð*. Related to 'quoth', a word not in use today but again found in Shakespeare. It is related to our PDE verb *bequeath*; try to work out what the meaning connection is.

(c) *wer* means 'man'. For those of you who know Latin, it will suggest a Latin word for man, *vir* (as in our *virile*). It may also suggest to you that 'man-animal' known as *werwulf*.

(d) There is a Scottish proverb which says 'many a mickel makes a muckle' (lots of small things add up to something big). But OE *micel* (*mycel*) meant 'great', not 'small', which makes the proverb a little mysterious… The *OED* describes the proverb as 'garbled'.

(e) *Stōw* means 'place', and there are a number of English place names that include the word: Felixstowe, for example. Another interesting example is Bristol ('the place of the bridge'), where the 'w' has become an 'l', following local dialect pronunciation. There is also a PDE verb *to stow* meaning 'to place' and usually used in relation to storing objects (e.g. on an aircraft). Then there is *stowaway*, of course…

Activity section

4A   Working with runes   AS

(a) Here are some words from the 'dead reeve passage', written in runes. What are they?

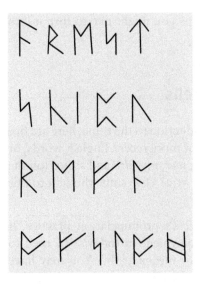

(b) Now put these words, from the same passage, into runes: *cōmon, hwæt, drīfan, wǣron*.

Answer section

Words for pronunciation in 4.2.1 and 4.2.2

Meanings are given in the order in which the words appear.

For consonant practice: witch; to choose; sedge; edge; to ask; to hop; raven; lived; sharp; fish; to shove.

For vowel practice: since; time/season; bird; to call; foul, to allow; water/sea; to send; bride/wife; tooth; truth; he; dark; cloud; to ask; never; thou/you; holy; hither; busy; to follow; father; man; back; wise; Latin; bench; transitory.

Activity 4A

(a) The words are: *ǣrest, scipu, rēfa, ofslōh*.
(b) Runic versions of the words:

Further reading

Most accounts of the OE language contain sections on graphology and sounds. Hogg (2002) is a short and accessible book, with sections on these areas in Chapter 1.

Mitchell and Robinson (2011) have longer, more detailed accounts.

Hogg's (1992) coverage is even more detailed, and includes discussion of the 'how do we know' issue we look at in 4.2.4.

Chapter 2 of Schendl (2001) looks at the kind of evidence that can be used to reconstruct historical versions of a language. The book as a whole is a useful short introduction to historical linguistics.

If you are interested in runes, Page (1987) is a good, short book to consult.

5 The Old English word-hoard

This chapter is about OE words. We look at how languages use native resources (like adding affixes or making compounds) as a way of creating new words. This was a particularly common process in OE. Borrowing words from other languages is another way of increasing vocabulary, and OE does this too, particularly from Latin and Old Norse. Here are some questions to explore before reading; sometimes the internet or other sources will help:

- Think of a few new words that have recently come into your L1. Where do they come from? Say whatever you can about the processes by which they came into your language.
- Some linguists divide adverbs into various categories. One that is mentioned in the text is 'adverbs of manner'. What are these? What other adverb categories are there?
- The work of the author Orosius is mentioned. Find out something about him. Also, if you happen to enjoy historical detective work, you may like (just for the fun of it) to find out whose body was brought to England in 1135, in an incident mentioned in CW5.2.
- 'Grammatical words' are mentioned, with pronouns and articles given as examples. What is a grammatical word? What other types of word are there (words which we would not call grammatical)?
- The etymologies of a number of words are given in the chapter. Find out something in advance about the meanings and histories of a few (or indeed all) of these: *puck, tor, brat, lobster, numb, anger, kirk, earl.*

5.1 How languages expand vocabulary

'I've gotta use words when I talk to you', says a character in T. S. Eliot's poetic drama, *Sweeney Agonistes*. Words really are right at the centre of language, and because they are so important, languages collect words. Their vocabularies grow. Sometimes it is a question of need. In times of development and expanding mental horizons, new ideas may be being explored, and new words will be needed to express them. Or perhaps the vocabulary growth will simply happen because of contacts with other languages.

In this chapter we will look at what OE words were like, and how the language developed its vocabulary. But before considering this, it is worth asking the question in general terms: how do languages accumulate new words? What ways are open to them to increase their word stock? One way of approaching this question is to think about a (if not *the*) major area of technological development in recent decades: electronic communication – the internet, the use of texting, the growth of social media. This development has, in all languages, led to new areas of vocabulary. Activity 5A (*OMG: what's happening to English today?*) invites you to think about this in relation to PDE. Do this before reading the following paragraphs, which discuss what the activity shows.

There are two major pathways to vocabulary expansion, which often intersect and combine. One is to create new words using what we can call 'native resources' – the means available in the language to invent new words. One very productive way of doing this is by **affixation**. **Affixes** are elements that can be put at the beginning or end of a word to create a new one. When the affix comes at the beginning of a word, it is called a **prefix**. The examples in Activity 5A show the prefix *un-* used to form *unlike* and *unfriend*. The activity also shows the prefixes *down-* and *up-* (in *download* and *upload*). We came across **suffixes** in CW3.1, where *-chester*, *-ham* and *-ton* (among others) were used to create place names. A second very productive method is by **compounding**, joining words together to form new ones. The activity's examples show that compounds sometimes actually create one word out of two, so *soft+ware* becomes *software*. Sometimes, though, two words are retained – as in *disk drive*. Or a hyphen can be used; *electronic-mail*, or (*e-mail*) does this (though it is also common today to find the hyphen left out). There is one particularly interesting type of compounding which creates what are known as **portmanteau** words. Here, just parts of words are joined together. So *web + log* becomes *blog*, and *iPod + broadcast* turns into *podcast*. Another method of word formation uses **functional shift** or **conversion**, where a word extends its usage into other parts of speech. An example is the word *Google*. It started off its young life as a noun, and you might be interested to use the internet to find out about its origin. Now people use it as a verb – you can 'google' something. *Trend* is the same; it is a noun that has now started to be used as a verb – the activity's example is the question *what's trending?* The activity also shows just how imaginative people can be in their word creations. Two examples – *LOL* ('laugh out loud'), and *OMG* ('Oh my God') – show how even abbreviations can become words.

The other major pathway is by borrowing words from other languages. *Wikipedia* is an example of this. *Wiki* is a word in the Hawaiian language meaning 'quick'. The activity includes another two examples of borrowing: *sudoku* (from Japanese), and *feng shui* (from Mandarin). The first is a good example of how a foreign word is introduced to describe something new; sudoku games were introduced from Japan, and it was natural to import the word with the game. Incidentally, notice that I had to go beyond the area of electronic communication to find examples of foreign borrowings into English. This is because so much of that field is dominated by English. Borrowings from English into other languages are much more frequent in this area. *To like* (in the Facebook sense) has become a French verb *liker*, and the English verb *click* has made its way into various languages – *cliquer* in French, *klicken* in German, *hacer clic* in Spanish. If your first language is not English, you may be able to think of other English words that have come into your language in the electronic communications area.

These two pathways – utilizing native resources and borrowing – provide us with a framework for looking at vocabulary expansion throughout the history of English. There is one important difference between the two methods. If they are to catch on, new words need to be readily understood, and the use of native resources generally makes this happen, because the word-formation rules are well tried. For example, I could invent a new word in PDE – let us say the word *unfindoutable*. You will never have come across it before, but I can be sure you will understand it, because you know what the constituent parts (*un* + *find* + *out* + *able*) mean. But this is often not true of foreign borrowings, which sometimes bewilder speakers who do not speak the source language. For example, imagine that for some reason I were to take the Norwegian word for 'to discover', which is *oppdage*, and use it to introduce a new word into English – say *unoppdageable* (meaning roughly the same as my other invention, *unfindoutable*). The word would be incomprehensible to anyone who did not know Norwegian. As we shall see in Chapter 15 (section 15.3), this lack of transparency of foreign borrowings was a big issue in Renaissance times, when **loanwords** (words coming into the language through borrowing) were extremely common.

In our look at OE words, two dictionaries will be particularly useful to you. One is the *OED*, and you might like to remind yourself of how to use it by looking again at CW2.3 (*The OED*). The other is the Bosworth-Toller Anglo-Saxon Dictionary (B-T), freely available online. You can find information about how to use this at CW5.1 (*An OE dictionary*).

5.2 Using native resources

5.2.1 Compounds

Compounding is natural to Germanic languages, and though we do it a lot in PDE, it is even more common in modern German. A rather extreme example is the word *Atomkraftwerkestandortesicherungsprogramm*. It means 'atomic-power-station-site-safety-programme'. If English had shown the same fondness for compounding as German, we might expect to have *farspeak* (a literal translation of the German word *Fernsprecher*) for 'telephone', *yeartime* for 'season' (*Jahreszeit*), and *houseshoe* for 'slipper' (*Hausschuh*).

The noun *word-hoard*, which appears in this chapter's title, is perhaps one you have not come across before – it is not really in use today – but you will probably have no trouble working out what it means. It joins together *word* and *hoard*, and is indeed an example of how compounding can lead to new words with fairly transparent (easy-to-work-out) meanings. A 'word-hoard' is, well, a 'hoard of words' – in this case, the 'vocabulary of a language'. The compound was indeed used in this sense until the word *vocabulary*, taken from Latin, appeared on the scene in this sense, centuries later. The actual OE form was *wordhord*, with *hord* meaning roughly what today's 'hoard' means – a stock, usually of something valuable. The use of *hord* in OE shows how amazingly productive native resources can be as a way of increasing vocabulary. Activity 5B (*A hoard of hords*) invites you to consider some compounds involving this word. Look at it before you read on.

Like *wordhord*, a few of the compounds in Activity 5B are very transparent, as long as you know the meaning of the individual parts. So there is *bōchord*, literally 'bookhoard', meaning 'library'. There is also *hordcleōfa*; once you know that *cleōfa* means 'chamber', the compound's meaning of 'treasure chamber' makes sense. Some compounds, though, are more opaque. *Hordweorþung* (literally 'hoard honouring') expresses quite an abstract and complex idea, meaning 'honouring a person by bestowing treasure'. A number of others are quite poetic, and indeed (as we shall see in Chapter 7, section 3), imaginative compounding was an important feature of OE poetry. So we have *grēothord*: *grēot* means 'earth' (and gives us our PDE word 'grit'). The compound means 'body', literally the 'hoard of the earth'. One of B-T's examples is *Grēothord gnornaþ gǣst hine fȳseþ on ēcne geard*: 'the body mourns, the spirit hastens to an eternal dwelling'. Then there is *brēosthord* (the 'hoard of the mind' = 'thought'), *feorh-hord* ('lifehoard' = 'soul'), and *mōdhord* = 'mind'. The word *mōd* in this last example means 'heart' or 'mind'. Like *hord*, this word was frequently used in compounds and, according to Baugh and Cable (2013: 60), there are over a hundred. Compounding was indeed highly productive.

OE compounds can result in various parts of speech – nouns, adjectives, verbs, adverbs – and they can be made up of various parts of speech. In the case of *wordhord*, we have nouns combining together to form a new noun; so it is 'noun + noun = noun'. Activity 5C (*Some OE compounds*) gives you the chance to take a good look at OE compounding. It involves working out the meanings of some compounds and seeing how they are made up.

Part (b) of the activity asks whether there is any generalization that may be made about the way the constituent parts relate to the 'result'. The answer is that it is the final part of the combination that determines the part of speech of the compound itself. So, for example, whenever the second constituent is an adjective, the compound will be an adjective. Another generalization, which the activity does not show, is that in the case of compound nouns, the final part determines the compound's grammatical gender (something discussed in the next chapter's CW6.1). An example given there is the word *wīfmann*. It means 'woman', but the noun is masculine because the final part (*mann*) is grammatically masculine. Incidentally, the small selection of compounds found in Activity

5C is representative of OE in one way – it shows that compound nouns and adjectives are the most common, with verbs coming in third.

As we have seen, compounding was common in OE. But some of the linguistic influences that affected English after the Norman Conquest of 1066 were less fond of this method, and for this reason, after that time – as Strang (1970: 333) puts it – 'the role of compounding in the language changed for good'.

5.2.2 Affixation

Another very productive way of forming new words in OE was by affixation (5.1 describes what this is). Many OE suffixes have made their way into PDE, and you will not have much difficulty recognizing them. Table 5.1 has examples. There are some OE words on the left, together with their PDE equivalents. On the right are related OE words with an added suffix. Identify the suffix in each case; for example, in 1 it is -*dom*. What are the PDE equivalents of these suffixes? What are the PDE equivalents to the words on the right (mostly they are easy to identify)?

Table 5.1 Suffixes in OE and PDE

1.	*biscop* (bishop)	*biscopdōm*
2.	*wīse* (wise)	*wīsdōm*
3.	*cild* (child)	*cildhād*
4.	*munuc* (monk)	*munuchād*
5.	*æfterfolgian* (succeed, follow after)	*æfterfolgere*
6.	*wrītan* (engrave, write)	*wrītere*
7.	*ceorl* (peasant, "churl")	*ceorlisc*
8.	*cild* (child)	*cildisc*
9.	gedeorf (trouble)	*gedeorfsum*
10.	*wyn* (delight)	*wynsum*
11.	*blind* (blind)	*blindlīc*
12.	*sōð* (true)	*sōðlīc*

You might like to do three more things before reading on. One is to look at the parts of speech involved in these examples. In 1, for example, *biscop* is a noun, and so is *biscopdōm*. So we can say that here -*dōm* is a suffix added to a noun to make another noun. Do this for the other examples. Then try and say as far as possible (not always that easy) what 'meaning' the suffixes have. What is the effect of adding -*dōm* to the word *biscop*, for example; what does -*dōm* mean? Finally, think of a few PDE words which carry versions of the suffixes – PDE words which use the -*dōm* suffix, for example. 'Kingdom' would be one instance.

Your answers to these questions will show that sometimes a suffix forms a new word with the same part of speech as the original one. It may change a noun into another noun, for example, as in examples 1 and 3 above. But suffixes are also used in OE to form different parts of speech. So in 2, *-dōm* is added to the adjective *wīse* to give a noun (*wīsdōm*). Number 12 in Table 5.1 has another example, this time showing an adjective changing into an adverb.

Sometimes you can only state the meaning of a suffix in rather vague terms. We can say, for example, that *-dōm* is used to describe a state, a position or a condition. In the PDE word *kingdom* it is a state, and in *boredom* a condition. *Hād* is rather similar. It is found in many PDE words as *-hood*: *motherhood*, *falsehood* and so on. The OE *-ere* has become PDE *-er*. It is commonly used to refer to a person involved in a particular activity, so it often makes nouns out of verbs. *Reader*, *writer* and *preacher* are PDE examples, and the OE equivalents are *raedere*, *wrītere*, and *predicere*. You will recall from 4.2.1 that OE 'sc' is pronounced 'sh'. So the suffix *-isc* was pronounced as it is written today: 'ish'. It changes nouns into adjectives, and means 'like'. So in PDE we have *foolish*, *apish*, *childish* and even *sheepish*. Incidentally, we can also use *-like* as a PDE suffix. In fact, today we have both *childish* and *child-like*, and you may wish to ask yourself how these two words differ in meaning. OE *-sum* has become PDE *-some*, and is found in *loathsome* and *fulsome*, among many others. It makes adjectives, usually (but not always) out of nouns. OE *wynsum* means 'pleasant', so one of B-T's examples – *wynsum stenc* – means 'pleasant odour'; you can see from the example that our PDE word 'stench' has rather different connotations! The suffix *-līc* is a particularly interesting one. Take a look at CW5.2 (*-ly: 'a prolific formative'*), which is all about it.

Prefixes, like suffixes, change the meaning of a word. But unlike suffixes, they do not change the part of speech. Add a prefix to a noun or an adjective and it remains a noun or an adjective. Or a verb: add the affix *dis-* to the verb *like*, to form *dislike*; the meaning has changed dramatically, but both the words remain verbs. You may like to ponder why prefixes do not change part of speech.

Prefixes are much used in OE. There is a verb *habban*, meaning 'to have'. If you add the prefix *æt-* you get *æthabban*, 'to retain'. The prefix *a-* gives *ahabban*, 'to abstain'. Then there is *onhabban* (also 'to abstain'), *behabban* ('to encompass'), *forhabban* and *ofhabban* ('to restrain'), *gehabban* ('to hold'), *oferhabban* ('to command'), *wiþerhabban* ('to resist'), *wiþhabban* ('to hold out against'), *ymbhabban* ('to surround'). An example of this last is the sentence *Ispania land is eall mid flēote ūtan (from without) ymbhæfd* – 'Hispania is completely surrounded by sea'.[1] If you want further proof of the productivity of OE prefixes – and if you have access to an OE dictionary (online or in book form) – take a look at the number of entries beginning with the prefix *mis-* or *un-*. If you want to find *mis-* in B-T online, go to 'Advanced Search'. Under 'Find headword that contains' enter *mis-* and you will be rewarded with a long list of words.

Sometimes the meaning of prefixes is very clear. You will have no trouble, for example, in working out why the prefix *under-* is used in PDE *underestimate*. But sometimes the meaning is less clear. What does the *under-* in PDE *understand* means? Or the *with-* in PDE *withdraw*? Activity 5D (*Exploring prefixes*) gives you the chance to explore the meanings and usages of some OE prefixes (and most of the frequent OE ones have in fact been mentioned in the last two paragraphs).

Activity 5D gives just some of the OE prefix meanings. *Be-* can be used to suggest the idea of 'around' or 'surrounding', so the verb *begān* means 'surround' (*gān* is 'go'), and *berīdan* means 'ride round'. But the prefix can also be a **deprivative**, carrying a sense of deprivation. The verb *behādian* describes what happens to a priest who is stripped of his ordained position (*hādian* means 'to ordain'). He is 'defrocked'.

Another interesting prefix is *for-*. It often acts as an intensifier, meaning something like 'completely'. Thus *bærnan* means 'to burn', and *forbærnan* 'to destroy by fire'. An OE translation of the Roman philosopher Boethius says *Nerōn hēt forbærnan ealle Rōme burh* – 'Nero ordered the city of Rome to be burned down'. *Fōrheard* means 'very hard', and shows the prefix being used to intensify an adjective – *heard* means 'hard'. Another example (which is not in Activity 5D) is *fordyslic* meaning 'very stupid' – *dyslic*, as you might guess, means just plain 'stupid'. You might expect *wiþ-* to mean 'with', but in fact it means 'against'. Thus *wiþcweþan* means 'to contradict' ('to speak against'). You can see the same sense present in the PDE 'withstand' – *wiþstandan* in OE.

You may think that the prefix *un-* has a clear meaning, but Activity 5D's examples show that it carries different shades of the negative theme. It can express the notion of 'not', and well as the idea of 'opposite'. So the opposite of *friþ* ('peace') is *unfriþ*, 'war'. The *Anglo-Saxon Chronicle* for 1001 reports on Danish attacks: *Hēr wæs micel unfriþ on Angelcynnes londe þurh sciphere* ('there were many hostilities in England because of the fleets'). Similarly the opposite of *bliss* ('happiness') is *unbliss*, 'sorrow'. But sometimes *un-* means 'bad' or 'evil'. So 'bad weather' is *unweder*. It can also be a **reversative**, describing the reversal of an action. Hence *unbindan, undōn unlūcan* and *untīgan*, mean 'to unbind', 'undo', 'unlock' and 'untie'.

In the next chapter, we will come across the prefix *ge-* used to form the past participle of verbs – CW6.3 is all about it. One of its uses is to suggest a finished action (in CW6.3 we will see it described as a 'completive prefix'). As an example: *siglan* means 'to sail', while *gesiglan* suggests 'to sail somewhere and arrive'. In one text (an OE translation of a Latin work by Orosius, possibly done by King Alfred), a traveller is described as sailing close to the shore so that *hē meahte on fēower dagum gesiglan* ('he would arrive by sail in four days').

When we were describing English 'in a nutshell', at the end of Chapter 1 (1.3), we said that it was 'basically a Germanic language'. This is particularly true, Kastovsky (1992: 294) comments, if we think about how OE enlarged its 'word-hoard'. There was some borrowing from other languages, as we are about to see. But Anglo-Saxon writers and translators seemed often to prefer to use the 'native resources' that their Germanic language provided to invent new words, rather than borrowing them from elsewhere.

5.3 Borrowing

Using native resources rather than borrowing has not been the rule throughout the history of English. As we shall see in Chapter 15, in Early Modern English, very large numbers of words were taken from foreign languages into English. PDE too shows a massive effect from linguistic borrowing. 'It has been estimated', Townend (2006: 73) says, 'that … as much as 70 per cent of the modern English lexicon is comprised of loanwords'. But, Townend continues, 'the comparable figure for the Old English lexicon is less than 5 per cent' In this section we will look at loanwords coming into OE from three sources: Celtic, Latin and Old Norse. One of the things we shall find is that it is often not a question of 'how many words', but of 'how few'.

5.3.1 Celtic borrowings

As we saw in CW3.1, there were place names that came from Celtic into English, including the names of rivers. This is not surprising, given that the land the Anglo-Saxons were inhabiting had been Celtic. But when it comes to ordinary words, the number of loanwords is extraordinarily small. They can almost be counted on the fingers of two hands. Table 5.2 shows some, with their meanings in mixed order underneath. Start with the meanings (a–j). Go through them in order, and try to find the matching Celtic-derived OE words (numbered 1–10). In most cases (though not quite all), this is fairly easy. As you do this, you may also be able to think of some other PDE words associated with the OE ones (**AS** – as you will have gathered by now, **AS** means that the *Answer section* deals with this activity).

Table 5.2 Some Celtic loanwords

1. *binn*	2. *torr*	3. *brocc*	4. *dun*	5. *luh* (*llyn*)
6. *cumb*	7. *drȳ*	8. *āncor*	9. *puck* (*pūca*)	10. *bratt*

a. badger	b. outcrop, peak	c. valley	d. dark coloured	e. basket, crib
f. hermit	g demon	h. lake	i. magician	j. cloak

Some of the few Celtic loanwords are interesting. We still today use the name 'brock' in relation to badgers (there are dozens of fictional badgers named Brock, including in the work of Beatrix Potter), and some of the craggy outcrops in SW England are called 'tors'. As we saw in CW3.1, according to some, *llyn* is the first element in the word 'London'. Overtones of 'demon' are present in Shakespeare's character Puck, in *A Midsummer Night's Dream*, and the word 'anchorite' is still used to refer to a religious recluse. *Drȳ* ('magician') is associated with our PDE word *druid*. Most interesting of all, perhaps, is the word *bratt*. In PDE a 'brat' is a badly behaved child. Some etymologists (though not all) think that OE *bratt* and PDE *brat* are semantically connected. As well as being a cloak, an OE *bratt* could be a 'rag', and perhaps the original human 'brat' was a child dressed in rags.

Why so few Celtic borrowings? The country which the Anglo-Saxons took over was occupied by Celts. The two ethnic groups must have come into a lot of contact over a long period of time, with intermarriages and shared interests. All in all, a situation in which you would expect copious linguistic borrowings. Before reading on, you might like to speculate why this did not occur.

In fact, speculate is all we can do. It really is a mystery. In fact, Crystal (2004: 33) calls it 'one of the great puzzles in the history of the language'. The most likely reason is that despite all the contact, the Anglo-Saxons regarded the Celts as inferior – people they had conquered and pushed out of their land onto the western fringes. One of the most important determinants of language influence is the relative perceived status of the languages. A language community that regards itself as 'inferior' is likely to borrow words from one regarded as 'superior'. In the same way, a linguistic community which feels 'superior' will not take words from a perceived 'inferior' one. Perhaps the 'superior' Anglo-Saxons felt it beneath them to borrow from the 'inferior' Celts. It was a very different situation from what occurred in France, where Celtic and Latin mingled happily to become French. Have you come across similar instances of much or little borrowing that can be explained in terms of perceived language status?

5.3.2 Latin loanwords

Celtic may not have been a language with much status, but Latin was very different. It was the language of an important empire, a civilization, and a religion. You might therefore expect the extent of borrowing to be greater than from Celtic, and so it was. Estimates of the total number of Latin loanwords coming into OE vary between 400 and 600. But what do these numbers mean? They are very much higher than the twelve or so words which came from Celtic, and you could indeed regard Latin borrowings in this period as the first great influx of foreign vocabulary into English. On the other hand, the loans were only a very small proportion of the total OE word-hoard. Durkin (2014) is a book all about loanwords coming into English. He estimates Latin loans at no more than 1.75 per cent of the OE vocabulary. This is a very small percentage. It shows that English, at this stage in its history, just did not borrow very much.

Words came from Latin into English by various routes. Before the Anglo-Saxons inhabited Britain, there were contacts between their Germanic homelands and the Roman Empire. Latin words came into their language, and they brought some of these with them to Britain. Second, Britain was itself part of that Roman Empire for a time, and conquerors always bring loanwords with them. Then there was the arrival of Christianity, and the religion's language was Latin. Given these various types of contact, it is not surprising that Latin loanwords should infiltrate into many aspects of life. Activity 5E (*Latin loanwords*) gives you the chance to explore these aspects. Why not do this activity now, before reading on.

Given that Augustine and his colleagues were missionaries with a religious intent, it is not surprising that many of the words coming into OE from Latin at that time were related to religion. Activity 5E words in this category are: *angel*, *anthem*, *abbot*, and *shrive*. Latin also had its influence on education and academia, with monks often teaching other subjects as well as religion. This gave words like *verse*, *school*, *(school)master*. There are other words in the activity showing that Latin reached into more general aspects of everyday life, with names for trees and plants (*lily* and *pine*, for example), as well as for food – *radish*, *mussel*, *oyster* and *lobster*. This last is from the Latin *locusta* meaning 'locust'; it came to apply to the crustacean because of a similarity in shape with the locust. The activity also contains the names of some animals (*cock*, *trout*, *turtle dove*), as well as tools and implements (*fork*, *pen* and *sickle*).

There is more than one way of borrowing a word, and one interesting method is called **loan-translation**, to form what are known as **calques** – literal translations. We have many of these in PDE. The phrase *devil's advocate* is a direct translation of the Latin *advocatus diaboli*. Similarly, we have *Stormtroopers* from the German *Sturmtruppen*, *blue blood* from the Spanish *sangre azul*, and the French *marché aux puces* has come straight into English as *flea market*. Perhaps you can think of some more in English or your mother tongue, using the internet or other resources to help.

Calques were popular in OE, perhaps because they involved stretching native resources rather than introducing foreign-sounding words into the language. Many of the calques came from Latin. So *benevolens* – literally 'well-wishing' – became OE *wellwillende*, and *unicornis* ('one horn') became *ānhorn*. It is interesting that in the case of both these examples, later ages were not so reluctant to adopt foreign loanwords directly: *benevolent* came in the fifteenth century, and *unicorn* in the fourteenth.

Like many borrowings, calques often help to express new ideas that have recently come to people's attention. This is what happened in OE with the introduction of Christianity, when many new concepts needed to find words. Hence we have Latin *evangelium* calqued as *gōdspel* ('good message', not 'God's message'), *trinitas* as *þrīnes* ('threeness'), *patriarcha* as *hēahfæder* ('high father'), and *Spiritus Sanctus* as *Hālig Gāst* ('Holy Ghost').

It can happen that when a borrowed word first enters the language it has to work hard to be accepted. One sign that a word has 'made it' is that the native word-formation strategies we saw earlier in this chapter start to be applied to it. It becomes a 'normal' word, and can form compounds, take affixes, become different parts of speech. You can see this process of 'anglicization' at work with many Latin borrowings. As an example, take the OE word *regol* meaning 'rule' or 'regulation', as well as a 'ruler' (the measuring instrument). It comes from the Latin *regula*, which had the same meanings. Once *regol* came into OE, compounds started to be formed. There are nouns like *regolbryce* ('breach of rules'), *regolweard* ('regulator'), *prēostregol* ('canonical rule'), and *rihtregol* ('canon'). There are also adjectives: *regolfæst* ('rigid'), *regollīc* ('according to rules'). There is also a verb *regolian*, which means 'to draw lines with a ruler'. *Regol* had made it.

5.3.3 Borrowings from Old Norse

We have just seen that a common function of Latin loanwords was to fill 'semantic gaps' – providing words for new concepts, many related to the 'new' religion, Christianity. Another language which gave English new words was Old Norse (ON), or 'Scandinavian' – the language spoken by the Vikings. As we saw in 3.1, these people arrived in the eighth century, and in the ninth, England was divided into Anglo-Saxon and 'Danelaw' territory. The two communities lived side by side for a long time, and once all the raping and pillaging was over, they actually got along quite well, having as they did similar ethnic roots.

In the case of Latin, the language's prestige was an important factor leading to linguistic borrowing. With ON, a more important factor was closeness, both in terms of ethnicity and of contact, and this created the conditions in which linguistic borrowings occurred. By and large, the ON loanwords were common words, describing things that the Anglo-Saxons were already familiar with – and already had words for. Very often, then, it was not a question of filling in semantic gaps, but of providing alternative ways of saying things that could already be said. Take, for example, the notion of 'feeling annoyance'. OE had the word *wrāð* (PDE *wrath*) to express this. There was also an ON word, *angr* meaning 'trouble', 'affliction', and this came into English, eventually meaning the same as our PDE word *anger*. We can call pairs of words like *wrath* and *anger* **synonym word-pairs**. Table 5.3 shows some more PDE synonym pairs derived from OE and ON. Notice that although all the pairs are semantically connected, they do not always mean anything like the same thing. *Shirts* and *skirts* are an example; it is likely that the etymological origin meant something like 'short garment', but today they refer to quite different items of clothing.

Table 5.3 Some synonym word-pairs

OE derived	ON derived
sick	*ill*
shirt	*skirt*
rear	*raise*
hide	*skin*
ditch	*dike*
rise	*raise*
craft	*skill*

Notice that three of the ON-derived words here begin with the prefix *sk-*. Many words in PDE with this prefix have ON origins, and often there is an OE equivalent which uses *sh-* instead. As well as *shirt* and *skirt*, we have *shin/skin*, *ship/skipper* (a 'shipper' – ship's captain), and *shatter/scatter* (this last word is written 'sc-' and not 'sk-', but the 'c' is pronounced /k/). We find other synonym word-pairs based on similar sound differences. Our PDE *church* comes from the OE word *cirice* (you'll recall from 4.2.1 that the 'c' could be pronounced [tʃ]). ON did not have this sound, and /k/ was used instead. It gives us *kirk*, the Scots word for 'church'. CW5.3 (*Place names and 's' sounds*) contains some more examples. And talking of place names, in England there are more than 1,400 of them with Scandinavian origins, mostly in the north and east (Danelaw areas). Activity 5F (*Old Norse place names*) invites you to explore some of these.

What happens when a language has two words with roughly the same meaning? One possibility is that one of the words will disappear or be relegated to a regional variety of the language. This latter is what happened in the *kirk* example above. Another example is the ON word *trigg*, which was a synonym word with *true*. It has really gone from the language, though it continued to be used in Northumbrian dialect, at least until the nineteenth century. Yet another example is the ON-related *nay*, a synonym word with *no*. *Nay* has now practically disappeared from standard English, though it does remain in occasional use in northern English dialects (again in 'Viking areas').

Nay and *no* are interesting synonym words because for a long time they existed side by side but were used in slightly different ways. In Shakespeare's time, for example, you could find *nay* used when the preceding statement or question was positive. When it was negative, *no* was used. This passage from *The Merchant of Venice* shows the distinction:

Bassanio: *Well, we shall see your bearing.*
Gratiano: *Nay, but I bar tonight. You shall not gauge me*
              By what we do tonight.
Bassanio: *No, that were pity.*

This illustrates the other solution to the 'two words for one thing' problem. Both the words survive but can develop different uses. This is true of all the synonym word-pairs shown in the table earlier. Sometimes the difference is quite transparent (*shirt* and *skirt* for example), but sometimes it is quite subtle – how, for example, would you characterize the difference between *wrath* and *anger*? You are invited to look through all the synonym pairs given in Table 5.3 and think about the semantic differences between them.

You might say that in the case of *nay* and *no*, both strategies occur. The words were for a while distinguished in use, and then one of them virtually disappeared. Another example is described in CW5.4 (*Niman and take*).

You may have noticed from the past few pages that borrowings often introduced nouns and adjectives, though you certainly do get verbs and adverbs as well. 'Grammatical' words – pronouns, articles and the like – often remain untouched by foreign influences. But there was one 'grammatical' area where ON made quite major and permanent inroads into English. This was with the third person plural pronouns. In PDE these are *they*, *them*, and the possessive *their* – all beginning with 'th'. In OE the forms began with 'h'; they were *hī* for 'they' and 'them', and *hira*, *heora* for 'their'. The 'th' forms were Scandinavian, and they spread down from the north of England, where the Scandinavian influence was greatest. It is interesting to plot their spread southwards. The 'movement towards *th-*' started in the OE period. *They* was accepted quicker than *them* and *their*, and in the *Ormulum*, the twelfth-century East Midlands document mentioned in CW5.4, we find a form of *they* but not *them* or *their*. Even in Chaucer's late fourteenth-century *Canterbury Tales* you find the *th-* form *they* together with the non-*th-* forms of the time: *hem* and *her*. There is one interesting exception. In one of Chaucer's tales, *The Reeve's Tale*, there are two students who come from the north-east of England, and their speech is full of northern characteristics. This includes a *their* form: *A wilde fyr on thair bodyes falle* ('may a wild fire fall of their bodies'), says one of them.

The spread of the *they* forms has several lessons to impart. One is that linguistic movements very often take a long time to complete, and do not always happen at the time you might expect them. Interestingly, as far as ON is concerned, it was after the 1066 Norman Conquest that ON borrowings in English increased. A similar 'delay' occurred with French borrowings. Though the Normans arrived in the eleventh century, it was not until the thirteenth that the quantity of French loanwords became significant. Another lesson is that one common direction of travel for new forms in English is north to south: we shall be meeting this again in the future. A third one is that for such fundamental grammatical forms as personal pronouns to have infiltrated from ON to OE, the contact between Scandinavian and Anglo-Saxon peoples must have been particularly intimate.

Another important fact about ON and OE is that the two languages, both being Germanic, had much in common. So much so that there was a degree of mutual intelligibility between them. So when an ON speaker met an OE speaker – a circumstance that will have happened many times on a daily basis – each could speak their native language and expect a degree of understanding. This is just what often happens today between speakers of Swedish, Danish and Norwegian. It may also have been that the constant interaction between the two groups of speakers led them to 'simplify' their speech a little to make themselves more comprehensible. This may well have been a contributory reason for something we will find in the next chapter, that OE grammar became 'simpler' – just in some respects and just to some extent – over time. This often happens when speakers of different languages are forced into contact, and the result can be the development of what is called a **pidgin** language, or a **creole**. It has in fact been argued that Middle English was a kind of creole, developed through the contact of OE and ON. To learn more about pidgins and creoles, and about this claim relating to English, take a look at CW5.5 (*Was English a creole?*).

Whether or not OE developed into a creole, it is valuable to appreciate that the linguistic situation of the time was a fluid one, with influences coming from various directions. CW5.6 (*Here lies Gunni*) gives another example of this.

ON died out in England by the eleventh century. But a version of it did continue to be spoken in the islands of Orkney and Shetland (to the north of the British mainland) until the seventeenth century. This version of the language was called 'Norn'. It is claimed that there are still some Orkney dialect words which show remnants of Norn, such as *felkyo* ('witch'), *speir* ('to ask'), and *kye* ('cattle'). You could also say that elements of Old Norse have survived in Tolkien's fictional works (*The Hobbit* and *The Lord of the Rings* were the two mentioned in 4.2.2). Some of the languages he invents for his characters have strong ON influences.[2] Like the rest of us, these characters 'gotta use words when they talk to each other', and their words are often ON. The language lives on in fiction at least.

Activity section

5A   OMG: what's happening to English today?

Electronic communications have led to some interesting areas of vocabulary growth. Here are some relatively new words or expressions in English. Be sure, first, that you know what they mean (the internet will help in cases of difficulty). Then note down the linguistic process involved in their creation (where the words 'come from', that is. Again, you may sometimes need the help of the internet):

LOL (and the plural *LOLz*)	to *unlike/to unfriend* (as used on a social media site like Facebook)
software	*download/upload*
electronic-mail (e-mail)	*blog*
Wikipedia	*OMG*
to google	to *trend* (as in *what's trending?*)
podcast	*disk drive*

And, just to add to the mix, here are a couple of recent words which do not have an electronic connection:

sudoku   *feng shui*

▓ 5BA hoard of *hords*

Here are some of the many OE words containing *hord*, which means 'treasure' as well as 'hoard'. What might they mean? Some clues are given, but you will also need an element of guesswork to do this. But even linguistic guesswork can be useful:

	Words	'Clues'
1	*bōchord*	*bōc* = book
2	*hordcleōfa*	*cleōfa* = cave, chamber
3	*hordweorþung*	*weorþung* = honouring
4	*brēosthord*	*brēost* = mind
5	*feorh-hord*	*feorh* = life
6	*grēothord*	*grēot* = earth (think 'grit')
7	*mōdhord*	*mōd* = spirit (associated with PDE 'mood')

▓ 5C   Some OE compounds

(a) Here are some OE compounds. Try to guess what they might mean. A glossary underneath gives you the meanings of some of the constituent parts. If you need further help, a list of the PDE meanings of the compounds is then given, with the words in a different order from the original list:

baec-hūs	*hunigswēte*	*wīdcūð*	*fōtādl*
geond-drencan	*woruldsnotor*	*scipwered*	*æfterfolgian*
ingang	*wīfmann*	*ærbeðoht*	*welgelīcwyrðe*
ealdfæder	*etelond*	*wīdsæ*	*mōdcræftig*
ofersceatt			

▓ Glossary

ādl, n. disease
cræftig, adj. strong
eald, adj. ancient
gang, n. journey
līcwyrðe, adj. pleasing
snotor, adj. clever
wīf, n. woman, female

bacan, v. bake
cūð, adj. known
etan, v. eat
geond, prep. over
mōd, n. mind
wered, n. company

beðencan, v. consider
drencan, v. drink
folgian, v. follow
hunig, adj. honey
sceatt, n. payment
wīde, adv. widely

PDE meanings

woman   gout   crew   bakery
pasture land   forefather   ocean   interest
entrance   premeditated   intelligent   world-wise
mellifluous   acceptable   celebrated   get drunk
succeed

(b) One way of categorizing compounds is in terms of 'constituent' and 'resulting' parts. The constituent parts of *word-hoard*, for example, are both nouns, and the result is another noun; it is 'noun + noun = noun'. The same is true of *word stock*. As another example, the first word in this activity, *baec-hūs*, is a verb plus a noun, forming a noun: verb + noun = noun. Go through the other words above categorizing them in the same way. Look closely at what you find; is there any generalization that may be made about the way the constituent parts relate to the 'result'?

(c) You may like to think of examples of these categories in PDE. Think, for example, of some 'noun + noun = noun' compounds in PDE, and so on.

5D   Exploring prefixes

Here are some common OE prefixes, with examples chosen to suggest some of their meanings. In many cases, the examples will provide no more than suggestions, and you are likely to finish the activity with 'hypotheses' rather than 'facts'. These prefixes are discussed in the text.

(i)   *be-*

There are two common meanings of this prefix.

Examples of the first:

begān = surround   *berīdan* = ride round, surround
bebūgan = flow around   *behindan* (preposition) = behind, back

Examples of the second:

bedælan = deprive   *behēafdian* = behead
behādian = defrock (a priest; *hādian* = ordain)

(ii)   *for-*

forbærnan = destroy by fire   *forheard* = very hard
forrotian = rot away   *forbītan* = bite through

/ = reject   *wiþfeohtend* = enemy
ʌn = contradict   *wiþgān* = act in opposition to
ʃan = hold out against *wiþstandan* = withstand

(ı., *un-*

There are three common meanings of this prefix.

Examples of the first:

unfriþ = war (*friþ* = peace)   *unhold* = unfriendly (*hold* = friendly)
unbrād = narrow (*brād* = broad) *unbliss* = sorrow (*bliss* = happiness)

Examples of the second:

ungiefu = evil gift   *unweder* = bad weather
undǣd = evil action   *unlagu* = bad law (*lagu* = law)

Examples of the third:

unbindan = unbind   *undōn* = undo
unlūcan = unlock   *untīgan* = untie

(v) *ge-*

geāscian = learn by asking   *gewinnan* = get by fighting
geæfnan = perform, accomplish *gesiglan* = accomplish a journey by sail

5E Latin loanwords

Here are some of the modern English words that came into OE from Latin, many at the time of the introduction of Christianity. Some scholars have categorized Latin loans into distinct groups; Durkin (2014) has over seventeen categories. One category, for example, is 'articles of clothing', and it includes the words *belt*, *cap* and *sock*.

Look through this list of words and identify six other categories. These are mentioned in the text. Incidentally, as with most categorizations, you will find items that will fit into more than one category; this is not something to worry about or agonize over:

angel	radish	lily	anthem	verse (in poetry)
school	abbot	cock	fork	(school)master
mussel	shrive	pine	oyster	turtle dove
sickle	trout	pen	lobster	

5F Old Norse place names

Places, particularly in the Danelaw area, often carry Old Norse names. Here are some ON suffixes which are particularly common in the north and east of England. They are in boldface in these six place names:

Grims**by**	Grime**thorpe**	Mickle**thwaite**
Lowe**stoft**	Trout**beck**	Swale**dale**

Use the internet (or some other source) to find out what these suffixes mean. Find the mentioned places on a map.

Answer section

Celtic words in 5.3.1

The matchings are: a/3; b/2; c/6; d/4; e/1; f/8; g/9; h/5; i/7; j/10

Further reading

Townend (2006) provides an excellent and approachable study of the multilingual context of the Anglo-Saxon period.

Kastovsky (1992) offers good broad coverage of the areas dealt with in this chapter.

Durkin (2014) is a scholarly history of loanwords in English, covering all periods dealt with in this book.

Notes

1 This example, together with some others in this section, are taken from the B-T dictionary.
2 The claim about Orkney dialect words is made on the website www.orkneyjar.com/orkney/ nornprayer.htm. To read about Tolkien's invented languages, take a look at https:// en.wikipedia.org/wiki/Languages_constructed_by_J._R._R._Tolkien.

6 OE grammar

A 'jungle of endings'

This chapter is about OE grammar. The language made great use of grammatical suffixes, or inflections, so this will be a main topic. In nouns and adjectives these give information about case, number and gender. OE verbs could also be inflectionally complex, and there were many different classes of them – some called 'weak' and some 'strong'. At the end of the chapter we look at word order, which in OE was less rigid than it is in PDE. We discuss one reason for this.

Some languages, like OE, are highly inflected, meaning that they use grammatical suffixes a lot. Is your L1 highly inflected? List some examples of your L1's inflections. Think also about word order in your L1. Identify some different word orders that your L1 uses. Answer these questions even if your L1 is English.

This chapter mentions quite a few grammatical concepts. Though the text sometimes supplies explanations, it would be useful to know something about these in advance. These include:

- various parts of speech: nouns, adjectives, articles, pronouns, adverbs, conjunctions;
- grammatical case. What is a case? What do the words nominative, accusative, genitive, dative mean?
- some concepts to do with verbs: what a tense is; the present and past tenses in English; what present and past participles are.

On a website about the learning of Latin, one teacher reports that his students 'seem to get lost in a jungle of endings'.[1] OE also has a 'jungle of endings' to get lost in. Our journey into this jungle leads us straight into its densest part: nouns and adjectives. We are going to find that in terms of endings, or **inflections**, OE is far more complex than PDE.

But we have to be very careful when we talk about language complexity. It is easy to be tempted into statements about one language being overall 'more complex' than another. But you often find that when Language A seems simpler than Language B in one aspect, Language B turns out to be simpler in some other way. For this reason, it is important that statements about complexity or simplicity must specify what aspect is being considered. We cannot really say that OE is overall more complex, or more simple, than PDE. What we can say is that in terms of inflections, OE has a more complex system than PDE.

6.1 Into the dense jungle: noun phrases

'Noun' is a grammatical concept you are probably familiar with, but you are possibly less so with the idea of a 'noun phrase' (often shortened to NP). Nouns are usually just one word. In the sentence *Nuns eat lettuces*, both the subject and object are nouns standing alone (*nuns* and *lettuces*). But often the subject or object of a sentence will be a phrase – including a noun but with other elements too. So in *Young nuns eat lettuces on which the devil occasionally sits*, the subject NP is *young nuns*, and the object is *lettuces on which the devil occasionally sits*. When discussing grammar we will often find ourselves needing to talk about NPs rather than just nouns. For example, the passive version of our second sentence is *Lettuces on which the devil occasionally sits are eaten by young nuns*. To form this passive, we move the object noun phrase (*lettuces on which...*) to the front. We apply the operation to the whole NP, not just to the noun *lettuce*.

6.1.1 Noun and adjective inflections in PDE

Chapter 3 (3.3) ended with the idea that OE is 'suffix-rich'. To explore this richness, it will be useful to spend some time contrasting OE with PDE, which is not at all rich in grammatical suffixes, and looking at what roles suffixes play in a language. Here are some PDE sentences to think about:

(a) *The young nun ate the lettuce.*
(b) *The devil attacked the young nun.*
(c) *The priest spoke to the young nun.*
(d) *The devil sat on the young nun's lettuce.*
(e) *The young nuns had a garden.*
(f) *She was the youngest nun in the nunnery.*

Concentrate on the nouns and adjectives in these sentences. Notice when they have suffixes and, equally importantly, when they do not. What role do the suffixes play? What are they there for? Do this before reading on.

Only the last three sentences have noun and adjective inflections. In (d) the -'s on *nun* indicates possession – it is 'the lettuce of the nun'. The case which expresses possession is known as the **genitive**, and we may say that in PDE -'s is a genitive inflection. In the first three sentences, *nun* is shown in other cases – the **nominative** (for the subject) in (a), the **accusative** (for the direct object) in (b), and the **dative** (for the indirect object) in (c).[2] There is no inflection on *nun* in any of these. So we can say that, as far as PDE nouns are concerned, the only **case inflection** is for the genitive.

But there is one other noun inflection in the sentences. It is in (e), where *nun* takes a final *-s*. This time the *-s* indicates plurality: *nun* = one nun, *nuns* = more than one. Singular and plural are referred to as **number**, and we can say that in PDE the noun inflection indicating plurality is usually *-s*. Usually, yes, but not always; perhaps you can think of some exceptions in PDE.

Looking now at the adjective *young*, the only inflection found is in (f). It is *-est*. This ending carries the idea of 'the most', and is referred to in grammar as the **superlative** form. There is in fact one other adjective inflection in PDE, not shown in our sentences. It is the **comparative** form *-er*, and it carries the idea of 'the more'. Notice that there are no other adjective inflections in our sentences. In fact, adjectives are not inflected for either case or number in PDE: nominative, accusative, genitive, dative, singular and plural; they are all the same.

All in all, we can conclude that noun and adjective inflections in PDE are very small in number. OE could not be more different. Before we look at OE inflections in detail, read through the 'lettuce story' in 4.3. Focus first on *nun*, *devil* and *lettuce*. You will find the OE nouns used in different cases. Identify the various forms, and say what cases are involved. Make sure you include genitives: there are two examples in the passage. Then look at the few adjectives in the story, and say where possible what cases they show.

6.1.2 'To the silly stones': noun and adjective inflections in OE

When I was learning Latin at school, we tackled noun inflections by learning lists of nouns with their various case endings. If you stopped to think what you were actually saying, it usually turned out to be something quite bizarre. *Mensa* was 'table', in the nominative; *mensae* was the dative, 'to the table', and – most bizarre of all – you even learned that the way to address a table (using the **vocative** case) was *mensa*, roughly translated into English as 'O table!' The image produced in the schoolboy imagination was of Romans dressed in togas holding long conversations with tables. But though the lists were semantically bizarre, they were full of grammar.

The same can be said about Table 6.1. It sets out some OE noun and adjective inflections. *Dola* in the table means 'silly'; *stān* is 'stone', *giefu*, 'gift', and *eāge*, 'eye'. The first word in each phrase is part of the definite article ('the' in PDE). 'Noun patterns' like these are called **declensions**. There is plenty of grammar in the table, but there is also bizarreness in plenty: *þǣm dolum stānum*, for example, means 'to the silly stones'; not a phrase OE speakers were likely to have uttered that often.

Look at the table and make sure you understand what it is showing, what the abbreviations mean, what each column and row contains. The dimensions you need to be thinking in terms of are case, number and gender.

Notice first how complex it all is, and how much grammar you need to know in order to produce a noun phrase in OE. Note particularly that adjectives as well as nouns change according to case, number and gender. As we have seen, PDE is much more inflectionally straightforward. But you may have come across

Table 6.1 Some OE noun and adjective declensions

		Masculine	Feminine	Neuter
Sing	N	se dola stān	þæt dole giefu	sēo dole ēage
	A	þone dolan stān	þæt dole giefe	þā dolan ēage
	G	þæs dolan stānes	þæs dolan giefe	þǣre dolan ēagan
	D	þǣm dolan stāne	þǣm dolan giefe	þǣre dolan ēagan
Plur	N	þā dolan stānas	þā dolan giefa	þā dolan ēagan
	A	þā dolan stānas	þā dolan giefa	þā dolan ēagan
	G	þāra dolra (dolena) stāna	þāra dolra (dolena) giefa	þāra dolra (dolena) ēagena
	D	þǣm dolum stānum	þǣm dolum giefum	þǣm dolum ēagum

similar complexity in another language. In German, for example, if a noun is nominative feminine plural, an accompanying adjective will have a nominative feminine plural inflection, and that inflection is likely to be different from (for example) the accusative, masculine singular one. Table 6.1 shows that OE was like German in this respect; and like Latin, with its 'jungle of endings'.

To come to terms with the details: think first about *nouns* and *case*. Notice that the noun inflection sometimes changes according to case. Note that in one declension the singular nominative and accusative are different, and that in other declensions, the accusative and dative are different. Then consider adjective forms; try to make statements generalizing how OE adjectives act in relation to case.

Then focus on *number*. Again our table shows that OE noun inflections for number are very much more numerous than in PDE. Note that the noun plural forms are different for each declension; also that they (as with singular nouns) change for the various cases. So, for example, the dative singular of *stān* is different from the dative plural; take a look at the table and identify these two forms. The adjectives are a little less complex, but remain a good deal more so than in PDE.

The other dimension is *gender*. As the table shows, OE nouns are categorized as masculine, feminine and neuter, and these are marked by different inflection patterns. How do adjectives behave in relation to gender? All in all, the OE gender system is a little alien to us today. Have a look now at CW6.1 (*Male stones and female doors*), which is all about it.

6.1.3 More declensions, more complexities

We have seen that the OE noun phrase was a complex beast. In fact, it was much more complex than we have shown. For one thing, Table 6.1 has just three declensions, but there were many more besides. The example of a neuter noun we gave was *ēage* ('eye'). We came across another neuter noun – *scip* – in the 'dead reeve passage'. It had an altogether different declension. Activity 6A (*Nominative and accusative ships*) gives you the chance to construct this declension from examples provided.

Adjectives were also more complex than Table 6.1 shows. In fact, there were two adjectival forms. The table gives the **weak** or **definite** form. This was used when the adjective followed a definite article, a demonstrative, or a possessive. When an adjective had none of these items in front of it, an altogether different, **strong** (or **indefinite**) form was used. Examples of weak sequences in PDE are: *the old man*, and *my old friend*, which in OE would be *se ealda mann, mīn ealda frēond*. Strong forms are found in: *an old man, old men (an eald mann, ealde menn)*. If you want to compare strong and weak declensions in detail, there is an entire strong declension at CW6.2 (*A strong OE adjective*).

Another difference between PDE and OE relates to pronouns. In PDE we have just singular and plural, but in PIE (Proto-Indo-European) there was also a **dual** number. This was used when just two entities were being referred to. The plural was reserved for 'more than two.' Some languages like Ancient Greek maintained the distinction, and it was also present in OE, but only really for first and second person pronouns. The forms *wit* and *git* meant 'we two' and 'you two'. For more than two, *we* and *ge* (the forerunner of Middle English *ye*) were used. Like grammatical gender, dual number in English was on the way out by the end of the OE period.

Then, finally, there is the humble definite article: humble at least in PDE, where there is just one form – *the*. But look at its forms in Table 6.1. It changes according to case, number and gender. It was quite a skill to be able to say *the* in OE. Let alone *to the silly stones*.

6.1.4 Complex, but becoming simpler: syncretism

OE's inflectional complexity comes from PG (Proto-Germanic), and ultimately from PIE. In fact, the number of cases potentially carrying different endings was larger in these earlier languages. They had not four but eight cases in both singular and plural – the other ones being **vocative** (used to address a person – or a table! – see the beginning of 6.1.2), **ablative** (expressing a variety of notions, including 'motion away'), **locative** (expressing 'place where') and **instrumental** (expressing a means). Take a look at Activity 6B (*A Proto-Germanic adjective*), which allows you to compare a PG adjectival declension with an OE one. Of course, looking at just one adjectival declension can be extremely misleading, but the comparison does suggest that while OE was a highly inflectional language, PG was even more so. The activity shows ten different forms in the strong version of OE *dola*, and five for the weak. The PG adjective *blindaz* has no fewer than fifteen strong forms.

Inflectional complexity was certainly an important feature of OE. But equally important is the fact that, over time, a process of inflectional simplification was taking place. In this significant way, OE stands between inflectionally more complex PG and inflectionally simple PDE. With this perspective in mind, take another look at the declensions in Table 6.1. This time notice, not differences, but similarities. Activity 6C (*Similarities, not differences*) suggests some specific points for you to consider.

The activity shows considerable overlap across noun cases. They show that the inflectional system was simplifying. The word used to describe this is **syncretism,** defined in the *Shorter Oxford English Dictionary* as 'the merging of different inflectional varieties of a word during the development of a language'. We shall find examples of syncretism at various points in this book; it is the process which plays a central role in making PDE the inflectionally simple language that it is today. Syncretism also plays a role in the loss of grammatical gender discussed in CW6.1.

But why does syncretism occur? Section 4.2.3 (in Chapter 4) suggests one answer – that the initial word stress of OE focused attention away from the ends of words, thus decreasing the importance that suffixes played. It is a theme we will return to later.

We are now about to move on to verbs. But, to cleanse the palate after mouthfuls of NP endings, and before the next course of verb inflections, here is a sorbet.

6.1.5   A riddle for a sorbet

The Anglo-Saxons liked riddles. One large collection of manuscripts, the Exeter Book, contains ninety-five of them. Tolkien produces some of his own in his fictional writing – in *The Hobbit*, for example.

OE riddles are mostly based on a 'tell me who or what I am' formula. The first person is usually used, and the riddle asks 'who or what am I?' The imagery is often vivid, and there are plenty of poetic compound nouns. The riddles are also full of double entendres; often something obscene seems to be being described, though the 'answer' given turns out to be innocent, and not obscene at all.

Read through this riddle once and write a list of the words whose meanings you can guess. Then use the translation below it to try and work out the answer to the 'what am I?' question. The *Answer section* will reveal all (**AS**).

Ic eom lēgbysig,   lāce mid winde,
bewunden mid wuldre,   wedre gesomnad,
fūs forðweges,   fȳre gebysgad,
bearu blōwende,   byrnende glēd.
Ful oft mec gesiþas   sendað æfter hondum,
þæt mec weras ond wīf   wlonce cyssað.
þonne ic mec onhæbbe,   ond hī onhnīgaþ tō mē
monige mid miltse,   þǣr ic monnum sceal
ȳcan ūpcyme   eadignesse.

'I am flame-busy, I play with the wind, wrapped in splendour, at one with the sky, eager to move forward, troubled by fire, a blooming grove, a burning ember. Very often companions pass me from hand to hand that men and women may kiss me proudly; then I rise up, and they bow to me. I increase their happiness, many with humility where I shall increase men's happiness'.

6.2 Verbs

6.2.1 Regular and irregular in PDE

Are PDE verbs as inflectionally simple as PDE nouns? To find out, we need to think about verb **conjugations**, the verb equivalent of noun declensions – you **decline** a noun, but **conjugate** a verb. Here are two PDE verb conjugations. What do they tell you? Table 6.2 shows a present and past participle. Do these terms mean anything to you? Look also at what the table shows you about verb suffixes in PDE; how many are there? When are they used?

Table 6.2 PDE verb conjugations

	Regular	Irregular
Present	work	sing
I	work	sing
You	work	sing
He, she, it	works	sings
we, you, they	work	sing
participle	working	singing
Past		
I	worked	sang
You	worked	sang
He, she, it	worked	sang
We, you, they	worked	sang
participle	worked	sung

The table shows, in the leftmost column, the different **persons** (*I*, *you* and so on). It also shows two **tenses**, known as the **present** and the **past**. The use of these tenses is complex, but as a working (over-)generalization we may say the present is used for present actions (*He works in London*), and the past for past actions (*He worked in London*). The **present** and **past participles** are used in other verb constructions; the present continuous aspect (as in *He is singing*) is described in 19.4.1, and the perfect aspect (*She has worked*), in 10.2.6. You can see that the verb patterns in Table 6.2 are inflectionally quite simple. There is only one person in the present that takes an inflection – an *-s* is used for *he*, *she* and *it* (the **third person singular**). The past remains completely unaltered according to person: the form for *I* is the same as the form for *they*. But there is one quite big difference between the conjugations for *work* and *sing*. Identify this before you read on.

Work can be described as a **regular verb** because the basic form of the present and past is the same. The only difference is that the past form adds the suffix *-ed*. But with *sing* the basic form changes: the past has a different vowel – *sing* becomes *sang*; and in the past participle, the vowel changes again – it is *sung*.

Because of these complications, we call *sing* an **irregular** verb. As we are about to see, OE has a distinction which is like (though not exactly the same as) the regular/irregular one. The terms used are **weak** and **strong**. *Work* is a weak verb, *sing* a strong one.

6.2.2 OE conjugations

Table 6.3 gives the same information for OE as Table 6.2 does for PDE. Take an initial look at it to be sure you are clear about what it shows. You might also like to record some preliminary impression about how Tables 6.2 and 6.3 compare. How, in other words, PDE and OE verbs are alike and unlike.

Table 6.3 Some OE verbs

	Weak		Strong	
Present	Hiēran (to hear)	Lufian (to love)	Bindan (to bind)	Crēopan (to creep)
ic	hīere	lufie	binde	crēope
þū	hiēst	lufast	bindst	crȳpest
hē, hēo, hit	hiērð	lufað	bindð	crȳpeð
wē, gē, hī	hiērað	lufiað	bindað	crēopað
participle	hiērende	lufiende	bindende	crēopende
Past				
ic	hiērde	lufode	band	crēap
þū	hiērdest	lufodest	bunde	crēape
hē, hēo, hit	hiērde	lufode	band	crēap
wē, gē, hī	hiērden	lufodon	bundon	crupon
participle	gehiēred	gelufod	gebunden	gecropen

The table's leftmost column will probably cause you no problems. The words *ic*, *þū*, *hē* are the persons, equivalent to PDE *I*, *you*, *he*. You came across several of these OE forms in the 'lettuce story'.

Concentrate now on the second and third columns. They give the forms associated with so-called weak verbs from two different classes. They show that 'he loves', for example, would be *hē lufað*, and 'they heard', *hī hiērden*. You may like to write down the different inflections associated with the different persons. The first person singular, *ic* form, has an *-e* ending, for example; what about the other persons? Because the two verbs come from different classes, there are slight differences between them; it is worth identifying what these are. The *Answer section* gives the various person inflections and the differences between the classes (**AS**).

Notice that in OE the past participle carries a prefix as well as a suffix; it is *ge-*. CW6.3 (*ge-*, *a 'completive prefix'*) talks about this. But the main point is how much more complex the system of verbal inflections is in OE, as compared to PDE. In fact, there are three main types of OE weak verb, and no fewer than seven classes of strong verb. We shall see later that (as with nouns and adjectives) there are signs of syncretism in OE verb conjugations. These help to move the system towards the inflectional simplicity we enjoy in PDE; but there is still a long way to go.

6.2.3 Strong verbs

Table 6.2's example of a PDE irregular (or strong) verb was *sing*. Verbs like this can cause problems for us, even today. I have just googled 'what is the difference between *sang* and *sung*?' and got 418 hits. The irregularity of the verb, with its changing vowel (from 'i' to 'a' to 'u') confuses people. Just in case these forms confuse you too, look at Table 6.2 to confirm what the difference is.

Strong verbs, because irregular, are particularly troublesome. The fourth and fifth columns of Table 6.3 contain two OE examples – *bindan* and *crēopan*. Before reading on, take a look at how these verbs differ from the weak verbs, and also from each other.

One inflectional difference between weak and strong shows up in the past singular, where the first and third persons of the strong verbs do not have an inflection, and there is an *-e* in the second person. But the heart of strong verbs is to do with the vowels in the base, or root, part of the word. There is very often more than one root vowel change in the conjugation. In the case of *bindan*, for example, the 'i' in the infinitive stays throughout the present, but in the past you find an 'a' for the first and third persons singular (*band*), and a 'u' for the other forms. The past participle keeps the 'u'. *Crēopan* is even more complicated, and there are five, not three, vowels involved: 'ēo', 'ȳ' 'ēa', 'u' and 'o'. In fact, strong verbs are usually described in terms of four parts: the infinitive, the third person singular past, the past plurals, and the past participle. For *crēopan* this gives: *crēopan, crēap, crupon, gecropen.*[3] What does it give for *bindan*? And what about the PDE verb *sing*?

Where do these vowel changes come from? They involve a linguistic process which takes us back to PIE. It is called **ablaut**, and was in fact one of the features that alerted nineteenth-century linguists to the similarities between many western languages and Sanskrit (we discussed this in 2.2). The term 'ablaut' was first used by Jacob Grimm (he of the fairy tales; 2.4 talks about him), and it describes regular vowel variations (or **gradations** as they are called), like the sequences we have seen here: 'ēo'→'ēa'→'u'→'o' in *crēopan*, and 'i'→'a'→'u' in *bindan*. Vowel gradations are most obvious in strong verbs, but you also find them linking verbs and nouns. For example, in PDE we have the verb forms *strike* and *struck*, but also the connected noun *stroke*, with another vowel. Our PDE verb *sing* is similar; along with *sing*, *sang* and *sung*, the noun *song* adds yet another vowel. Try to think of some more examples of vowel gradations in PDE; irregular/strong verbs will most readily come to mind, but you might also find some verb–noun gradations too.

We have mentioned that there are seven main classes of OE strong verbs. Here they are:

Table 6.4 The seven OE strong verb classes

Class	Infinitive	Past singular	Past plural	Past participle
I	rīdan ('ride')	rād	ridon	geriden
II	clēofan ('cleave')	clēaf	clufon	geclofen
IIIa	findan ('find')	fand	fundon	gefunden
IIIb	helpan ('help')	healp	hulpon	geholpen
IV	stelan ('steal')	stæl	stǣlon	gestolen
V	tredan ('tread')	træd	trǣdon	getreden
VI	scacan ('shake')	scōc	scōcon	gescacen
VII	blōwan ('blow')	blēow	blēowon	geblōwen

To what classes do *bindan* and *crēopan* belong? If you would like to develop a clearer idea of how vowel gradation works, write down the sequence for each class. For example, Class I has 'ī'→ 'ā'→ 'i' → 'i', as in *rīdan, rād, ridon, geriden*. By the way, the past participial *-en* inflection has not completely disappeared from PDE. Sometimes it remains in a participle, as in *broken*, and sometimes it appears in adjectives, like *drunken*. Think of some more *-en* adjectives in PDE; for some (though not all), you may be able to associate them with verbs.

We have already seen that there are strong verbs in PDE. To explore this more, look at CW6.4 (*PDE 'strong' verbs*), which considers PDE vowel sequences in verbs, and contains an activity.

If you want to continue to look at OE verbs, 4.3's 'lettuce story' can reveal a little more. Start by making a list of the story's verbs. Then:

(a) Find examples of infinitives, to confirm what you have already read, that they mostly end with *-an*.
(b) There are quite a few words beginning with *ge-*, though not all of them are past participles. Identify the ones which are.
(c) Find examples of third person singular past-tense forms ending in *-te* or *-de*.
(d) One of the ways of recognizing strong verbs is that they do not have these *-te* or *-de* endings. Find some examples of what look like strong verbs in the story.

The *Answer section* contains comments on each of these points (**AS**).

To finish this section, take a look at CW6.5 *(To be: a 'badly mixed-up verb')*. It is about a verb which, from many points of view, is a very 'special' one indeed.

6.3   Word order

Word order is very important in PDE. You could say it is a question of life and death in these PDE examples:

(a)   *The hunter killed the ox*
(b)   *The ox killed the hunter*

In (a) *the hunter* is the sentence's subject (in case terms it is the nominative). That tells us he is the one that does the killing. But in (b), *the hunter* is the object, and this time he ends up dead. How do we know? The difference is not shown by any inflection (it is the same word *hunter* each time). It is shown by word order. In PDE, the subject usually comes before the verb, and the object after. So in (a) we know that the hunter (mentioned before the verb) does the killing, and the ox (mentioned after the verb) is killed.

In OE, inflections often carry some of the information conveyed by word order in PDE. Sentence (a) would be *hunta abrēoteð oxan* in OE. It is the *-a* inflection on *hunta* that tells us the word is the subject of the sentence, and hence does the killing. If the hunter were the object, the word would be *huntan*, with the accusative *-an* inflection. In the same way, we know that *the ox* is not the subject, because the OE nominative form is *oxa*, not *oxan*. Because inflections carry this information, word order is not so important in OE as it is in PDE. In fact, all the word orders in sentences (c) to (f) would be possible in OE, and they would all mean the same thing. It is the hunter that kills, and the ox that dies every time. The word order in (c) is Subject-Verb-Object (SVO); in (d) it is Verb-Subject-Object (VSO); in (e) it is SOV, and in (f), OVS:

(c)   *Hunta abrēoteð oxan*   (d)   *Abrēoteð hunta oxan*
(e)   *Hunta oxan abrēoteð*   (f)   *Oxan abrēoteð hunta*

Our example sentences show how much flexibility there was in OE word order. In PDE, by far the most common order is SVO, as shown in sentences (a) and (b). What about in OE? Though the order OVS found in (f) is theoretically possible, it does not in fact occur in OE to any extent. But the other three – SVO, VSO and SOV – are there. The 'lettuce story' shows this clearly. Spend a moment going through the story to find examples of each of these three orders; if you try this, you will need to consider indirect objects as well as direct objects under the category 'O' for 'object'.

So OE's word-order flexibility is possible because it is inflections that express the grammatical relations we have been discussing. To realize the importance of this to the development of English, it helps to make the same point the other way round: as inflections disappeared from the language, fixed word order became important to express those grammatical relations that had previously been expressed inflectionally. This important point is developed in 10.2.4.

The 'lettuce story' also gives an idea of how frequent the various orders are in OE. There are very few examples of the order which is so common in PDE: SVO. *An nunne ... eōde inn on hyra wyrttūn* ('a nun ... went into her garden'), and *Ic sæt mē on ānum leāhtrice* ('I sat me on a lettuce') are two. There are a few more instances of the VSO order. *Þā geseah heō ǣnne leāhtric* ('there saw she a lettuce') is an example. In PDE we would have SVO: 'there she saw a lettuce', or 'she saw a lettuce there'. What may surprise you is that by far the most common order is SOV. It is found in *Heō þā hine genam* ('she then it took'), and also in *faeder Equitio … wæs gebeden þæt hē … mid his gebedum hire gehulpe* ('Father Equitius was asked that he with his prayers her help').

When were the various OE word-order possibilities used? VS(O) – Verb-Subject, with or without a following Object – quite often occurred when a sentence began with an adverb, particularly *þā* ('then' or 'where'). The example we have just seen is *þā geseah heō ǣnne leāhtric*. 'VS(O) after an adverb' is still sometimes found in Shakespeare. For example, Hotspur in *Henry IV, Part 1*, says *Today will I set forth*. It became less common soon after Shakespeare's time, but there are some remnants of it in PDE. Some adverbs like 'scarcely' absolutely require VS(O). We say *Scarcely had he arrived …* and cannot say **Scarcely he had arrived*. You also find PDE sentences like *Up jumped the man*. As for SOV, one common use was in OE subordinate clauses, often starting with a conjunction like *þæt* ('that'). Hence *faeder Equitio … wæs gebeden þæt hē … mid his gebedum hire gehulpe*. Also, it was often found when the object was a pronoun, as in our earlier example: *Heo þā hine genam* ('she then it took').

The fact that SOV was so common in OE tells us something about the language's parentage and its family relations. 'Remembering to put the verb at the end' is something that people learning German – a family relation to OE – often find difficult to remember, and one of the times this happens in German is in subordinate clauses. In fact, PG (Proto-Germanic) – the common parent of OE and German – was predominantly an 'SOV' language: among those in the world that are called **verb-final languages**. That word order more or less disappeared from English during the Middle English period, though again you do find the odd example in Shakespeare. For example, in *A Midsummer Night's Dream*, Snug the Joiner, dressed up to act in a play, says *Then know that I … Snug the Joiner am*. Between PG's SOV and today's SVO, OE occupies a transitional stage.

Activity section

6A Nominative and accusative ships

(a) The OE for 'ship' is *scip*, and you will recall that 'sc' is pronounced [ʃ]. Here are some PDE sentences containing the word 'ship', together with what the OE form would be. The task is to fill in the table below to show the whole declension for the word *scip*.

The ship arrived.	(scip)
He walked to the ship.	(scipe)
They slept in the ships.	(scipum)
He saw the ship.	(scip)
The ship's sails were huge.	(scipes)
The ships attacked the soldiers.	(scipu)

The ships' sails were huge.   (scipa)

The soldiers attacked the ships.   (scipu)

Singular	N
	A
	G
	D
Plural	N
	A
	G
	D

(b) Two of the nouns in the 'lettuce story' are *deōfol* and *leāhtric*. Both are masculine, and both follow the *stān* model, though (as the form *deōfle* in the story shows) the second 'o' of *deōfol* is dropped when endings are added. Work out the complete declensions for both these nouns (**AS**).

6B   A Proto-Germanic adjective

The PG adjective *blindaz* meant 'blind'. Here are its strong forms.[4] 'I' stands for 'Instrumental', a case mentioned in 6.1.4:

	Masculine		Feminine		Neuter	
	Singular	Plural	Singular	Plural	Singular	Plural
N	blindaz	blindai	blindo	blindoz	blinda	blindo
A	blindano	blindanz	blindo	blindoz	blinda	blindo
G	blindas	blindaizo	blindaizoz	blindaizo	blindas	blindaizo
D	blindammai	blindaimaz	blindazoi	blindaimaz	blindammai	blindaimaz
I	blindana	blindaimiz	blindana	blindaimiz	blindaizō	blindaimiz

Count the number of different forms in these paradigms and compare them with the number of forms preferably in the strong declension of OE *dola*, which you will find in CW6.2.

6C   Similarities, not differences   AS

Some specific points to consider about Table 6.1:

- Look first at the nouns. List points where forms are the same *across case*. For example, the nominative and accusative singular masculine are the same.
- Staying with *case*, do the same for adjectives. For example, the accusative and genitive singulars carry the same suffix.
- Then look at adjectives *across gender*. For example, in all genders the genitive singulars carry the same suffix.

Answer section

The riddle in 6.1.5

The answer is 'tree', or 'wood'. As in much OE poetry, 'tree' has overtones of the Christian cross, and this explains the riddle's last lines.

6.2.2   Person inflections and class differences

Table 6.3 shows that the person inflections are, for the present -e (associated with ic, the 'first person'), -st (with ðū, second person), -ð, and -að (for all plural persons). The past inflections are -de, -dest, -de, -den/-don (for all plural persons). Sometimes you find a 't' instead of a 'd' – so the third person past of cēpan ('to seize') is cēpte. The differences between the classes are that there are vowel changes in the 'lufian class' of verb. The 'i' in first person present lufie becomes an 'a' in the second and third persons. And 'o' makes an appearance in the past.

6.2.3   Verbs in the 'lettuce story'

(a) The story has two -an infinitive forms: clypian and æthrīnan, and there is also the irregular dōn.
(b) Past participial ge- is in gegrīpen, gedreht, gecȳðed, gebeden.
(c) The third person singular past -te or -de endings are found in the forms gelyste, gewite, næfde and dorste.
(d) There are many strong verb forms in the story, including (from just the first few lines) eōde (from gān meaning 'to go'), geseah (from seōn, 'to see'), and genam (from niman, 'to take' – you will recall that this verb made an appearance in Chapter 3's 'dead reeve passage'). The number of such verbs here tells a story – that there were many more strong verbs in OE than there are irregular ones in PDE.

Activity 6A

(b) Here are the declensions with the cases given in the order N, A, G, D:

deōfol, deōfol, deōfles, deōfle; deōflas, deōflas, deōfla, deōflum.

leāhtric, leāhtric, leāhtrices, leāhtrice; leāhtricas, leāhtricas, leāhtrica, leāhtricum.

Activity 6C

Here are some of the similarities: the nominative and accusative masculine singular forms are the same, and this is also true for the neuter. In all genders, the nominative and accusative plurals are the same. In the feminine declension, the accusative, genitive and dative are the same, and so are the nominative, accusative and genitive plural. As for adjectives, the -*an* suffix makes a large number of appearances throughout, and there are quite a few similarities across gender, especially in the masculine and neuter declensions.

Further reading

There are many detailed accounts of the OE language. Hogg's (2002) account is short and accessible.

A longer, more detailed account is found in Mitchell and Robinson (2011).

Notes

1 The website is https://joyfullatinlearning.wordpress.com/tag/exercise/.
2 'Cases' are to do with relationships between words in sentences, and are usually associated with inflections. Since there are so few inflections in PDE noun phrases, it does not mean much to talk about cases in PDE. But words like 'nominative' and 'dative' are useful to us, because they express notions that are associated with inflections in OE.
3 The conjugation of *crēopan* used here is the one found in B-T; some of the forms have variations. Notice that there is a vowel change in the verb's present tense singular, where two persons have 'ȳ'. The vowel gradations associated with ablaut chiefly affect the infinitive, third person singular past, past plural, past participle, and so this vowel change does not appear in the sequence.
4 The forms of the adjective *blindaz* were taken from the Wikipedia entry on Proto-Germanic Grammar. The forms given are from the strong declension.

7 OE literature

'A syzygy of dipodic hemistichs'

This chapter – its title is explained in section 7.3 – takes a brief look at OE literature. After an initial consideration of the literature as a whole, there are some 'Rough Guides' to a few important works, providing no more than basic information. The final section focuses on a few important characteristics of OE poetry.

By way of preparation, think about what you already know (if anything!) about OE literature. Do you know the names of any works? Are there any characteristics that you associate with the literature of the period?

7.1 A rich and significant literature

The reason why some people study a language is to have access to its literature. Even when you are interested in a language for its own sake, one of the rewards is to have the pleasure of that access. It is often in literature that a culture's feelings, aspirations and thoughts are best expressed. You do not have to be a literature specialist to appreciate and enjoy good writing.

Perhaps your knowledge of OE literature is confined to knowing (or indeed just having heard tell of) the epic poem *Beōwulf*. But there is much more, in what Baugh and Cable (2013: 69) regard as 'one of the richest and most significant [literatures] of any preserved among the early Germanic peoples'. They argue, interestingly, that in the development of literature, prose generally comes later than poetry. It is therefore remarkable, they say, that English had an impressive body of prose as early as the ninth century, when most of the rest of Europe scarcely had any poetry.

OE poetry covers a wide range of genres – the heroic, the historical, the religious, the elegiac. There are even, as we saw in 6.1.5, riddles written in verse. As far as prose is concerned, there are historical records, homilies, and a number of translations from Latin. King Alfred, incidentally, is sometimes called the 'father of English prose'. He had a major involvement in translations, and generally in facilitating the production of prose.

At the beginning of the Anglo-Saxon period, people's beliefs were largely Germanic pagan – with gods like Thor and Woden existing in a world very much akin to the one familiar to many today from Tolkien's *Lord of the Rings* and Wagner's *Ring* cycle. Important to that world-view is the 'Germanic heroic spirit', a set of beliefs which emphasized the importance of revenge, and of fighting bravely against heavy odds. It puts forward a rather pessimistic view of the world in which (to use a phrase mentioned in 4.2.2) *līf* is indeed *lǣne* – 'life is transitory'.

But in the middle of the period, a new, gentler, less fierce world-view appeared – Christianity. Given how different these two world-views were, it is surprising that they did not come into more conflict. As it is, the literature of the period shows the two views interacting in fascinating ways. Thus there are full-blooded pagan Germanic stories with little elements of Christianity creeping in. And there are Christian texts where more pagan, Germanic elements are discernible. You will see examples of this in the next section.

The following section offers you a 'Rough Guide' to just three works of the period. You will find 'Rough Guides' to three more on the companion website. The CW also gives information about the main manuscript collections in which OE works are found (CW7.1 *Manuscript collections*). For each work mentioned, both here and on the CW, this information is given:

- **background**: any important background information, including what genre the work represents. Information is sometimes also given about where the manuscript is found.
- **authorship**: who wrote it, and when.
- **content**: what it is about.
- **value**: some noteworthy characteristics of the work.
- **quotations**: some lines which are noteworthy, give a good 'feel' for the work, or have some other interest. Translations are given, often with punctuation added to make the meaning clearer.

Though in many cases the dates of composition can only be guessed at, the Guide considers the works in rough order of composition.

7.2 'Rough Guides' to three works

Beōwulf

- **background**: A major heroic epic (the first in English). It survives in a tenth-century manuscript, part of the *Cotton Codex* (mentioned in CW7.1). Though it is a pagan Germanic story, there is a strong overlay of Christian ideals.
- **authorship**: Unknown, probably written in the eighth century.
- **content**: It describes two events in the life of the hero Beōwulf. He was a Geat (the 'land of the Geats' is now Götaland in Sweden). He kills the monster Grendel, who has been attacking the hall of the Danish king Hrothgar,

then Grendel's mother, who seeks to avenge her son. Fifty years later, Beōwulf, who has become king of the Geats, kills a troublesome dragon, but is himself also slain.

- **value:** A story about a fight between mortals and superhuman monsters; the style is brilliant, and provides a picture of the Germanic heroic age.
- **quotations:**

  (a) In this quotation, Beōwulf (the person being described in the first line) is returning home in triumph to the Geats' court and its king Hygelac, having slaughtered Grendel and Grendel's mother. There, rings (spoils of war) were being shared out. The quotation reveals several features of OE poetry which will be discussed in the following section. Because it will be referred to then, two translations are given. The one on the right of the text is word-for-word, in which some of the more poetic expressions have less poetic meanings given in brackets. The one below the text is free, and at this stage it is enough to look at that one:

Gewāt him ðā se hearda mid his hondscole	Went he then the hardy man with his band of companions
sylf æfter sande sǣwong tredan	himself along the sand on the sea-plain [shore] walking,
wīde waroðas woruldcandel scan	the wide shore; the world's candle [sun] shone,
sigel sūðan fūs hī sīð drugon	the sun hastening from the south; they made their way
elne geēodon, tō ðæs ðe eorla hlēo	eagerly went, to where the noblemen's protector,
bonan Ongenþēoes burgum in innan,	the slayer of Ongentheow, from within his stronghold,
geongne gūðcyning gōdne gefrūnon	the young war-king, they heard that the good man
hringas dǣlan. Higelāce wæs	rings was sharing out. To Hygelac was
sīð Bēowulfes snūde g ecȳðed	the journey of Beowulf quickly made known,
þæt ðaēr on worðig wīgendra hlēo	that there in the enclosed homestead, the protector of warriors,
lindgestealla lifigende cwōm	the shield-companion (comrade in arms) living came
heaðolāces hāl tō hofe gongan	from the war-play (battle) unharmed, going to the court

'Then the hardy man himself, with his band of companions, went along the sand, walking along the shore, the wide shore. The sun shone, hastening from the south. They made their way, travelling eagerly, to where – they had heard – the protector of noblemen, the slayer of Ongentheow, the young war-king, was sharing out rings from within his stronghold. Hygelac was soon informed of Beowulf's journey. He, Hygelac, the protector of warriors, a comrade in arms, came living, unharmed from battle, to the court.'

(b) The next quotation well expresses aspects of the 'Germanic heroic spirit', where importance is given to glory, and to avenging the death of loved ones. At this point in the story, Beowulf is consoling Hrothgar after the attacks of Grendel's mother. The translation below the passage is word-for-word; you may like to produce a freer one:

> Ne sorga, snotor guma   sēlre bið æghwaēm
> þæt hē his frēond wrece   þonne hē fela murne
> ūre æghwylc sceal   ende gebīdan
> worolde līfes: wyrce sē þe mōte
> dōmes aēr dēaþe   þæt bið drihtguman,
> unlifgendum   æfter sēlest.

'Do not grieve, wise man. Better it is for each man that he his friend avenges than that he greatly mourns. Each of us shall the end experience in the world of life. Achieve he who may glory before death. That is for the warrior, unliving, afterwards best.'

There are a number of recordings available on the internet of parts of *Beōwulf* being read in OE. One example, worth a listen, is https://www.youtube.com/watch?v=_K13GJkGvDw.

Anglo-Saxon Chronicle

- **background:** A historical text, written in prose. There are nine manuscripts existing in whole or part. The best known is the Peterborough Chronicle, produced after 1116 when a fire in the Peterborough monastery destroyed an earlier version.
- **authorship:** Various unknown monks and scribes. In the 890s, Alfred played an important role in encouraging its assembly.
- **content:** A record of historical events from 60 BC till AD 1154. Early entries are very short and in Latin. Among the highlights are: the arrival of Hengest and Horsa (449), the story of Cynewulf and Cyneheard (755), the description of Alfred's last wars against the Danes (893–7), the Battle of Brunanburh (937).
- **value:** Important as a historical record, but it also has linguistic significance as a record of the developing language. It contains some literary texts, including the poem *The Battle of Brunanburh*.
- **quotation:** This extract from the year 449 describes the arrival of Hengest and Horsa, mentioned in 3.1:

And on hiera dagum Hengest and Horsa, fram Wyrtgeorne gelaþode, Bretta cyninge, gesōhton Bretene on þǣm stede þe is genemned Ypwines-flēot, ǣrest Brettum tō fultume, ac hīe eft on hīe fuhton.

'In their days Hengest and Horsa, invited by Vortigern, king of the Britons to his assistance, landed in Britain in a place that is called Ipwinesfleet [a small creek in Kent]; first of all they were to support the Britons, but they afterwards fought against them.'

The Seafarer

- **background:** An elegy; recorded in the *Exeter Book*. The twentieth-century American poet Ezra Pound made a loose translation of the poem's first part.
- **authorship:** Unknown, pre-tenth century.
- **content:** An old seafarer reflects on his life at sea. This leads to thoughts on the transience of life – that '*lif is laene*' theme again: see quotation (b) below. The latter part of the poem is overtly Christian, looking forward to heaven after all the hardships of life.
- **value:** Lots of symbolism, using the life at sea to represent the challenges of a Christian life.
- **quotations:**
(a) A rather gloomy picture of the seafarer's lot...

> *Nāp nihtscūa,*   *norþan snīwde,*
> *hrīm hrūsan bond,*   *hægl fēol on eorþan,*
> *corna caldast.*   *Forþon cnyssað nū*
> *heortan geþōhtas*   *þæt ic hēan strēamas,*
> *sealtȳþa gelāc*   *sylf cunnige –*

'night-shadows darken, from the north it snowed, frost gripped the ground, hail fell on the earth, the coldest of grains. For that reason, now the thoughts of my heart are oppressed, that I myself should have to explore the high streams, the tumultuous motion of the salt waves.'

(b) ... but Christianity offers a solution to this life's transience:

>   *Forþon mē hātran sind*
> *Dryhtnes drēamas*   *þonne þis dēade līf*
> *lǣne on londe.*

'For this reason, hotter for me are the joys of the Lord than this dead, transitory life on earth.'

Our 'Rough Guides' do not cover nearly all the important OE literary pieces. The three on CW are CW7.2 (*Widsith*), CW7.3 (*The Dream of the Rood*), and CW7.4 (*The Battle of Maldon*). Activity 7A (*More OE 'Rough Guides'*) suggests you create a few more 'Rough Guides' of your own.

7.3 Hemistichs, dipody and syzygy

In this section we will look at some important characteristics of OE poetry. *Beōwulf* and *The Seafarer* are both poems and yet, you notice, there are no rhymes. The *Shorter Oxford English Dictionary* defines rhyme as a 'correspondence of sound between … the endings of words, especially when these are used at the ends of lines of poetry'. Usually these 'correspondences' involve a final vowel and consonant – *hat* rhymes with *cat* because both end with an [æ] and a [t]. But although there are no rhymes, there are some 'correspondences of sound' occurring within these lines. Before reading on, consider what these correspondences are. Look, for example, at the first three lines of *Beōwulf*, quote (a).

The correspondences are to do with the beginnings, not the ends, of words. Glance through all the *Beōwulf* and *The Seafarer* lines, and you will find plenty of examples where two or more words begin with the same consonant. This is known as word-initial **alliteration**, and it is an important characteristic of OE poetry. The reason why it occurs is to do with the point made in 4.2.3 about stress. There we saw that in OE, like in other Germanic languages, the stress generally came on the first syllable of a word. With the stress in that position, it was natural to create 'correspondences of sound' on the beginnings of words. The development of 'end rhymes', which we are today much more used to, came about when – later in the development of the language – stress patterns became more variable.

Our *Beōwulf* quotation (a) gives us a useful starting-point for looking at other important characteristics of OE poetry, including the way that alliteration operates in it. If you wish to work out some of the characteristics for yourself, look at Activity 7B (*Syzygy and other things*) before reading on.

The *Beōwulf* and *The Seafarer* quotations show that lines are generally divided into halves, with a 'break' (called a **caesura**) in the middle. The word *hemistich* used in this chapter's title refers to this characteristic: a *hemistich* is a half-line of verse.

Even though you may not know exactly how to recognize stressed syllables in OE, a quick look at our quotations may suggest to you that half-lines usually contain two stressed syllables. The second line of the *Beōwulf* passage (a) gives a good example: *sylf æfter sande sæwong tredan*. The half-lines are **dipodic** (with two **feet**, or **metrical units**), each having two stressed syllables. The name *syzygy* can be used to describe this pattern: the *OED* defines this as a 'combination of two feet in one metre'. Hence the chapter's title; it comes from Fry (2007): 'You could say, if you loved odd words … that a line of Anglo-Saxon poetry is "a syzygy of dipodic hemistichs"'.

As for alliteration, a very common pattern is for it to fall on the first, second and third stressed syllables. *Sylf æfter sande sæwong tredan* (*Beōwulf* quotation (a)) shows just this. Other poetry extracts in our 'Rough Guides' show the same thing. Alexander (1970) calls it 'the BANG, BANG, BANG – CRASH! rule' – four stressed syllables with the first three alliterating.

What might be called 'figurative variants' are another common feature of OE poetry. Often something is described in various ways using similar patterns of words. There are examples in the *Beōwulf* passage (a), and the word-for-word translation will help you locate them. Thus, in the space of three lines, Hygelac is described as *eorla hlēo* (the noblemen's protector), *bonan Ongenþēoes* (the slayer of Ongentheow) and *geongne gūðcyning* (the young war king). Very often the figurative variants are compound nouns, which, as you will recall from 5.2.1, were a common feature of OE). These have been called **kennings**. Thus in the *Beōwulf* passage (a), the sun is described as the *woruldcandel* – the 'world's candle'. Similarly, the word *heaðolāces* (literally 'war-play') is used to describe 'battle'; and *sǣwong* ('sea-plain') is used for 'shore'. Two more examples of kennings (both from *Beōwulf*, but not in the 'Rough Guide' quotations) are: *seglrād* ('sail-road') and *hronrād* (whale-road) – both meaning 'sea'.

7.4 Reading more OE poetry

If you would like to dip a little further into OE literature, there are various modern translations of *Beōwulf*, the best-known piece. The poet Seamus Heaney has, for example, done one (Heaney, 2000). Or perhaps one evening, when *nāp nihtscūa* ('night-shadows darken'), you might also take a look at one of the very short poems – *The Dream of the Rood* is just 156 lines long, and *The Seafarer* only 124.

Activity section

7A More OE 'Rough Guides':

Use the internet or other sources to write your own 'Rough Guides' to some or all of the works below. Use the same headings as in the text: background/authorship/content/value/quotations – though for some entries you may not find something to say under every heading. If you can work together with others, you might share the load, doing one 'Rough Guide' each, and ending up with several which together give a more detailed picture of the period's literature. The works are:

The Battle of Brunanburh: a historical poem along the lines of *The Battle of Maldon*;

Judith: a religious work, like *The Dream of the Rood*. Found in the same MS as *Beōwulf*;

The Wanderer: an elegy in the manner of *The Seafarer*, with a consistent Christian perspective;

Boethius Consolation of Philosophy: The Latin original of this highly influential philosophical work by the sixth-century Roman philosopher Boethius was translated into OE by King Alfred.

7B Syzygy and other things

(a) Look first at the OE text of the *Beōwulf* quotation (a). You will notice that each line is divided into two parts. Usually each part has the same number of stressed syllables. How many stresses fall into each half-line? What about the half-lines in the other 'Rough Guide' poetry quotations; do they follow the same pattern?

(b) Look at the alliteration in the *Beōwulf* quotation (a). In many lines (though not all) the alliterating words are in the same place in the line. Identify this common pattern. Find other examples of this pattern in the other poetry quotations.

(c) Now look at the word-for-word translation of the *Beōwulf* quotation (a) as well as at the original text. The passage has a few examples of what might be called 'figurative variants', where something (or someone) is described a number of times using different words. The word for 'sun' (*sigel*), is, for example, used once, and then given another name – 'world's candle (*woruld-candel*). Identify some other examples of figurative variants in the *Beōwulf* and *The Seafarer* passages.

(d) If you are feeling in creative mood, you may like to invent some 'figurative variations' of your own (in PDE or another language), along the lines of calling the sun the 'world's candle'. '(Native) country' could be 'life seat', and – more prosaically – 'computer' might be 'mind machine'. Let your imagination run wild.

Further reading

Mitchell (1994) – *An Invitation to Old English and Anglo-Saxon England* – contains (as its title suggests) much information on OE and the Anglo-Saxons. There is a section on literature which includes extracts from poems and prose.

A collection of OE text, not all of them 'literary', is available in Marsden (2004).

Another anthology, covering both Old and Middle English, is Treharne (2000).

Donoghue (2004) offers an intriguing account of the literature based around important cultural concepts.

Part III
Middle English

8 Lo, England into Normandy's hand

The invasion of the Normans in 1066 was a significant event in both historical and linguistic terms. It is generally taken to be the beginning of the Middle English (ME) period, which continued up to 1500. This chapter will give you some general historical background. Then it focuses particularly on one major linguistic theme: the relationship, which changed over the period, between English and the language the Normans brought with them: French. Towards the end of the chapter we will look at a passage from the best-known English author of the time, Geoffrey Chaucer, chosen to provide us with a starting-point for our detailed consideration of ME in the chapters that follow.

Some things to think about before reading:

- Are you aware of any events (apart from the Norman invasion) which took place in England during the period 1066 to 1500? What are they? What effect (if any) might they have had on the English language?
- Some events and people to find out about in advance: The Hundred Years War between France and England; William the Conqueror; the 'articles of accusation' against Richard II.
- If you do not know already, find out where Normandy is. If you were planning to invade England from Normandy, where would you cross the Channel? Find out where in fact the Norman fleet landed.
- 8.3 talks about the linguistic phenomenon of 'code-switching'. What is this? Have you come across examples of it in your own experience?
- In 8.4 the expression 'lingua franca' is used. What is a lingua franca?

8.1 Men, noble and low: a first look at ME

It is likely that Robert of Gloucester, who lived in the second half of the thirteenth century, was a monk. He was author of part of a chronicle describing the history of Britain, starting with its founding, which was – according to legend – by Brutus, the grandson of Virgil's Aeneas. Below are some lines from the *Chronicle of Robert of Gloucester*. They describe the linguistic situation in England after the Norman Conquest of 1066. The passage provides you with a 'first look' at Middle English (ME). Many scholars regard the Middle English period as starting in 1066 and finishing around 1500 – a period of over 400 years. As you would expect, the language changed a great deal in that time, and for this reason the period is sometimes divided into an Early and a Late stage (EME and LME). Though the process of change from one to the other was a gradual one, some put the demarcation line at 1300, and this places Robert's *Chronicle* towards the end of the EME period. Later in this chapter (8.5) we will look at an example of LME. But here first is Robert of Gloucester:

Normandy's hand passage

Þus com, lo, Engelond in-to Normandies hond:
And þe Normans ne couþe speke þo bote hor owe speche.
And speke French as hii dude atom, and hor children dude also teche.
So þat heiemen of þis lond, þat of hor come.
Holdeþ alle þulke speche þat hii of hom nom:
Vor bote a man conne Frenss me telþ of him lute.
Ac lowe men holdeþ to Engliss, and to hor owe speche ȝute.

...

Ac wel me wote uor to conne boþe wel it is.
Vor þe more þat a mon can, þe more wurþe he is.

You will doubtless recall (possibly with some pain) that to understand the OE 'dead reeve passage' in 3.2 required a lot of effort. You will probably find the passage above (let us call it the 'Normandy's hand passage') very much easier to understand. Use this glossary to help work out what the passage says. It is only a partial glossary, calculated to be enough for you to understand the sense. If you want a full translation, there is one in the *Answer section* (**AS**).

couþe, knew how to	*speche*, language
hii, they	*dude*, did, had (= caused)
atom, at home	*hor*, their, them
heiemen, noblemen	*holdeþ*, keep to, retain
þulke, that	*nom*, take
vor, for	*conne/can*, know(s)
telþ, esteem	*lute*, little
ac, but	*ȝute*, yet, still
wote, know	*me*, man, one
uor, for	*wurþe*, valued

Once you are confident about what the passage says, take a moment to register a few initial impressions about its language. Are there any features that particularly strike you? How does it compare with PDE? And with OE? Are there EME words in the passage that you have found in your brief exposure to OE?

One final question. Look back to 3.3 where three basic aspects of OE are listed. Are these also present in the EME of the 'Normandy's hand passage'?

The first basic aspect of OE listed in 3.3 is that '*Old English is … English*'. This is even more true of EME, and your first reaction to the passage may well have been that the language looks very much more like PDE than OE did. The EME passage really is recognizable as English as we know it. There are, it is true, some curious spellings. But often it is possible to work out what the PDE equivalents are. So EME *teche* is PDE 'teach', *hond* is 'hand', and *lond* is 'land'.

But also, as you might expect, there are many ways in which EME and OE are similar. You will have noticed that two of the letters – the thorn (þ) and the yogh (ʒ) – are still there. And there are some OE-sounding words. You may recall from 4.3's 'lettuce story' that OE *ac* means 'but', and this word is here too. OE *þæt* makes an appearance as *þat*; and *com*, meaning 'came', appears both here and in the 'lettuce passage'.

The second aspect mentioned in 3.3 is that *Old English is suffix-rich*. In this respect, EME is quite different. Focus on the nouns in the 'Normandy's hand passage', and identify how many suffixes you can spot. There is a possessive form (*Normandies*), and some plurals – regular ones ending in -*s* (Normans), and irregular ones like *men* (in the compound *heiemen*), and *children*. Noun possessives and plurals are among the few grammatical inflections remaining in PDE. Again, we will be exploring this at length in a later chapter (10).

The third and final aspect mentioned is that *Old English is Germanic*. An example given was the word *nam*, a past-tense form of the verb *niman*. As it happens, the equivalent also appears in the 'Normandy's hand passage', though the form there is *nom*; the EME infinitive form is *nimen*. Your instinct may or may not tell you that there are other Germanic-based words in the passage. In fact, there is almost nothing but. Why not take a few words from the passage – concentrate on verbs perhaps –and use the internet or some other resource to check on their origins. Germanic is what you will overwhelmingly find. It is particularly in this respect that this EME passage differs from the LME one we will look at in 8.5, where we will find that a substantial French dimension has come into the lexis. Very much more of that in the next chapter.

Now, after this 'first look', here is some history.

8.2 1066 and all that

It was in 1066 that England came 'into Normandy's hand'. But there had been Anglo–Norman links before that. Edward the Confessor, who was king until 1066, was half Norman, and spent the early part of his life in Normandy. When he was king, many of his advisors were Norman. He died childless. Harold was elected and crowned in January 1066. But Duke William of Normandy (known now as 'William the Conqueror') felt he had a claim to the throne, and he supported this claim with an invasion. Harold was killed (by an arrow through his eye) at the Battle of Hastings, and William was crowned king of England on Christmas Day, 1066.

In a sense, William's conquest was a second Viking invasion, because Normandy had been invaded by the Vikings at the same time that those same Scandinavians were making inroads into England, as described in 3.1. The word 'Normans' means 'Northmen'.

As is natural following any invasion, the conquerors brought with them a retinue of their own people to take over important posts. A new nobility of Normans was introduced into England. There were Normans in high church positions, Norman merchants, Norman artisans. Important trading towns like Norwich developed French quarters; Norwich's 'French Borough' was a colony of French traders set up to establish commercial links with the 'locals'.

As the 'Normandy's hand passage' says, the Normans also brought their language with them – a dialect of French which developed into what is known as Anglo-Norman. It was used by the royal court in England (William himself could not speak English), by the nobility (which was now largely Norman anyway), and by the upper classes. Also, as the passage says, the 'low' classes – ordinary folk – continued to use English.

After a brief period of rape and pillage, while William was establishing his authority, things calmed down and the Normans and English started to trade together, to mingle, and to intermarry. But linguistic separation continued. The Normans and upper classes stayed with French and the non-upper-class English continued with English. Language use was determined by social class, not by ethnic origin. French was the language with status and authority, and because of its lack of status, English became diverse, with no one standard version developing. Dialects abounded. In fact, the surviving early ME texts 'document widespread variation unrivalled in any other period of the language before or since'.[1] You might like to think about what kind of effect the lack of a standard will have on the development of a language.

The intercourse between Normandy and England was two-way. The English nobles established themselves in Normandy as the French nobles did in England, and the two states became closely linked. But all this began to change in the early thirteenth century. King John, who reigned from 1199 till 1216, fell in love with the beautiful Isabel of Angoulême, and terminated his existing marriage in order to marry her. The marriage displeased Philip of France, because Isabel was already promised to Hugh de Lusignan, whose feudal lord was Philip. War ensued. In 1204, Rouen (Normandy's capital at the time) surrendered and the region, which up till then had been a separate Duchy, became a part of France. Suddenly the nobles had to decide whether to settle in Normandy or England. There was also increasing commercial competition between England and France, particularly over the managing of one of England's prime commodities – wool. The English court's attitude towards the growing separation also caused trouble. The king continued to favour Norman connections, and the English barons became displeased at such favouritism. This led to the so-called Barons' Wars, between 1258 and 1265. It also created much anti-foreign sentiment in England, a sense that the 'locals' – the English born and bred – were receiving second-rate treatment compared with the foreigners. Here is a verse from a political song of the period:

> Thus the nation is wasted, the land destroyed,
> A foreign nation grows strong and rises up,
> While the native man grows worthless.[2]

Hostility and rivalry between England and France continued into the fourteenth century. France was thought to be interfering with English attempts to control Scotland, and this was one of the reasons for the outbreak of the Hundred Years War (1337–1453).

The separation from France, and the strengthening attitudes of dislike towards the French, had significant linguistic consequences. French was changing from being the language of aristocrats to the language of unfairly favoured intruders. Then it became the language of the enemy, and indeed some even accused the Normans of actually trying to eradicate the English language. These events and attitudes played an important role in re-establishing English.

There were other, social, changes that led in the same direction. It was the lower and middle classes who were using English, and their condition was improving. The 1215 Magna Carta, forced on King John by the Archbishop of Canterbury and the barons, restrained the power of the monarch and was the beginning of a move towards democratization. It was followed in 1258 by the Provisions of Oxford, an agreement which placed government into the hands of a council, picked partly by the barons. The medieval systems of serfdom and villeinage, in which workers were controlled entirely by their lords, was on the way out. Then there were two disastrous events which, ironically, indirectly improved the status of English even more. One was The Great Famine of 1315–17. Bad weather destroyed harvests, and millions of workers throughout Europe perished. The other was the plague, known as The Black Death, which struck in 1348–51. The population was devastated, with around 30–40 per cent of the English being killed. The lower classes were particularly badly hit; for one thing, they had less access to quarantine, which could be life-saving. As a result of these disasters, workers became scarce, their value increased, and they also became more aware of that value. Thirty years after the end of the Black Death, in 1381, came the Peasants' Revolt. Though this was quashed, the position of workers became stronger. So too did that of the middle classes, with merchants and craftsmen setting up guilds to look after their interests. As the power of these classes grew, so did the status of the language they spoke – English. Eventually, even the upper classes found themselves having to change from French to English.

It is possible to track the increasing role of English through a number of dates. Table 8.1 gives some of them, and there is an activity later in this chapter which involves using these dates:

Table 8.1 English spreads

- English began to be used in schools in 1349.
- The 1362 Parliamentary 'Statutes of Pleading' decreed that future lawsuits should be in English.
- In 1362, Parliament opened in English for the first time.
- The London guilds started to use English from the 1380s.
- The first known will written in English was dated 1383.
- In 1384, John Wycliffe's Bible was completed – the first complete translation into English.
- The articles of accusation, which finally led to the downfall of Richard II, were written in English (as well as Latin; 1399). Incidentally, Shakespeare's play *Richard II* tells this story.
- Henry IV, who came to the throne in 1399, was the first king since the Conquest who spoke English as a mother tongue.
- Henry IV's coronation speech was in English (1399).
- London brewers used English in 1422 (because they did not 'in anywise understand' Latin and French).
- The late fourteenth century saw the first examples of personal correspondence written in English. The celebrated 'Paston letters' were started in 1422.
- Parliamentary documents show that, before 1423, most petitions were in French. By 1489, they were all in English.

8.3   A very curious letter

In the early 1400s, a group of Welsh rebels, led by the Welsh ruler, Owain Glyndŵr, tried to take Wales and the bordering English county of Hereford (their rebellion is part of the plot of Shakespeare's play *Henry IV, Part 1*). Richard Kyngston, Dean of Windsor, was severely alarmed by this threat. He wrote a letter to the king in 1403 telling him of the rebellion and urgently asking for reinforcements. Here is the main part of the letter. It is not necessary to understand much of it to consider what, you might think, would be a simple question to answer: what language is it written in?

Please a vostre tresgraciouse Seignourie entendre que a-jourduy apres noone … q'ils furent venuz deinz nostre countie pluis de.cccc des les rebelz de Owyne, Glyn, Talgard, et pluseours autres rebelz des voz marches de Galys … Warfore, for goddesake, thinketh on your beste frende, god, and thanke hym as he hath deserued to yowe! And leueth nought that ye ne come for no man that may counsaille yowe the contrarie … Tresexcellent, trespuissant, at tresredouté Seignour, autremeny say a present nieez. Jeo prie a la benoit trinité

> que vous ottroie bone vie ove tresentier sauntee a treslonge durré, and sende yowe sone to ows in help and prosperitee: for in god fey, I hope to almighty god that, yef ye come youre owne persone, ye schulle haue the victorie of alle youre enemyes ... Escript a Hereford, en tresgraunte haste, a trois de la clocke apres noone, le tierce jour de Septembre.[3]

French or English? Before reading on, go through the letter, identifying the parts that are English. One section is almost entirely English, and other sections are predominantly French, though containing some English words. Identify these words.

The first few lines – up to *de Galys* – are mostly French, though they include some apparently English words. *Noone* ('noon') is one of them, *countie* ('county') is another. Then follow a few lines of English, up to *the contrarie*. Then there is more French. But suddenly, in the middle of a sentence, beginning with the words *and sende yowe*, there is a return to English. The last sentence (from *Escript a Hereford*) is a most curious mixture of French and English. Look particularly at the delightful expression *en tresgraunte haste*: in modern French the first two words would be 'en très grande', meaning 'in very great'. Followed by the English *haste*. Can you suggest any explanation as to when French or English is used in this letter?

The letter is an example of what is known as **code-switching**. This is where a speaker will switch from one language to another, sometimes even in the middle of a sentence. It often occurs in communities where more than one language is in common use. Thus Polish workers living in Britain may code-switch from English to Polish; Spanish speakers living in the United States may switch from Spanish to English, and French Canadians – French speakers surrounded by large English-speaking areas – may find themselves putting English words into sentences which are otherwise French. An example of this is the French Canadian lady who says 'Je suis une Canadienne-française I guess.'[4]

There can be a number of reasons why people proficient in two or more languages will code-switch. Sometimes who you are talking to will make you decide what language to use, and even what you are talking about may be relevant. In some cases, a speaker will find that they are not sufficiently competent in one of the languages to express something, and will switch languages to make themselves clear. This is perhaps what happens to Richard Kyngston; or perhaps his letter shows that he feels he should be writing in French, but every so often he gets fatigued by the effort, and reverts to English. Whatever the case, what is important is to realize that the linguistic situation in medieval England is one ripe for code-switching to occur, with both French and English in circulation (as well, incidentally, as Latin). CW8.1 (*A macaronic poem*) contains two verses from a trilingual poem, with lines in English, French and Latin – the word 'macaronic' means mixing various languages.

8.4   English re-established

French was regarded by many throughout Europe as a cultivated and elegant language, as well as being one which, like Latin, played a role as a European lingua franca. There were certainly conservative forces in England determined to keep French and Latin in use. It is said that fellows of Merton College, Oxford, were accused of the heinous behaviour of talking English (rather than Latin) at meals, and also (intriguingly) of wearing 'dishonest shoes' – one wonders just what makes a pair of shoes 'dishonest'![5] That was in 1284, and Oxford colleges were still requiring Latin or French at meal times in the fourteenth century. But for the various reasons mentioned in 8.2, French was fighting a losing battle, as is suggested by the appearance of a number of manuals intended to help speakers of English with French, treated as a foreign language. One of these is described in CW8.2 (*Boterfiles and gnattes*).

In the fourteenth century, English was fully restored as the language of England. When French was used, it was because of its status as the language of a cultured society, rather than as the result of invasion and occupation. A standard, accepted form of English became established. It was not based on the West-Saxon model which was the standard form of OE, but on the East Midlands and London dialects, because these were the areas of the country which were prospering economically. After 1430, the model which became the basis for the English we use today was described by the term 'Chancery English'. It was the model used by the scribes who prepared royal and governmental documents and who worked in the London Chancery. It was also the type of English favoured by William Caxton. He is an important figure in the history of English, because he set up the first printing press in London in 1476. There is more about him in 13.2.

This chapter contains a lot of history. If you are a person who finds the chronology of historical events difficult to remember, Activity 8A (*Timeline*) may help; it asks you to produce a timeline for important dates mentioned in 8.2 and 8.4. Take a look also at CW8.3 (*A collection of passages*), which is quite a substantial activity. It contains some passages relevant to topics raised in those sections.

As you will have gathered, a major theme of the history of this period revolves around relations with France. In the next few chapters we will look in more detail at ME. In previous ones we have more than once had to consider the influence of conquering neighbours on English. Remind yourself what kinds of influences these are. What kind of influence would you expect French to have had on English?

8.5   Chaunticleer and Russell

In Chapter 4, we used the 'lettuce passage' as the starting-point for exploring the nature of OE. The passage we will use in the same way for ME is introduced here. The emphasis at this stage is on understanding what it says. The 'linguistics' of the passage will come in the following chapters.

The passage is taken from by far the best-known work of English ME literature, occupying a place comparable to *Beōwulf's* in OE literature. That work is Chaucer's *Canterbury Tales*. It was written at the end of the fourteenth century, and thus falls within the LME period, unlike the EME 'Normandy's hand passage' we have already looked at. The *Tales*, which are described in more detail in 11.3, are a collection of over twenty stories, told by a group of pilgrims to divert themselves on the long walk from London to Canterbury. The characters are a mixture of social classes and professions, and *The Tales* thus offer a rich pageant of society at the time. The storytelling is a competition, the prize for the best story being a free meal in London when the pilgrimage is over.

We are not told who wins that free meal, but a sure contender is the Nun's Priest, a person whose job involved acting as confessor to nuns. His story represents a genre popular in the Middle Ages – the beast fable. The main protagonists are a fox and a cock. In Chaucer, the fox is called Russell, perhaps because of his russet-coloured coat. In other versions of the story, the bird involved is a crow, and indeed you may be familiar with one of Aesop's Fables, 'The Fox and the Crow' which tells a similar story. In Chaucer, the bird is a cock called Chaunticleer – a common name for cocks in fables. The name comes from the Old French *chanter cler* – 'to sing clearly', an appropriate name because Chaunticleer is indeed something of a male diva.

In the part of the *Nun's Priest's Tale* relevant to us, Chaunticleer and Russell meet. The fox flatters the cock to put the bird off its guard, making Chaunticleer close his eyes and 'sing' (crow, that is). As soon as Chaunticleer's eyes are closed, Russell grabs him and carries him off, intending to have him for dinner. But Chaunticleer responds by persuading the fox to open his mouth, thus allowing the bird to escape. 'Do not believe flattery' is the message, as the short moralizing passage in the middle of our extract makes clear.

To keep the extract down to size, some parts are omitted from the middle. Read through the 'Chaunticleer passage' and try to grasp its sense. The likelihood is that you will understand the gist, but not every word. You might also like to produce your own rough translation of the passage (or even just part of it):

Chaunticleer passage

> This Chauntecleer, whan he gan him espye,
> He wolde han fled, but that the fox anon
> Seyde, 'Gentil sire, allas! wher wol ye gon?
> Be ye affrayed of me that am youre freend?
> Now, certes, I were worse than a feend,
> If I to yow wolde harm or vileynye!
> I am nat come youre conseil for t'espye,
> But trewely, the cause of my comynge

Was oonly for to herkne how that ye synge.
For trewly, ye have as myrie a stevene
As any aungel hath that is in hevene.'
[... ....]
This Chauntecleer his wynges gan to bete,
As man that koude his traysoun nat espie,
So was he ravysshed with his flaterie.
Allas! ye lordes, many a fals flatour
Is in youre courtes, and many a losengeour,
That plesen yow wel moore, by my feith,
That he that soothfastnesse unto yow seith.
Redeth Ecclesiaste of flaterye;
Beth war, ye lordes, of hir trecherye.
This Chauntecleer stood hye upon his toos,
Strecchynge his nekke, and heeld his eyen cloos,
And gan to crowe loude for the nones.
And daun Russell the fox stirte up atones,
And by the gargat hente Chauntecleer,
And on his bak toward the wode him beer,
 For yet ne was ther no man that hym sewed.

Here are two things to do in relation to this passage:

(a) Among the words and phrases which may cause you problems are:

stevene	*losengeour*	*Ecclesiaste*	*for the nones*
atones	*gargat*	*hente*	*sewed*
youre conseil for t'espye			

At the very least try to find something to say about these words and phrases. What parts of speech are the words? What kind of thing do they refer to – what sorts of objects or persons? What kinds of actions? Try to make specific guesses at meanings.

There is a full translation of the 'Chaunticleer' passage, should you need it, in the *Answer section* (**AS**).

(b) Like many writers of the time, Chaucer's use of personal pronouns does not always make it immediately clear who is being referred to. Go through the passage identifying all the personal pronouns (*he, I, yow* and so on), as well as the possessive forms (*his, my*, etc.). Specify which characters each refers to.

In preparation for the following chapters, you might now like to look through the passage again, recording any aspects of the language that catch your attention and seem interesting.

Activity section

8A   Timeline

(a) You may be a person who finds it easier to remember historical facts and dates if you see them in a table. If so, put dates and events into the table below. All the information you require is given in 8.2 and 8.4. If you prefer, you could go through the sections and produce your own timeline of important events, without using this table – make sure the dates are in chronological order, though.

Event	Date
	1066
John loses Normandy	
	1215
Provisions of Oxford	
	1258–65
Great Famine	
	1337–1453
Black Death	
	1381
Caxton sets up printing press in London	

(b) To make your timeline a little richer, find dates for the following, and add these. Not all are mentioned in the chapter. If any of these events or people are new to you, you might like to find out something about them, using the internet or other sources. The dates are given in the *Answer section*:

- The poet Chaucer's approximate dates
- John's marriage to Isabel
- The Battle of Agincourt (during the Hundred Years War), where the English won a victory
- The approximate dates of a French hero during the Hundred Years War – Joan of Arc.

Answer section

Section 8.1

A translation of the 'Normandy's hand passage':

'Thus came, lo, England into Normandy's hand: and the Normans knew how to speak only their own language, and spoke French as they did at home, and also had their children taught it, so that noblemen of this land, who came from among them, all keep to the same language that they took from them; for unless a man knows French, men do not esteem him much. But low men keep to English, and to their own language still… But men know well that it is good to know both, because the more a man knows the more valued he is.'

Section 8.5

A translation of the 'Chaunticleer' passage:

> This Chaunticleer, when he saw him
> He would have fled, except that the fox immediately
> Said, 'Gentle sir, alas! Where would you go?
> Are you afraid of me, who am your friend?
> Now, certainly I would be worse than an enemy
> If I were to do you harm or wrong
> I have not come to spy on your secrets
> But really, the cause of my coming
> Was only to listen to how you sing
> For truly, you have as pleasant a voice
> As any angel in heaven.'
> [...]
> This Chaunticleer began to beat his wings
> As one that could not perceive [suspect] his betrayal
> So much was he ravished by his flattery
> Alas, you lords, many a false flatterer
> Is in your courts, and many a deceiver
> Who pleases you much more, by my faith,
> Than he who tells you the truth.
> Read Ecclesiastes on flattery;
> Beware, you lords, of their treachery.
> This Chaunticleer stood high on his toes,
> Stretching his neck, and kept his eyes closed
> And began to crow loudly for the occasion
> And Sir Russell the fox started up at once,
> And caught Chaunticleer by the throat,
> And bore him on his back towards the wood
> For there was as yet no-one pursuing him.

Activity 8A(b)

Chaucer's dates. c. 1343–1400; John's marriage to Isabel, 1200; The Battle of Agincourt, 1415; Joan of Arc's dates, c. 1412–1431.

Further reading

For a (non-linguistic) historical look at the period, the relevant chapters of Schama (2000) provide a lively account.

Baugh and Cable's *A History of the English Language* first appeared in 1951. Its sixth edition (2013) still provides an excellent historical account focusing on issues relevant to the English language. Chapters 5 and 6 are the relevant ones here.

Chapter 2 of Holmes (2013) has a section dealing with code-switching. A recent article by Schendl (2015) focuses particularly on code-switching in medieval English literature.

Notes

1 The quotation is from Fennell (2001: 108).
2 The song is found in Wright (1996), and is cited by Machan (2003: 50), whose translation this is.
3 This version of the letter is taken from Trotter (2000).
4 The French-Canadian quotation is taken from Swann (1996).
5 Baugh & Cable (2013: 134) say this, for example.

9 'The English tongue ... honourably enlarged and adorned'

ME words and pragmatics

The first part of this chapter is about ME lexis. As we saw in Chapter 5, OE preferred using native resources rather than borrowing as a means of vocabulary development. ME was very different, and many loanwords came into the language. We take a detailed look at these. Not surprisingly, after the Norman Conquest, French was the major source of new words, but words were also taken from the Low Countries and particularly too from Latin – a language which still enjoyed much status in various spheres. As we will see, loanwords helped to make English vocabulary particularly rich. The last part of the chapter looks at two areas associated with ME pragmatics: terms of address, and swearing. You may be surprised to find how much the 'rules of use' associated with these areas have changed since ME times.

Some things to do before reading:

- The concepts of denotation and connotation are discussed. What do these terms mean?
- Loanwords are a major theme of this chapter. Why do languages borrow words?
- In this chapter, you will be asked to explore the origins of various words. As a way of preparing for this, you may be interested to choose one or two words from the opening paragraphs of this chapter, and explore their origins and histories. For this you will need access to an etymological dictionary and/or to the internet.
- This chapter looks at the pragmatics of swearing. What kinds of ways of swearing are used in your first language? Do they use words that refer to sex, or religion, or some other taboo area?

9.1 Native versus borrowed

In 1422 the Brewers Company decided to adopt English as their language of communication. The reason they gave was that 'the English language, hath in modern days begun to be honourably enlarged and adorned'. How was this enlargement and adornment achieved? We have seen that OE was fond of using its own 'native' resources – particularly compounding and affixation – to develop its store of words (the word-hoard). Though there was borrowing, especially from Old Norse, taking words from other languages was not a major strategy. ME was dramatically different. It borrowed. Compounding and affixation did not disappear, but the amount of borrowing from other languages, particularly French, was huge. As Baugh and Cable (2013: 163) put it: 'the number of French words that poured into English was unbelievably great. There is nothing comparable to it in the previous or subsequent history of the language'. Their estimate has the number of new French words during the ME period as 10,000, with, incidentally, about 75 per cent of these still in use today.

There are both social and linguistic reasons for this sudden change of focus onto borrowing. On the social side, England was coming into contact with various other countries, especially France, helped by the particularly outward-looking attitudes of the royal courts. Contact is, of course, the necessary prerequisite for borrowing. Also, as we shall see in the next chapter, there was a dramatic decrease in inflections during the ME period, and that made it easier for new words to come into the language. OE had suffixes that marked nouns, verbs, adjectives and other parts of speech. Foreign words had to adopt the right endings before they could be accepted as nouns, verbs, or adjectives. With the endings that mark parts of speech disappearing, it was much easier for 'cuckoo words' to clamber into the nest.

Looking at ME words has been made a great deal easier for us because of major lexical resources now available online. One of these is known as the 'Middle English Compendium'. CW9.1 (*Working with the MEC*) says something about this free resource, and shows you how to use it online.

9.2   Loanwords

9.2.1   Borrowing from French

In the years after the Conquest, the variety of French that had influence in England was the Norman version. It was the language of the conquerors, and words of the sort that the conquered are likely to pick up from the conqueror were taken from Norman French (NF). As we saw in Chapter 8, Normandy became a part of France in the early 1200s, and the French of Paris, called 'Central French' (CF), became the linguistic norm. With this shift of linguistic power came a widening of the scope of borrowing – not just words for the conquered, but words dealing with other areas of life. These changes occurred slowly, but some put the dividing line at 1250.[1] Before that time, the number of words borrowed was relatively small. The flood occurred thereafter. Activity 9A (*Dating first occurrences*) invites you to use the *OED* to find when some words first appeared. Do just Part (a) at the moment.

Baugh and Cable's (2013) pre-1250 examples of 'conqueror-type words' include Activity 9A's *baron, noble* and *servant*. The other words in the activity (*empire*, *manor* and *priory*) are post 1250. Sometimes different versions of words were borrowed, one from NF and another from CF. NF had the sound [w], while in Central French [g] was used – so our word *war* comes from NF, while it was CF that led to the modern French word *guerre*. NF gave us the 'w words' *warranty* and *warden*. Later, 'g' versions came into English – in the form of *guarantee* and *guardian*. Then there is *wile* and *guile*.

1250, when the floodgates opened, was almost two hundred years after the Conquest, and it continued until 1500 – over 400 years since the invasion. Why did it take so long for so many French words to come into English? Think about this before reading on. Now would also be a good time to do Activity 9A, part (b), which asks you to use the *OED* to count new words coming into English in specific years.

One reason for the 'delay' is just that some linguistic changes do take a long time to become established. But there are also more specific reasons. One is that, as we saw in 8.4, in the 1300s, English was once more becoming the language of England. That meant that many of the upper classes and noblemen who had previously communicated in French were having to use English. Doubtless they often had problems with their new language, and naturally had to resort to French-based words to make themselves understood. It is rather ironic that the re-establishment of English was partly responsible for the introduction of so many French words. A second reason is that there was still doubtless a degree of 'snobbery' involved in the use of French-sounding words. Peppering one's speech with French loanwords marked you as 'upper' in class terms.

French vocabulary crept into every area of English life, though there are some areas where it is particularly heavily represented. Strang's list (1970: 253) gives a feel for the extent of the borrowing. It includes:

> names of people, with their kinds, classes, ranks, temperaments and offices, terms for finance, property and business, for building and for the equipment of homes, for law and social organization, religion, war, the arts, clothing and food, entertainment, hunting, animals, especially foreign, science and medicine; nouns are dominant, but there are many verbs and adjectives, and some other forms.

Another way of appreciating the extent of French borrowing is to use the *OED*'s facility to look up words on given topics. The relevant word to click on the *OED* page is 'Categories'. This shows you the topics for which the dictionary has this facility. Choose one of the topics related to one on the list above. For example, since 'hunting' is on the list, I chose 'Hunting, fishing and shooting'. Clicking on this led me to a list of 2,776 words. I decided to focus on the first twenty only. I found that ten (exactly half) were given French etymologies (though not, admittedly, all appearing during the ME period). Among the other ten, three were from Latin, and the rest from a variety of other languages. You may wish to try another of the *OED* categories, which might, like the hunting entry, suggest just how common French borrowing was.

Yet another way of appreciating the number of loanwords is to look at samples of ME and see just how many words have French origins. But how do you recognize a French-derived word? It is not always easy; have a look at CW9.2 (*How to recognize a French connection*), which offers some hints.

Armed with such (admittedly rather general) rules of thumb, return to our old friend Chaunticleer, in his 8.5 passage. This will give you a good idea of just how many French words were coming into the language. In the first eleven lines (up to the break in the middle), there are at least ten French (or in some cases possibly Latin-derived) words – *espye, gentil, sir, allas, affrayd, certes, vileyne, conseil, cause,* and *aungel.* That is almost one per line. Look now at the next eight lines, up to *Redeth Ecclesiaste of flaterye* (or you can go further if you wish). Make a list of words that you think might be of French origin. What are the reasons for your suspicions? Then, if you have access to the *OED* online, look them up to confirm these suspicions (AS).

Incidentally, exploring the history of words can be great fun. If you feel like a short digression in this direction, take a look at CW9.3 (*Exploring word histories*), which suggests a way of spending an entertaining half-hour ... or afternoon.

Often when French words came into the language, there already existed 'native' Germanic words with roughly the same meaning. These produce synonym word-pairs of the type we came across in 5.3.3 with Old Norse loanwords. One of the most memorable synonym pairs there was *skirt* and *shirt.* Activity 9B (*Words, alike and similar*) introduces some ME examples.

The first synonym word-pair in the activity is *rise/mount.* The first word is from the OE *rīsan.* The second comes from the NF *monter.* There are words in today's Romance languages (2.3 will remind you that these are languages descended from Latin) which are the same – there is a *montare* in Italian, and a *montar* in Spanish. The word is ultimately associated with the Latin *mons,* meaning 'mountain'. All the other words in the activity make up similar pairs. There is *ask/question, goodness/virtue, fear/terror, freedom/liberty, likelihood/ probability, beginning/commencement, worship/adoration, doom/judgement, hearty/cordial, stench/odour, calf/veal, ox/beef, sheep/mutton* and *pig/pork.*

Part (b) of the activity asks you about differences in denotation or connotation between the two lists. The animal/food examples have a clear difference. The Germanic words (*calf, ox, sheep* and *pig*) refer to the animals, while the French-derived ones are the names of the equivalent meats – *veal, beef, mutton* and *pork.* Behind this difference is the suggestion that the more 'sophisticated' words are from French – not just the animal, but the animal's meat prepared for eating. 'More earthy versus more sophisticated' applies to some of the other word-pairs, particularly *stench* versus *odour.* It is the same difference between *sweat* (which is what horses do, from the OE *swǣtan*) and *perspire* (which is what men do – the word is from French, though admittedly it did not come into English until the seventeenth century). Women, of course *glow* – a far more refined description, even though the word is Germanic! There is also in some pairs a clear difference of formality: compare *ask* with *question, beginning* with *commencement*. The celebrated Danish linguist Otto Jespersen (1905) is one who discusses 'the differences that have developed in course of time between two synonyms when both have survived, one of them native, the other French. The former is always nearer the nation's heart than the latter, it has the strongest associations with everything primitive, fundamental, popular, while the French word is more formal, more polite, more refined and has a less strong hold on the emotional side of life.' Other examples from Jespersen are *help/aid*, *deep/profound* and *lonely/solitary*.

But, you might say, languages do not need two words for the same thing, and this is just what the creation of synonym word-pairs provides. In such cases, one of two things tends to happen. The first is that one of the word-pair falls out of general use (sometimes surviving in a dialect). Such was the momentum of French borrowing that it was often the Germanic equivalent that disappeared. An example is the ME word *athil*. It meant 'noble', and comes from the OE adjective *æðele*. The French part of the word-pair was *noble*, and this word won the day – the last *OED* citation for *athil* is 1525. Another example is the OE *leōde*, meaning 'people'. It kept going till the fifteenth century, but NF *pople* arrived in the fourteenth century, and is now our PDE 'people'. A second outcome is that both members of the synonym word-pair survive, but differentiate themselves in terms of meaning, often on the level of connotation. As we have just seen, there are some typical directions in which word-pair members tend to go. The French words often become more formal or 'sophisticated', for example.

It is worth pondering for a moment the overall effect of synonym word-pairs, and the quantity of borrowing behind them. It led not just to a huge enlargement of the vocabulary but also to its sophistication. Different words came to be used in different contexts, by different sorts of people. Linguists use the word **register** for this kind of variation, defined by the *Shorter Oxford Dictionary* as 'a variety of a language or a level of usage, as determined by degree of formality and choice of vocabulary, pronunciation, and syntax, according to the communicative purpose, social context, and social status of the user'. You see this particularly clearly in Chaucer's *Canterbury Tales*, where a wide range of people tell a whole spectrum of different stories – from the sublime to the ridiculous and back again. 'Here is God's plenty' is what Dryden later said about the poem. The vocabularies of the storytellers and their tales demonstrate different registers, and these can be differentiated partly as a consequence of the rich lexicon of English that was developing, including those synonym word-pairs. Horobin and Smith (2002) give a good example of how Chaucer changes his register according to speaker. In his poem, *The Parlement of Foules*, different groups of birds make speeches. The noble birds of prey use plenty of French-derived words. The humble waterfowl use more earthy language. There are some French words in their speech, but not so many.

The way that members of synonym word-pairs come to develop different meanings touches on the general topic of semantic change – a subject which was mentioned at the beginning of this book, in 1.2. Words change meaning, and the history of a language plots these. When we were looking at OE, you may have found that the considerable differences between OE and PDE made you very aware that you were dealing with what was almost another language. Because ME is much more like PDE, this feeling of 'differentness' (or 'dissimilitude', if you prefer a word with a Latin/French suffix) may disappear ... and this can be dangerous. The danger at the semantic level is that ME words may look familiar – just like PDE words – but may in fact have changed meaning over the centuries. As we saw in 1.2, these words are called false friends. An example often used is the PDE word *silly* – in fact it came up in Activity 1C. Today it means 'foolish', 'lacking in common sense'. The OE word was *sælig*, and it meant 'blessed' or 'happy' – if you speak German, you will have come across their word *selig* meaning just that. How do you get from 'blessed' to 'foolish'? An important stop on the journey is the sense developing in the fifteenth century of 'innocence and undeserved suffering' – nice, positive attributes, but unfortunately just a stone's throw from the potentially less positive 'weak' and 'vulnerable'. When the 1611 King James Bible talks of 'silly women' (2 Timothy iii.6) perhaps it means 'vulnerable', not 'foolish'. But the sense of 'foolish' was around at that time, and when Hippolyta in Shakespeare's *A Midsummer Night's Dream* describes something as *the silliest stuff that ever I heard*, she really does mean 'foolish'. The play was written around 1595. Activity 9C (*Some ME false friends*) gives you the opportunity to explore some other false friends from the ME period.

It is not only words, but also parts of words (affixes) that came from French into English. Activity 9D (*Some suffixable inflections*) looks at some of these. It is based around words which were introduced in an earlier activity (9B, *Words, alike and similar*).

Some of the words in Activity 9B have Germanic suffixes which were very productive in OE and were used in ME too. They are -*ness*, -*dom*, -*hood*, -*ship*, -*ing* and -*y*. As the examples given show, the first four of these could be used to create abstract nouns from adjectives. The suffix -*ing* (and its variant -*ling*) had a number of functions. One was to describe an action, making a noun out of verbs – like *wedding* and *beginning*. The suffix -*ling* can mean 'belonging to a particular group'. So a *hireling* is one who is hired. Added to an adjective, it may mean 'having the quality of'. Thus *darling* is someone who is 'dear'. The suffix -*y* also carries the general meaning 'having the quality of' and it can be added to a noun to make it an adjective. So *hearty* is 'full of heart', *icy* is 'as cold as ice'. *Sandy*, *sugary*, and *mouldy* work in the same way.

But the words in Activity 9B also show that another whole set of French-derived suffixes came into use. Those in the activity are -*ment*, -*(i)ty*, -*tion*, -*(i)al*, and -*our*. The first of these, -*ment*, is used to make an abstract noun out of a verb (or sometimes out of an adjective). Hence *commencement* out of *commence*. Similarly, -*our* also creates abstract nouns describing states or conditions – so the adjective *candid* becomes *candour*. Nouns of 'state or condition' are also formed by the -*(i)ty* suffix, with *pure* becoming *purity*. The suffix -*tion* is often added to a verb to create a noun describing an action (as indeed is shown by *action*, from *act*). One of the meanings of *-(i)al* is to indicate 'related to', so *cordial* means 'related to the heart'. As this paragraph shows, Germanic and French suffixes were used in comparable ways, and were thus sometimes 'in competition' with each other. The activity's examples *likelihood* and *probability* show that.

One test that a suffix has to pass to become truly part of the language is to attach itself to words from different origins than its own. So when a French-derived suffix starts to be attached to a Germanic-derived word, it really has become accepted. This happens late in the period (in the fourteenth and fifteenth centuries, for example) with some French suffixes. One example is the word *eggement*. It comes from the ON verb *eggen*, meaning 'to egg on, instigate'. So you have an ON root plus a French suffix. The word no longer exists today, but is in Chaucer's *Man of Law's Tale* (1386): *Thurgh wommans eggement, Mankynde was lorn* (lost). The reference, presumably, is to Adam and Eve.

In linguistics, the word **productive** is used to describe an element that is, in the *OED*'s definition, 'readily or frequently used in the formation of new words'. For a suffix to become productive in this sense, it needs to have a clear and useful meaning. The French-derived suffix *-able* meets this criterion, and so became popular, so much so that in Late Middle English (LME) you find it attached to Germanic root words. Thus we find *believable*, which is Germanic *believe* plus French *-able*; (the word is something of a false friend, though, because it meant 'trustworthy', which is not quite our modern meaning). There is also in ME the strangely modern-sounding *doable* – 'capable of being done'. Again, the root word is Germanic. An interesting example of a word that no longer exists is *derkable*. Here the French suffix has been added to the verb *derken* (from OE *deorcian*, meaning 'to darken'). The adjective, used in 1475, means 'liable to be misled'. One Reginald Pecock's dismal thought in 1475 is that *Ech man is... derkeable and temptable in his resoun*. Back to Adam and Eve again, perhaps...

The same 'acceptability criterion' works the other way round. A French-derived word has become well and truly part of English when it starts taking Germanic suffixes. Thus the ME word *peine* (PDE 'pain', from AN *peine*) starts to take the Germanic *-ful* suffix towards the beginning of the fifteenth century, to give *peinful*. Then Germanic *-ness* is added to make *peinefulnes* The adverb *peinfuli* – with the Germanic *-ly* ending follows shortly. The first citation dates in the *OED* for these are: *painful* (1395), *peinefulnes* (1400), *peinfuli* (1440). You can see that once a word has become accepted, it can multiply forms quickly. There are plenty of other examples, including *gai*, meaning 'joyous' – an Anglo-Norman word first cited in 1225. Once that was 'in', *gainesse* and *gaili* followed hard on its heels.

9.2.2 Borrowings from Flanders, Holland and north Germany

England had flourishing trade relations with the Low Countries, and there were large numbers of Flemish settlers in England and Wales. Part of the attraction was high-quality wool, which the weaving trade in those countries had need of. But there were also seafaring interests in common, as well as artistic ones – Dutch art at the time was flourishing. Loanwords from the Low Countries reflect these interests, with words like *nap* (a woolly material), *skipper*, and *easel* entering the language. Among other interesting imports are *bouse*, to 'drink deeply', which gives us PDE *booze*, and ME *snacchen*, (*snakken* in Middle Dutch). It meant 'to snap', or 'bite' (used for a dog), and it gives us our word *snack*. Again, you find words which show mixed pedigrees. Here are two examples which join Low Country root words with the French-derived suffix *-ard*. This ending sometimes means 'someone who does something too much'. The Middle Dutch verb *doten* meant 'to be crazy, silly', and with the *-ard* suffix this gave *dotard*, meaning 'a fool'. The second example has a particularly interesting history. It is the word *lollard*, from the Dutch *lollen*, meaning 'to mutter'. The word was first associated with the members of pious religious orders who seemed to spend a lot of their time 'muttering' prayers or parts of religious texts. These 'mutterers' were called 'lollards'. The word came to be associated with followers of the religious reformer John Wycliffe. He was a dissident who can be seen as a precursor to the Protestant Reformation. In the linguistic world he is known as a translator of the Bible into English, thus making it available to all those who could not read Latin. His supporters were 'the Lollards'. You will find more about them in CW13.1 (*Translating the Bible*).

9.2.3 Latin borrowings

In fact, Wycliffe and the Lollards were responsible for borrowing a large number of words from another 'donor language' – Latin. According to one estimate, they introduced more than a thousand. Many Latin words came into the language through religious or literary texts, and a large number are still with us today, including *distract, magnify, pulpit, subordinate* and many, many more.

In the fifteenth century, a literary movement arose which was celebrated for what is called **aureate diction** – highly ornamented language with a high proportion of words which are Latinate (meaning Latin-like, or derived from Latin). An author much associated with this was John Lydgate, a monk at Bury St Edmonds in Suffolk. Here is what his contemporary John Metham said about his style:

> Eke Ion Lydgate, sumtyme monke off Byry,
> Hys bokys endyted with termys off retoryk
> And halff chongyd Latyne, with conseytys off poetry
> And crafty imagynacionys off thingys fantastyk

(*endyted* = composed, *chongyd* = changed, *conseytys* = conceits, *crafty* = skilful)

The phrase 'half changed Latin' very elegantly sums up aureate diction. A group of Scottish poets known as the 'Scottish Chaucerians' were also particularly associated with the movement, the best known being William Dunbar and

Robert Henryson. Here are two lines from the opening stanza of Dunbar's poem, *The Golden Targe*. They describe a sunrise:

> Up sprang the goldyn candill matutyne
> With clere depurit bemes cristallyne

These lines give a clear sense of the ornamentation tendency – 'goldyn candill' is a rather elaborate way of describing the sun. *Matutyne* is a Latin word referring to the Christian service called 'Matins', which takes place early in the day. So the word just means 'morning'. *Depurit* (from Latin or perhaps Old French) means 'purified'. You will probably have no trouble understanding the word *crystalline*, coming from French and ultimately Latin.

As with Low Country loanwords, it is not surprising that a number of aureate terms have not made it today, or are in extremely rare use. You might like to use internet and dictionary resources to try and track down the meaning of some of these (AS):

equipollent   dispone   abusion   mansuete   ancilee

The introduction of quantities of Latin words into the language added another register to a vocabulary already becoming rich. It sometimes led to synonym word-pairs becoming synonym word-triplets, with Latin terms being added to the Germanic and French counterparts. Activity 9E (*Identifying synonym word-triplets*) looks at some.

In the Activity 9E examples, the Latin-based words are the more literary, more ornate-sounding ones. So the prosaic-sounding Germanic *rise* compares with the rather lofty Latin *ascend*, and the same can be said about Germanic *ask* and Latin *interrogate*. It would be wrong to generalize this and conclude that all Latinate words coming into English have these characteristics, but a significant number do. It is even true today to say that sometimes in order to sound formal and sophisticated one chooses Latin-based words. The point is well made in an extract from the BBC comedy series *Yes, Prime Minister* (from the 1980s). A main character in the series is the civil servant Sir Humphrey, who often speaks in an intentionally obscure, Latinate way. Here is how he tells his Minister why he wants to leave the department:

> the relationship, which I might tentatively venture to aver has not been without a degree of reciprocal utility and even perhaps occasional gratification, is approaching the point of irreversible bifurcation and, to put it briefly, is in the propinquity of its ultimate regrettable termination.

The minister asks Humphrey to try to summarize 'in words of one syllable'. His summary uses short, simple, Germanic words: I'm on the way out', he says.[2] In the light of what we said earlier about French and Latin suffixes, take a look through Humphrey's first response and notice how many of them are used there.

The activity examples also show that, in general (but not always), the Latin words come into the language slightly later than the French ones. Typical from this point of view are Germanic *fire*, French *flame* and Latin *conflagration*. The *OED* first citation dates are 825, 1384 and 1555 respectively.

Latin borrowings and aureate diction look forward in several ways to future chapters of this book. One is that they had a distinctly literary feel, with links to Chaucer and the Scottish Chaucerians, and Chapter 11 is about literature. But also, these borrowings look forward to the next period in the history of English – the Early Modern English period, associated in part with the Renaissance – that time when the classical cultures of Greece and Rome, and their languages, became a prime focus of attention, if not an obsession. The fascination with aureate diction looks forward to this. It is the precursor to something we will discuss in Chapter 15 – **inkhorn terms**. These were fantastic, elaborate, highly ornate words and phrases coming into English, often from Latin. Aureate diction takes a step in that direction.

9.3 Some ME pragmatics, by goddes bones

In the early pages of this book (section 1.2), the linguistic area of pragmatics was mentioned, and in CW1.1 we looked at various ways of 'saying hello' at different points in the history of English. You might have been surprised to find historical differences. '"Saying hello" is "saying hello"', you might have been tempted to argue, 'it's always the same, so there is no need to look at that in a history of English'. But CW1.1 shows you would be wrong. You might have the same initial reaction in relation to the two pragmatic areas we shall look at now: how Middle English people addressed each other ('terms of address'), and how they cursed or swore. In both cases, you will find differences between then and now. The justification for studying pragmatics historically is that language use changes historically.

9.3.1 Terms of address

Chaucer is without doubt the best-known poet of the ME period. We mentioned earlier (9.2.1) that his work is particularly revealing linguistically because he offers such a mix of characters, social classes and language registers. This is particularly true of *The Canterbury Tales*, a poem in which (you will recall from 8.5) stories are told by a number of people going on a pilgrimage. Because Chaucer's characters are so socially diverse, his works are very useful for the pragmatic study of 'terms of address'.[3]

At one point in *The Canterbury Tales*, the 'master of ceremonies' (the innkeeper, named Harry Bailey), invites the Prioresse to tell the next tale. He addresses her as *My lady prioresse*. The elements of this term of address are: the possessive *my*, a title (*lady*), and her occupation (*prioresse*). These elements occur in the order: 'possessive + title + occupation'. There are a number of other elements that can occur in terms of address. Activity 9F (*Forms of address*) focuses on terms of address in Chaucer and invites you to identify some of these other elements. For the moment, look just at parts (a) and (b).

The activity shows that, as far as titles are concerned, the ones found in Activity 9F are *sir(e)*, *maister*, *madame*, *dame* and *lady*. Like today, *Sir* could refer to a person who has been knighted, but it was also a polite general form of address. Notice that it could be put in front of either an occupation (*sir Cook*) or a first name (*sir John*). Incidentally, '*sir* + first name' was a conventional way of addressing a priest. *Maister* had a variety of meanings, many still used today. It could refer to someone in authority, to an expert (as in our PDE phrase *a master cook*) or to a teacher. But it could also be used as a polite way of addressing an inferior (as in the activity's *maister Nicholay*). For women, *madame* was a particularly elevated title. The Prioress in *The Canterbury Tales*, a character very conscious of her social position, is known as 'Madame Eglentyne'. The wives of Chaucer's artisans (the haberdasher, carpenter and others) also aspire to it: *It is ful fair to been ycleped* [called] *'madame'*, they feel. *Dame* is another title to aspire to. Symkyn, the miller in Chaucer's *Reve's Tale*, has a wife who *dorst no wight* [person] *clepen* [call] *hire but 'dame'*. It is used for a woman of rank, the mistress of a household, or simply as a respectful form of address. As today, *ladie* (*lady*) could be used specifically for the wife of a knighted husband, or as a more general polite address form, sometimes followed by an occupation (as in *lady Prioresse*).

As far as occupation is concerned, in ME it is usually prefixed by a title like 'sir', and when you find it without (as in the activity's *squire*, and *frankeleyn*) this is rather more direct, less polite. The activity also shows that you can address someone by mentioning their relationship to you; the activity has *suster Alisoun*, and *wif*, *spouse* and *cousin* are also common: *go dear spouse*, says one of Chaucer's characters. As in PDE, first names can indicate familiarity, intimacy, solidarity, but also inferiority. Use of both first and surname is rare – *Herri Bailly* is the example in the activity. Often a first name or relationship will be accompanied by a possessive (*my*) or a term of affection (like *deere*), both of which will make it less 'bare'. Thus in the activity you find *gentil Roger* and *my Criseyde*. Using the pronoun *thou* in front of 'occupation' (as in *thou preest*) was rather rude. As our discussion reveals, there are some ME forms of address that have similarities with practices today. But there are also differences. Now is the time to look at parts (c) and (d) of Activity 9F, which asks you to think about these differences.

Perhaps you will have noticed that the most common address forms in PDE are not really represented on the ME list. These are *Mr* and *Mrs*. *Maister* is of course the origin of *Mr*, though we do in fact have a form *Master*, little used nowadays and reserved for young male youths. Notice that ME *maister* is followed by a first name – *maister Nicholay*. Title + first name is not generally used in PDE. You cannot today say 'Mr John' or 'Mrs Mary'. The same is true for other titles like *Professor* and *Dr. Sir* is an interesting exception in PDE when it is used for a knighted person. If a name follows, it must be a first name and not a surname. It is *Sir Winston* but not *Sir Churchill. Sir* is also commonly used today by service providers (like shop assistants) as a form of address, and of course in letters ('Dear Sir'). In PDE we do not use occupations as terms of address. In some European languages you can say the equivalent of 'Mr Barber', or 'Mrs Teacher', but not in English. Rather as in ME, 'first name + surname' is not very common today. Some people use it in correspondence when they do not know their correspondent ('Dear John Smith'), and it is sometimes used to express surprise or annoyance ('John Smith, you should be ashamed of yourself!'). Family relationship address terms (sister, brother, etc.) are hardly ever used. Nor is the possessive, and terms of endearment are altogether rare.

Perhaps you will come out of this section rather surprised at how complex terms of address are in PDE as well as in ME. Hopefully, you will also be convinced that language use does indeed change with time. We will find the same in the next area we will look at...

9.3.2 Swearing

Being foul-mouthed in fifteenth-century England really was quite different from being foul-mouthed today. Activity 9G (*A string of oaths*) invites you to think about the differences, as well as to classify some oaths found in Chaucer.

Hughes (1991) – an entire book on the fascinating topic of swearing – characterizes the Middle Ages as a period when 'an astounding volume of religious asserveration, ejaculation, blasphemy, anathema and cursing, both personal and institutional, fraudulent and genuine, poured forth...' (p. 55). There are estimated to be at least 200 different types of oaths in the works of Chaucer, and by far the most common were on Christ's (or God's) body – Hughes speaks of the 'grisly invocation of Christ's body, blood and nails in the agony of the Crucifixion'. *By goddes bones* and *by Goddes precious herte* are examples from the activity. Perhaps the most foul-mouthed characters in Chaucer are the three young blades who are the protagonists of his *Pardoner's Tale*. About them the storyteller says: *And many a grisly ooth thane han they sworn/And Cristes blessed body they al torente* [tore into pieces]. The activity includes six oaths like this, including a rather pretentious one in Latin – *by corpus dominus*, says the innkeeper, doubtless trying to show off with his learned profanity. The activity also includes two examples referring to Christ's cross, one being the rather poetic *for Cristes sweete tree*. Christ's mother, the Virgin Mary, is also in the list of oaths, as are other Christian saints (Cuthbert, Thomas and Ronan). It is entirely in character that the rather amorously inclined Wife of Bath elevates Venus, the goddess of love, to a sainthood, and talks about *sainte Venus*. All these examples are from *The Canterbury Tales*, but the activity includes three from Chaucer's poem

Troilus and Criseyde, a story with a classical setting. Appropriately enough, the oaths here refer to non-Christian characters: Mars, Jove and Venus. Another two oaths in the activity's list might be called 'family related' – *by my fader soule*, and *by thy fader kyn*.

Part (b) of Activity 9G asks you about the difference between ME and PDE swearing. A main one is that in many modern English-speaking societies, swear words are sexual obscenities, an element that was largely missing from the ME foul mouth. Our emphasis on such obscenities would doubtless puzzle a medieval time-traveller who turned up in today's society. Similarly, you may be puzzled by the ME oaths which to us may seem relatively harmless. Certainly there are many words that today have lost their force, but which in ME times were really quite rude – like *wretch, churl, shrew, foul, lousy*.

The dire punishments meted out to medieval swearers suggests that however harmless some expressions may seem today, they were not so then. Hughes tells of one person who believed that swearers should be 'branded upon the face with a hot iron for a perpetual memorial of their crime'. He also mentions a monk named Dan Michel who denounces swearers as being 'like mad hounds that bite and know not their lord'. (1991: 60). At the same time, alongside many expressions which today we find rather mild, you do in ME on occasions find some of today's taboo words used without compunction. In the *Prologue* to *The Canterbury Tales*, for example, Chaucer talks about *A shiten shepherde and a clean sheep*. And there are some worse ones we will not dwell upon. It is clear that the words and topics a society regards as taboo change with time.

Activity section

9A   Dating first occurrences

(a) 9.2.1 mentioned 1250 as the date after which French loans increased dramatically. Here are some words with French pedigrees that came into English during the ME period. Look the words up in the *OED* – CW2.3 shows you how to do this. Note the dates of the first citations, and separate the words into 'pre-1250' and 'post-1250'. Note also the ME forms of the words:

baron	*priory*	*servant*
noble	*manor*	*empire*

(b) Here is a way of using the *OED* online to gain an impression of the increasing number of new words coming into the language. Go into the *OED* and click on 'advanced search'. One of the options you are then given is to find 'date of entry'. If you put in a date, you will be given a list of all the words which have a first citation from that year. Put in a year before 1250 – say 1230. You will be given a list of 'new' words, plus a number of how many there are. In the case of 1230 the number is 164. Now do the same for a post-1250 date – say 1330, a century after 1230. The figure for new words goes up to 817. Choose some other dates, before and after 1250, and compare the figures.

Click on some of the words listed for both 1230 and 1330 (or for other dates you choose). The likelihood is that many of them will have French origins.

9B Words, alike and similar

Here are some Germanic-derived PDE words, with ME versions given in brackets. Below the table are PDE 'synonym words' (with related, though rarely exactly the same, meanings). They all have French origins.

(a) Write the French-derived words in the boxes beside their Germanic synonym equivalents. The 'answers' are given in the text.

Germanic words	French-derived PDE words	ME equivalents
rise, n (*rese*)		
ask, v (*axien*)		
goodness, n (*godenesse*)		
fear, n (*fere*)		
freedom, n (*fredome*)		
likelihood, n (*liklihod*)		
beginning, n (*begynnynge*)		
worship, n (*worschippe*)		
doom, n (*dome*)		
hearty, adj (*herty*)		
stench, n (*stenche*)		
calf, n (*kelf*)		
ox, n (*oxe*)		
sheep, n (*seop*)		
pig, n (*pigge*)		

commencement	*question*	*pork*	*veal*
liberty	*mount*	*terror*	*mutton*
cordial	*virtue*	*beef*	*odour*
judgement	*probability*	*adoration*	

(b) As you have seen, the synonym words do not mean exactly the same thing. Some denote different things, some are different in terms of connotation. For each pair, say what the difference is. Based on these examples, can you make any tentative generalizations about the different denotations/connotations between Germanic- and French-derived words?

(c) If you have access to the *OED*, look up the French-derived words, and write the ME versions in the box beside each. Where the *OED* gives more than one possible spelling, just select one. For example, one of the ME forms given for the noun *mount* is *montt*.

9C   Some ME false friends   AS

(a) Here are some PDE words. Two examples of associated ME words are given
for each. What do these words mean today? What about the ME words (you
will sometimes have to rely on guesswork)? There is a short glossary below
the examples.

    (i) **gentle**
- *In Southwerk / at this gentil hostelrye / That highte the Tabard* (Chaucer)
- *He was a verray, parfit, gentil knight* (Chaucer)

    (ii) **adventure**
- *A gret ston ... Fel doun, of sodein aventure / Upon the feet of this figure* (Gower)
- *Wrong went my whele, But who may be ageyns hap & aventure?* (Beryn)

    (iii) **cunning (adj)**
- *Þis was a kunnynge astronomer* (Higden's Polychronicon)
- *Iram sente to hym ... schippis and schippe men kunnyng of the see* (Wycliffite Bible)

    (iv) **meat**
- *So that [ye] hafe a lessone redde before yowe euery daye in tyme of mete.* (William Alnwick)
- *he sente Unto the Senatour to come...To sitte with him at þe mete.* (Gower)

    (v) **courage**
- *With-outen drede and fayntnesse of corage* (Secreta Secretorum, anonymous)
- *Redy to wen, den on my pilgrymage / To Caunterbury with ful deu-out corage* (Chaucer)

    (vi) **sad**
- *It ys ordeyned ... that ther be electe and chosen ... sadde and dis-crete persones ... to sitte ... as Juges.* (Ordinances of Worcester)
- *Hyt was a howse of nunes. Of dyuers orderys ... But not welle gouernede. Aftyr the rewle of sad levyng* (Why I Can't Be A Nun)

    (vii) **or**
- *He was dede or ever kynge Uther came to her.* (Malory)
- *Or he deye he shalle be long kynge of all Englond.* (Malory)

    (viii) **nice**
- *He was nyce & ne couþe no wisdom* (Robert of Gloucester)
- *He that is not a grete clerke Is nyse & lewde to medle with that werke.* (Norton)

hostelrye, inn, tavern	*highte*, was called
whele, good furtune	*hap*, fate
wenden, go on foot	*coupe*, knew
rewle, rule, governance	*lewde*, unskilled

(b) In 9.2.1, we describe the 'pathway' by which *silly* went from 'blessed' to 'foolish'. Can you see any pathway that might account for the meaning changes in (i) to (viii) above? When you have tried to do this, and if you have access to the *OED*, look up the words and see if your pathway was the actual one.

(c) For some more examples of false friends, use the MED to look up these words – CW9.1 tells you how to use this resource:

harlot	*clerk*	*courteisie*	*baiten*

Among the meanings given, find any ME ones different from the one in use today.

9D Some suffixable inflections   AS

(a) Activity 9B contains a number of Germanic and French synonym words. Some of these carry suffixes characteristic of their language of origin. List the suffixes, and think of some PDE words which use them.

(b) Suffixes are usually used to create specific parts of speech. For example, the Germanic suffix *-ness* creates nouns, usually out of adjectives. Go through the suffixes on your list; try, where possible, to make some statements about what parts of speech they are used to create.

(c) Although it is often difficult to specify the exact 'meaning' of a suffix, you can often make some general (if rather vague) statement about its sense. Thus *-ness* is often used to express an abstract idea (as in *goodness* and *cleanliness*). Are there any other suffixes on your list which you associate with particular senses? (You will almost certainly not be able to find meanings for them all.)

(d) Moving beyond Activity 9B now, here are some more French-related suffixes which came into ME. Using PDE words to provide you with examples, think about the parts of speech involved, and about their general meanings. If you have access to the *OED*, you could use this to help you.

-ant	*-ous*	*-esse*	*-able*	*-ard*	*-ive*

9E   Identifying synonym word-triplets   AS

(a) Write the Latin-based words (listed under the table) in the rightmost box
    next to their Germanic and French synonyms. Do the Latin words differ in
    terms of style/tone from their Germanic and French counterparts?

Germanic	French	Latin
rise (v)	mount	
ask (v)	question	
fast (adj)	firm	
fire (n)	flame	
fear (n)	terror	
holy (adj)	sacred	
kingly (adj)	royal	

trepidation	interrogate	ascend	regal
consecrated	conflagration	secure	

(b) If you have access to the *OED*, look up some of the triplets in the table above
    (all the words: Germanic, French and Latin), and find out the dates of the first
    citations. This will give you an idea of the chronology of these various addi-
    tions to the language. Note that when the *OED* says 'OE' instead of giving a
    date, it means that the citation date is uncertain but within the OE period.

9F   Forms of address

(a) As the text mentions, the three elements of *My lady prioresse* are: 'posses-
    sive', 'title' and 'occupation'. Here are some more forms of address from
    Chaucer. For each example, write down what elements are used and the
    order in which they occur. There is a short glossary under the examples:
    • *Cometh neer quod he / my lady Prioresse / And ye sire clerk*
    • *my Custance / wel may thy goost haue feere*
    • *Custance answerde / sire / it is cristes might*
    • *deere cosyn / Palamon quod he*
    • *Bifore the court / thanne preye I thee sir knyght*
    • *Now knowe I, dere wyf, thy stedfastnesse*
    • *Now telle on, gentil Roger by thy name*
    • *My deere doghter Venus / quod Saturne*
    • *my Criseyde, allas, what subtilte*
    • *if it may don ese / To thee sir Cook*
    • *Alayn, thou is a fonne*
    • *Madame, quod he, ye may be glad and blithe*
    • *Go deere spouse / and help to saue oure lyf*
    • *What, frankeleyn! pardee, sire, wel thou woost*

- *And therfore / Herry Bailly / by thy feith*
- *And seyde / deere suster Alisoun*
- *Com neer, thou preest, com hyder, thou sir john*
- *Where is youre fader / o Grisildis he sayde*
- *My lorde the Monke quod he be merry of chere*
- *Thise Marchantz / han hym toold / of dame Custance*
- *hayl maister Nicholay / Good morwe*
- *Squier, com neer, if it youre wille be*

goost, spirit	*subtilte*, deception	*don ese*, gives pleasure
fonne, fool	*frankeleyn*, landowner	*pardee*, by God
thou woost, you know	*merry of chere*, content	*marchantz*, merchants

(b) Though you will not be able to make firm judgements, do you have any intuitions about which are the more and less polite of these forms of address? Are there any on the list that seem particularly polite, or the opposite – a little blunt or rude?

(c) Now consider these ME forms of address in comparison with PDE ones. Which of the elements would not be used in PDE? Which combinations are not found? Are there any common PDE forms not found in the examples above?

(d) Some specific questions about PDE (you may already have answered some of these above):
   (i) When do we use 'sir'. And what about 'madam'?
   (ii) Do you ever find 'Mr' followed by a first name? What about a surname?
   (iii) When do we use 'first + surname'?
   (iv) Do we ever mention an occupation in a form of address? What about a family relationship?
   (v) Is the possessive 'my' ever used? What about terms of endearment?

9G   A string of oaths

(a) Here are some Chaucerian oaths. Put them into categories according to who or what is being sworn by. For example, the first is 'by a part of God's body'. There is a glossary below:
- *by goddes bones*
- *by the Crosse*
- *by seint Cutberd*
- *by my fader soule*
- *by thy fader kyn*
- *by Mars, the god that helmed is of steel*
- *for Cristes sweete tree*
- *by corpus dominus*
- *for cristes moder deere*
- *by the blisful Venus that I serue*
- *by Seint Ronyan*

- *by nayles and by blood*
- *for Joves name in hevene*
- *by Seinte Marie*
- *by Goddes precious herte*
- *by the blood of Crist*
- *by seint Thomas of Kent*

Cutberd, Cuthbert	*fade*, father's	*heled*, with a helmet
tree, here = cross	*corpus dominus*, body of the lord (Latin)	*modr*, mother
Roynan, Ronan (an Irish saint)		

(b) How they swore in medieval England and how we swear now are really quite different. How would you describe the difference?

Answer section

9.2.1 French words in the Chaunticleer passage (lines 12-19)

At least the following are candidates for being of French origin: *traysoun, espye, revysshed, flaterie/flaterye/flatour, allas, courtes, losengeour, plesen, feith*.

9.2.2 Aureate words

As we have seen, it is sometimes difficult to say whether a word comes into the language from French and Latin. This applied to some of the words asked about:

equipollent, 'equipped with equal power'
abusion, 'abuse'   *mansuete*, 'gentle'

dispone, 'set in order'
ancilee, 'handmaid'.

Activity 9C

Here are some (but not all) the meanings of the words in ME:

(i) *gentil*, of noble birth; (ii) *aventure*, fate, chance (think PDE *peradventure*); (iii) *cunning*, skilful, knowledgeable; (iv) *mete*, food, meal; (v) *corage*, heart, desire; (vi) *sad*, serious; (vii) *or*, before (like the archaic word *'ere*); (viii) *nice*, foolish, sluggish.

Activity 9D

(d) *-ant*, verb to adjective, sometimes expresses an agent (e.g. *repellant*)
-ous, often noun to adjective, meaning 'characterized by' (e.g. *dangerous*)
-esse, noun to noun, female (e.g. *hostess*)

-able, verb to adjective, sometimes 'able to be' (e.g. *believable*)
-ard, noun from adjective, sometimes derogatory (e.g. *dullard*)
-ive, verb to adjective, 'having the nature of' (*productive*)

Activity 9E

Here are the triplets, and the dates of first *OED* citations:

Germanic	French	Latin
rise (v) OE	mount 1300	ascend 1382
ask (v) OE	question 1470	interrogate 1483
fast (adj) 888	firm 1611	secure 1548
fire (n) 825	flame 1384	conflagration 1555
fear (n) OE	terror 1480	trepidation 1625
holy (adj) 1000	sacred 1380	consecrated 1549
kingly (adj) 1382	royal 1400	regal 1375

Further reading

Crystal's informative and highly readable history of English (2004) includes a chapter (No. 7) on ME lexis.

Burnley (1992) offers a more detailed and comprehensive account of ME vocabulary.

Durkin (2014) – also given as 'Further reading' for Chapter 5 – includes a long section on ME borrowings.

As well as having a chapter on vocabulary, Horobin (2013) considers pragmatics, including 'terms of address' and 'swearing'.

Traugott (2012) is a chapter dedicated to ME pragmatics and discourse.

McEnery (2009) is a book all about swearing in English, and it has a historical dimension to it.

Notes

1 The date is suggested by Baugh & Cable (2013), but there are those who argue against the significance of that date, Rothwell (1998), for example.
2 The *Yes, Prime Minister* quote is from Lynn & Jay (1989: 16). It is cited in Culpeper (2015: 44).
3 Much of what follows in this section (9.3) is based on the account of Horobin (2013).

10 'Lighter ... than the old and ancient English'

The complex system of inflections which we found in OE largely breaks down during the ME period, and in this chapter we will see the process of syncretism gaining momentum. Also, many strong (irregular) verbs became weak (regular). The terms **synthetic** and **analytic** are discussed, and the conclusion is that English in this period is moving towards being a more analytic language. The chapter also looks at pronunciation, and involves a comparison between ME sounds and **received pronunciation (RP)** today. Some things to do before reading on:

- There are quite a few linguistic concepts brought up in the chapter. Find out something about: synthetic and analytic languages, relative clauses, transitive and intransitive verbs, the perfect and the progressive aspects.
- It would also be useful to look back to earlier sections of the book which deal with topics that come up again here. Particularly: 6.2.3 on OE strong verbs; 6.1.3 on strong and weak adjectives in OE; 6.3 on word order in OE.
- Section 10.3 introduces the concept of received pronunciation (RP). Find out about this. If you speak RP, identify some of the characteristics associated with the accent. If you are a non-RP native-English speaker – or if your L1 is not English – can you identify an accent which is regarded as the accepted standard in your language? Is it associated with any geographical area or group of people?
- It is well worth looking at CW10.1 (*Making sounds and writing them down*) before reading this chapter. It contains information about phonetic transcriptions (which the chapter contains), as well as about how consonants and vowels are produced and classified in English.
- One literary work that is mentioned in this chapter is the *General Prologue* to Chaucer's *Canterbury Tales*. Find out something about this *Prologue*.

10.1 'Lightening up' the language

The Middle English period was a time of great linguistic change. There were two main ones. One was to do with vocabulary, and, as we saw in Chapter 9, a whole torrent of loanwords entered the language. The other broad change was to do with inflections. Though OE was inflectionally simpler than PIE (Proto Indo-European, mentioned in 2.2), the process of syncretism was beginning to rid OE of inflectional complexities. It is perhaps the single most important characteristic of ME that this process of syncretism continued. The result was that, to use a phrase of Caxton's, the language became 'lighter … than the old and ancient English', at least as far as inflections were concerned.[1]

10.2 Grammar

10.2.1 Nouns phrases with a 'new look'

It was in the noun phrase that some of the largest changes took place, so we will begin there. You can assess the simplification process for yourself by looking back to Table 6.1 (in section 6.1.2). This gave the declensions of *se dola stān*, *þæt dole giefu* and *sēo dole ēage*. Very complex. Now compare it with Table 10.1 below which shows the NP in Chaucer's time (he died in 1400, in the latter part of the ME period). The OE adjective *dola* ('silly') in Table 6.1 has been changed to the ME *olde* ('old').

Table 10.1 The ME noun phrase

Sing	N	the olde stoon	the olde yift(e)	the olde eye
	A	the olde stoon	the olde yift(e)	the olde eye
	G	the olde stoones	the olde yiftes	the olde eyes
	D	the olde stoon(e)	the olde yift(e)	the olde eye
Plur	N	the olde stoones	the olde yiftes	the olde eyen
	A	the olde stoones	the olde yiftes	the olde eyen
	G	the olde stoones	the olde yiftes	the olde eyen
	D	the olde stoones	the olde yiftes	the olde eyen

To do the OE/ME comparison in detail, concentrate initially on the nouns, then on the adjectives (both the tables show the weak forms), and finally on the definite articles. In each case compare the OE and ME declensions, specifying exactly what changes have occurred. The three categories you will find yourself thinking about are of course case, number and gender. Do some counting: for example, how many different forms are there for *stoon*, and *yift(e)*, and *eye*, in comparison with *stān*, *giefu* and *ēage*?

Now focus on ME alone and try to come up with statements about how ME nouns, adjectives and articles 'work', based on the examples given in Table 10.1. When are the various forms you have noted used?

The tables clearly show how inflectionally simple ME has become. The OE noun *stān* has six different OE forms, while *giefu* and *ēage* have four. The ME *stoon* and *eye* have three forms, and *yift(e)* just two. The only ME case inflection is for the genitive, which has *-es*. Notice also that the considerable OE gender differences have disappeared.

ME plural forms had a 'new look' too. OE plurals had six nominative and accusative forms overall – Bennett and Smithers (1982) give as their examples: *dagas* ('days'), *scipu* ('ships'), *giefe* ('gifts'), *suna* ('sons'), *guman* ('men'), *bēc* ('books'). In ME the number was reduced to two. In the cases of *stoon* and *yift(e)*, the inflection *-(e)s* is used. But look at the plural form of ME *eye*. It is *eyen*, and it comes from the OE plural form *ēagan*. Nouns like these with plurals ending in *-an* were a common class in OE, and on the journey to ME, the *-an* became *-en*. In Early ME, these two plural forms, *-es* and *-en*, co-existed. The first was dominant in the north, the second was found in the south. We have seen before (in 5.3.3, for example) that 'north to south' language movement sometimes occurs, and this is a case in point; *-(e)s* gradually moved southwards. By 1250, this form was used throughout the Midlands, and by the fourteenth century, it was down into the south. But in Chaucer you do find some remaining *-en* forms: for example, *foon* alongside *foes*, and *toon* as well as *toes*. Some remnants of *-en* survived even longer. You find a version of *eyen* (*eyne*) in Shakespeare, as when a character in *Antony and Cleopatra* talks of *Plumpy Bacchus with pink eyne*. A dominant *-(e)s* ending and an occasional *-en* one is just what we find today for plural nouns. In PDE, *-(e)s* is by far the most common inflection (in *stones*, *gifts*, *eyes*, for example). But there are even today some irregular plural forms, and among these is the *-en* – not found in *eye* any more, but in PDE *men* and *oxen*.

You may remember that in OE there were two adjective forms, strong and weak. They were discussed in 6.1.3. What happened to the distinction? Well, it is still there in ME, though it was on the way out by the time of Chaucer. The strong forms are not shown in our table, and they are easy to describe: the *-e* inflection is used throughout the weak form and in the strong plural. The suffix is dropped in the strong singular, and there are no gender differences. CW6.2 (*A strong OE adjective*) shows the OE strong declension. If you count all the weak and strong versions of the OE *dola*, the total is ten. The ME *old*, weak and strong, has only two. Even simpler is the ME definite article. All the forms like *se*, *þone*, *þæs*, *þæm* have become just *the*. Overall, the noun phrase really did have a 'new look'.

10.2.2 The causes for syncretism, and an 'indeterminate' vowel

Why did these simplifications occur? Section 6.1.4 mentioned one reason for syncretism, that the Germanic stress pattern placed stress on the first syllable of a word. This helped to draw attention away from word endings, which is of course where suffixes dwell. It is worth looking now in a little more detail at what initial word stress did to other, unstressed, syllables in a word, particularly to their vowels. In English (but not in all languages), vowels that are not stressed can change their pronunciation. You can see this at work in PDE. Think about the word 'but'. Imagine that for some reason you wanted to emphasize this word when speaking – perhaps when saying 'Yes, I agree with you. BUT, on the other hand…'. You would probably pronounce the word [bʌt], with the same vowel found in 'shut'. Usually, though, *but* is unstressed, as in the sentence 'Russell is clever, but so is Chaunticleer'. Then the vowel is generally not [ʌ] but [ə] – like the first vowel in the word 'afoot'. This vowel [ə] is an interesting one. Technically it is known as **schwa**, but it has also been called 'the indeterminate vowel'. Sometimes it is described as 'weak', and we may say that in our 'but' example, the [ʌ] is **weakened** to [ə].

Schwa played its part in the ME loss of inflections. To see the process at work, we can look at the plural forms of the noun OE *stān* ('stone'). As Table 6.1 shows, these were *stānas, stāna* and *stānum*. With the stress on the first syllable, the unstressed plural endings became less distinct from each other. The final unstressed vowel became weakened to schwa, written as an 'e'. This gives *stanes, stane* and *stanem*. Another consequence of unstressed endings was that the 'm' on *stānum* was dropped, and that left just two forms: *stanes* and *stane*. Later, another process came into operation. People came to think of *-s* as the way to form plurals. So *stane* became *stanes*, and this became the sole plural form. It eventually gave us PDE plural *stones*.

There is another factor that contributed to the decrease in inflections. We mentioned in 8.2 that English was spoken by the lower classes. Their small amount of education did not expose them to teachers laying down prescriptive sets of rules about language use; they did not have prescriptive statements drummed into them at school: statements perhaps like 'the dative singular feminine of a strong adjective should end in *-re*, while the weak form takes the *-s* suffix'. Prescriptive statements can help a lot to preserve some linguistic complexities, and when these are not given, the result can be simplification. So it comes about that we have partially to thank lack of education for the relative inflectional simplicity of English today. It is a reason that is also relevant when we come to consider another area of ME grammar where big changes occurred: verbs.

10.2.3 Verbs

ME verbs are complicated. As Lass (1992: 125) puts it 'the story of the verb during Middle English is enormously involved, and nearly impossible to tell coherently'. Just how involved it is does not really become apparent when you look at the 'weak' verb (the terms 'weak' and 'strong' were first used for verbs in 6.2.2). To enable you to compare OE and ME verbs, the conjugation of OE *lufian*, taken from Chapter 6 (Table 6.3) is given again below. The ME *loue* (also meaning 'to love') is given too. The simplifications and syncretism from OE to ME are not so great as they are for nouns and adjectives, but you can see that there are some.

Use Table 10.2 to list what they are. You can also use the table to take a look at the personal pronouns. How do they compare with the PDE pronouns?

Table 10.2 OE and ME verbs compared

	OE lufian		ME louen
Present			
ic	lufie	I	loue
þū	lufast	thou	louest
hē, hēo, hit	lufað	he, she, it	loueth
wē, gē, hī	lufiað	we, ye, they	loue
Participle	lufiende		louyng
Past			
ic	lufode	I	louede
þū	lufodest	thou	louedest
hē, hēo, hit	lufode	he, she, it	louede
wē, gē, hī	lufodon	we, ye, they	louede
Participle	gelufod		yloued

You cannot fail to notice from this table just how close to today's English ME is becoming. This is clear when you look at the pronouns as well as the verb forms. The only difference between the ME and PDE forms is *thou* (which is hardly used now), and *ye*, which has become *you*.

The complicated side of ME verbs becomes apparent when you turn to the strong verbs. You will remember that there was a large store of OE strong verbs – 6.2.3 will remind you about these. One difference between OE weak and strong verbs lay in the past-tense forms. The weak ending in OE was *-ode*, which became *-ede* in ME – leading to our PDE *-ed*. In strong verbs, the root vowel usually changed, so the 'ī' of *rīdan* ('ride'), became 'ā' in the past singular *rād*. Bearing this in mind, take a look at Activity 10A (*Verbs, strong and weak*), which focuses on some ME verbs. What this activity shows is discussed in the next paragraph.

All the verbs in Activity 10A were strong in OE. But, as the activity reveals, in ME they existed in both strong and weak forms. Take the OE verb *helpan*, for example. In OE it had the forms *healp*, *hulpon* and *holpen*, showing the changing root vowel associated with strong verbs. Now look at the ME verb *helpen*. It also has a 'strong form'; the activity gives the part participle *holpen*, with the vowel change from 'e' to 'o'. But there was also a weak form coming into use. The past tense *helpide* has the same vowel as the infinitive, and is marked by the suffix -(*i*)*de*, associated with weak verbs. *Helpide* became today's 'helped'. The same can be said about all the other verbs in the activity. *Climben* ('to climb') has a strong form *clomben*, after the OE, but you also find *climbed*. Strong *welk* stands alongside weak *walked*, *loughe* beside *lawghed*, and *shoon* with *shynede*. What is happening is that in ME, a large number of OE strong verbs were in the process of becoming weak. And weak is what they are today. With one possible exception, all the verbs in the activity are now weak (or 'regular'). The possible exception is *shine*. Today this generally remains strong, as it was in OE – the PDE simple past and past participle is *shone* (though, notice, we would prefer *He shined his shoes* rather than (*)*He shone his shoes*). But even with this verb there was an attempt in ME to make it weak; alongside strong *shoon* we find weak *shynede*.

The 'movement towards weak' was well under way in ME. According to one estimate, nearly a third of the OE strong verbs died out in the Early Middle English (EME) period, with the process reaching its height in the fourteenth century.[2] If it were not for the simplifying effect of ME, we would have many more irregular verbs today; the list of verbs which were once strong and are now weak includes *ache, bow, brew, burn, glide, mourn, row, step,* and *weep*. One reason for this movement is the powerful force of analogy – the process whereby 'exceptions' often tend to fall in line with rules. Hence irregular verbs tend to become regular. Remember also the point made earlier about the lower classes and education. Once again we have perhaps to thank the relatively uneducated for the simplifications they were making to the language.

But look at the dates of the sources to Activity 10A's examples. They suggest that the changes we have been discussing did not occur overnight. Strong verbs did not give up the fight without a battle, and for a very long time, strong and weak forms co-existed before the eventual victory of the weak. 'Help' is a good example. *Helpide* may have occurred in ME, but the 'strong' form *holp* lasted at least into Shakespeare. For example, Gloucester in *King Lear* says: *Yet, poor old heart, he holp the heavens to rain.*

Though weak usually wins out over strong, there are a few verbs in PDE which have kept both strong and weak forms. One is *weave*, with both *wove* and *weaved* as past forms. *Hang* is an interesting case. There are some – possibly conservative – British English speakers today, including myself, who use *hung* as the normal simple past, but *hanged* when the form of capital punishment is being spoken of – for me, a coat is *hung up*, but a man is *hanged*. We also today find some strong past participles used as adjectives. So *swelled* is the normal past participle of *swell*, but *swollen* can be used as an adjective. So too *molten*.

As well as OE strong verbs becoming weak in ME, there were other changes that occurred to the strong verbs. If you are interested in some of these, look at CW10.2 (*Strong verbs behaving badly*), which shows how the seven classes of OE strong verbs listed in 6.2.3 (Table 6.4) were becoming mixed and simplified in ME.

10.2.4 Word order

Word order is an important topic in the study of ME. As we saw in 6.3, OE word order was quite flexible. In the 'lettuce story', for example, we found SVO, VSO and SOV. The one that is most common in PDE is SVO, and that was in fact the least frequent order in the story. Next came VSO, but the most common was SOV. This order, in which the verb comes at the end, has led some to call OE a verb-final language.

ME – which after all developed from OE – continues to show some word-order flexibility. This is particularly true in poetry. If a poet wants to create a rhyme, or maintain a particular rhythm, using 'poetic licence' to change normal word orders is one way of doing it. Chaucer's 'Chaunticleer passage' gives examples of some of the more common conventions of ME word order, and Activity 10B (*Word order and Chaunticleer*) explores these. To do this activity, and to make sense of the next paragraph, you will need to refer back to 8.5's 'Chaunticleer passage'.

A number of the sentences in the passage show our common PDE word order of SVO (though often the O is an indirect object). So *many a fals flatour / Is in youre courtes*, and *Chauntecleer stood hye upon his toos* do not seem at all odd to us. But the SOV order, so common in OE, is also there, as in the line: *This Chauntecleer his wynges gan to bete*. The passage also shows that in sentences with a modal or auxiliary verb, the main verb may be delayed until the end of the clause. This is what happens in *whan he gan him espye*. A subordinate clause can also send the verb to the end. For example, *He that soothfastnesse unto yow seith* is a relative clause, with *that* meaning 'who', and the verb comes at the end. The tradition of OE as a verb-final language is being maintained here. Another pattern that the passage shows is found when the object (or indirect object) is a pronoun. It is put before the verb: *I to yow wolde harm or vileynye*, says Russell.

What about VSO? We call it **inversion** when you have VS instead of SV. In ME, this can happen after the word *ne*, which is used to introduce a negative. An example is the line *For yet ne was ther no man that hym sewed* (rather than **yet ne ther was*). You also find inversion in questions beginning with a so-called **wh-word** (like *where* or *when*, which begin with a *wh-*). Hence *wher wol ye gon?* Inversion can also occur after an adverb (like *so* meaning 'thus'), or an adverbial clause (like *by the gargat*). The subjects *he* and *Chauntecleer* come after the verbs *was* and *hente* in the lines: *So was he ravysshed with his flaterie*, and *[he] by the gargat hente Chauntecleer*.

You might like to think about which of these word-order conventions continue into PDE. We have already seen that by far the most common order today is SVO. Of the situations we have considered above, almost the only one where PDE deviates from this SVO order is in *wh-* questions. Here, as in ME, we use inversion – we say *where are you going?* rather than **where you are going?* We mentioned in 6.3 that there is also a PDE remnant of the 'inversion after an adverbial' convention. When the adverbial is a 'restrictive' or negative one, PDE continues to use inversion. In 6.3 the example given was with *scarcely*. Other examples are *seldom*, and *at no time*: we say *seldom have I seen him work* and *at no time was she in danger*. You simply cannot say **Seldom I have seen him work*, or **at no time she was in danger*.

The 'Chaunticleer passage' illustrates that, as in OE, there was some flexibility about ME word order. But partly because it is poetry and not prose, the passage does not fully illustrate one very important point about ME word order. It is that overall the language was moving quickly towards being what it is now – a predominantly SVO language. Here is how Fischer (1992: 371) puts it: 'I do not think it is too bold to state that we are dealing here with a major restructuring, one in which the language, which was largely verb final, changed into one that is clearly verb non-final.' The change was becoming evident early in the ME period. In his study on the topic, Mitchell (1964) looks at the Late OE text of the *Peterborough Chronicle* and compares it with continuations of the *Chronicle* written in the 1122–54 period (which makes it EME). He finds some interesting statistics. In subordinate clauses, the instances of SVO orders increases from 41 per cent to between 72 and 88 per cent. These figures are quite dramatic ones. They suggest just how fast English was 'becoming SVO'. Because the 'Chaunticleer passage' does not illustrate this important trend so well, take a look at CW10.3 (*Covering your head*). It contains a prose passage which makes the point much more clearly. That passage also shows – in general and not just for word order – how much like PDE LME had become.

10.2.5 Synthetic and analytic

A 'major restructuring'? Can the change to SVO really be regarded as so important? A recent editor of the *Peterborough Chronicle* (Clark 1970: lxix) certainly believes so: 'before our eyes', he says, ' English is beginning to change from a synthetic language to an analytic one'. These words, **synthetic** and **analytic**, hold the key to the importance of word order, and we need to spend some time on them.

A good place to start is back with the nun and her lettuce. In 6.1.1 we looked at two ways of expressing possession in English. They were:

(a) *The nun's lettuce*
(b) *The lettuce of the nun.*

In (a), you might say that the idea of 'nun' and the idea of 'possession' are brought together in the one word: *nun's*. In (b) there are two separate words that do the same thing: *nun* captures the idea of, well, 'nun', and there is a separate word, *of*, which expresses the possession element. One definition of 'synthetic' given in the *OED* is 'involving synthesis, or combination of parts into a whole'. In our example, the 'combination of parts into a whole' is shown by the elements *nun* and *-s* combining to make one word. 'Synthetic' has come to be used in linguistics to describe a language which tends to use inflections to show grammatical function. One meaning of the word 'analytic' in the *OED* is 'characterized by the use of separate words ... rather than inflections to express syntactical relationships'. *Of the nun* is, you might say, an analytic expression, and an analytic language is one that tends to have single words to express discrete ideas.

Is PDE a synthetic or analytic language? Well, both sentences (a) and (b) are good PDE sentences, so we have to say that English today is both synthetic and analytic. In fact, no language is entirely synthetic or analytic. All we can say is that a specific language tends towards one or the other, or that one language is more synthetic or analytic than another. Bearing this in mind, we can certainly state that OE was quite synthetic, and Chapter 6 shows this very clearly. PDE, on the other hand, is relatively analytic. ME stands in the middle. It is the stage of the language in which synthetic moves towards analytic. It is quite a big move. Which is just what Mitchell and Clark are saying.

It is common for analytic languages to use prepositions to express grammatical notions, in the way that *of* is used to express 'possession' in sentence (b). You may remember that in 6.1.1 we discussed the dative case, used to express indirect objects. It is often associated with a *to* phrase in analytic PDE, while in synthetic OE you did not need the preposition because the inflection signalled the dative form. One sentence in the 'lettuce story' shows this well. In *Hwæt dyde Ic hire* ('what I did to her'), the dative is signalled by an inflected form (*hire*) in the OE, while the PDE translation needs the preposition *to*. Incidentally, talking of the dative, you may be interested in a rather rare and strange use of it that grew up in the ME period. It is called the 'ethic dative', and is described in CW10.4 (*A particularly moral dative?*).

But there is more to being analytic than using prepositions. Word order also plays a very important role. You may remember from our discussion in 6.3 that OE used inflections to show grammatical relations in sentences like *Hunta abrēoteð oxan*, translated as 'the hunter killed the ox'. This is the synthetic way of doing things. In ME, where inflections were on the way out, word order took over some grammatical roles. Using word order rather than inflections to 'do their grammar' in this way is a central characteristic of analytic languages. And for word order to fulfil its grammatical roles, it must be stable. Though exceptions will always be permitted, one order must become the norm – precisely so that language users are able to distinguish subjects from objects, for example. Word-order flexibility has to be dramatically curtailed, and this is just what happens in ME. The stable, relatively 'inflexible' form which became the norm was SVO.

10.2.6 More verb forms

In this book we have dealt with the present and past tenses. These tenses are marked, in OE, ME and PDE, by inflections – in a 'synthetic way'. So in PDE you know that *He loves* is present and *He loved* is past, because of their suffixes. Some languages mark other tenses by suffixes. In Italian, for example, the first person future tense of the verb *cantare* ('to sing') is *Io cantero*. It is the *-ero* suffix that signals the future here. The English route is more analytic. One (but not the only) way of expressing future time uses the modal verbs *will* and *shall* – *I will/shall* sing. It is easy to see how *will* came to be associated with futurity. The OE verb was *willan* and it expressed not futurity but volition: so 'I will sing', meant 'I want to sing' or 'I would like to sing'. This is just a small semantic step away from expressing something that is going to happen in the future.

There are several other English verb forms which use auxiliaries, in the analytic manner, rather than suffixes. One is used to express **perfect aspect**. In PDE we do this by using part of the verb *have* followed by the past participle – in *He has walked there*, for example. Like the use of *shall/will* to express futurity, this form was not really present in OE. It really only came into use in the 1400s. It is right there in what are surely Chaucer's most famous lines – the opening of the *General Prologue* to *The Canterbury Tales*: *Whan that aprill with his shoures soote / The droghte of march hath perced to the roote*. There are in fact four examples in the first paragraph of that poem, and a future activity (11A in Chapter 11) asks you to locate these.

You may have come across a similar way of expressing perfect aspect in another language, like French. In some languages, and on some occasions, the auxiliary used is the equivalent of *be* rather than *have*. In French you say *J'ai vu* (*I have seen*), but *Je suis venu* (literally 'I am come'). The (rather vague) rule of thumb is that *be* is used after 'verbs of motion'. ME too uses both *be* and *have*. The exact conditions under which one or the other is used are hard to specify precisely. According to one formulation, *be* is used with intransitive verbs (verbs which do not take a direct object), and *have* with transitive ones. So in Chaucer's *Knight's Tale* you find *Whan he **was come** … un to the toun*, but elsewhere in the same poem *Juno … **hath destroyed** … al the blood / Of Thebes*. Sometimes the same verb is found with both auxiliaries. Again in Chaucer there is *we **ben entred** into shippes bord* (*The Miller's Tale*), but *ye **have entred** into myn hous by violence* (*The Tale of Melibeus*). This variation may simply be evidence of the system in transition, though one attempt to explain the difference says that *be* is used to emphasize the 'state resulting from the action' (something like 'here we are on board the ship' in the above example), while *have* in *have entred* emphasizes the action itself.

The use of *be* as well as *have* persisted into EME times and beyond, but today we use *have* exclusively. Why did *have* 'oust' *be*? One theory is that *be* was already in use as an auxiliary, for example in the passive. *Be* is also used in another verb construction which, analytically, uses this auxiliary rather than inflections. This is the **continuous aspect** (as in *I am singing*). We will consider this in 19.4.1, and CW19.2 (*The continuous aspect in PDE*) looks at its use today. You may wish take a quick look at CW19.2 now.

The ME period also saw the development of the so-called **historic present** tense. This is when a present tense is used to describe past actions. CW10.5 (*The past in the present*) describes this.

10.3   Sounds ... and what happened to Chaunticleer

Nouns and verbs, synthesis and analysis, inflections and word order apart, what happened to Chaunticleer? We left him in the jaws of Russell, about to be consumed for dinner. His owner and various other characters – human and animal – learn of his capture and follow Russell into the woods, creating a hullabaloo. Chaunticleer realizes that to escape, he must persuade Russell to open his mouth. He does this by suggesting that the fox should remonstrate with the pursuers and tell them to go away. In the extract below, Russell opens his mouth to speak, Chaunticleer seizes the opportunity and escapes into a tree. Russell is now left to work out how to lure Chaunticleer back down from the tree and into his jaws again. But Chaunticleer has learned his lesson:

> The fox answerde, 'In feith, it shal be don.'
> And as he spak that word, al sodeynly
> This cok brak from his mouth delyverly,
> And heighe upon a tree he fleigh anon.
> And whan the fox saugh that the cok was gon,
> 'Allas!' quod he, 'O Chauntecleer, allas!
> I have to yow,' quod he, 'ydoon trespass
> …'.
> 'But, sire, I dide it in no wikke entente,
> Com doun, and I shall telle yow what I mente'
>
> (*delyverly* = quickly, nimbly; *wikke* = bad)

We can use this passage to explore an aspect of ME we have not so far touched upon: what it sounded like. CW10.6 (*Chaunticleer escapes*) contains a reading of the passage. Listen to it a few times and try to identify characteristics that distinguish it from modern-day pronunciation (in whatever version of English you are most familiar with).

Once you have done this, here is a phonetic transcription of the passage you can use to help identify more characteristics (it is also reproduced in CW10.6 for convenience):

> ðə fɒks ænswɜːrd 'in faiθ it ʃæl bei dɒn'
> ənd æz hei spaːk ðæt wɜːrd æl sɒdeɪnliː
> ðɪs kɒk braːk frəm ɪz muːθ dəlivrɜːliː
> ənd haɪx əpɒn ə treɪ hei flaɪx ənɒn.
> ənd wæn ðə fɒks saʊx ðæt ðə kɒk wəz gɒn
> 'əlaːs' kwəʊt hei 'əʊ ʃæntəkleɪr əlaːs
> iː hæv tʊ juː kwəʊt hei iːdɒn trespaːs
> …'.
> 'Bət siːr, iː dɪd ɪt ɪn nəʊ wɪk əntentə
> kɒm duːn, ənd iː ʃæl tel juː wɒt iː mentə'

How does this compare with today's pronunciation? To help you answer this, CW10.6 also contains an audio version of the passage read by me in my PDE accent. This accent is the one known as **received pronunciation**, or **RP**. It is a particular variety of PDE British English pronunciation, originating in the English southern counties and accepted by some as a 'standard'. Here is the transcription (also in CW10.6):

> ðə fɒks ɑːnsəd 'ɪn feɪθ ɪt ʃɑːl biː dʌn'
> ənd æz hiː speɪk ðæt wɜːd ɔːl sʌdənli
> ðɪs kɒk brəʊk frəm ɪz maʊθ delɪvrəli
> ənd haɪ əpɒn ə triː hiː fluː ənɒn.
> ənd wen ðə fɒks sɔː ðæt ðə kɒk wəz gɒn
> 'əlæs' kwəʊθ hiː 'əʊ ʃæntəklɪə əlæs
> aɪ hæv tʊ juː kwəʊθ hiː iːdʌn trespæs
> ...'
> 'bət saɪə, aɪ dɪd ɪt ɪn nəʊ wɪk əntent
> kʌm daʊn, ənd aɪ ʃæl tel juː wɒt aɪ ment'

Of course, a transcription like this is of restricted value for comparison purposes, partly because some of the words in the text no longer exist, or have changed out of recognition – how do you pronounce *delyverly* or *fleigh* in RP? The answer is, you do not. But you may find it interesting to compare transcriptions from different historical times in detail, and this can draw attention to points of interest.

The following paragraphs discuss some of the ways in which these two phonetic transcriptions – the ME and the RP – differ phonetically, in a way that at the same time encourages you to think about some aspects of modern pronunciation. If you would like more chance to identify these ME/RP differences for yourself, do Activity 10C (*Chaunticleer tricks Russell*) before reading on.

First to the consonants:

(a) In our ME transcription, the 'w' in *answerde* is pronounced, as it was in the OE verb from which it comes – *andswarian*. In RP this is silent. In fact, in the ME period, some 'w's' were on the way out. Thus the OE *swa* lost its 'w', the 'a' became an 'o', to give us our modern 'so'. On the other hand, 'w' seems to have remained pronounced in words like *write*.

(b) It is likely that the 'r' was pronounced in *answerde*, *sire* and *Chauntecleer*. In my version of PDE we do not pronounce it in these words. In fact, RP does not normally pronounce 'r' in word-final position, or before another consonant (in *car* and *cart* for example). But the pronunciation of 'r' differs from variety to variety of English. Does this apply in the variety you know? There is a more detailed consideration of RP 'r' in Chapter 14 (14.4.1).

(c) Another interesting ME consonant is represented by the phonetic symbol [x]. In phonetic terms it is a **velar fricative**. 'Fricative' means that in producing the sound the air flow is constricted; 'velar' means that where this constriction takes place is in the area of the soft palate, or velum. Consult CW10.1 if you are not familiar with this way of classifying consonants. This sound is not found in standard British today, but is the sound at the end of the German (and Scottish) word *loch*. In ME it was often, as in this passage, how the letters 'gh' were said.

Think about 'gh' today. These letters are sometimes silent, as in *brought*, and when they are pronounced they are notoriously odd. Alongside *brought* we have *though* and *enough*, where they are pronounced quite differently. You may be able to think of some other odd pronunciations for today's 'gh'.

(d) In OE the initial letters of 'whan' and 'what' would once have been written 'hw', and the 'h' would have been pronounced, but it seems likely that by Chaucer's time these have become silent. Notice that the consonants have also reversed their order in spelling – 'hw' has become 'wh'.

(e) The passage does not show some other letters which are silent today but which were pronounced in ME. One is the 'g' in *gnat*, and another the 'k' in *knight*. And while we are on the subject of 'silent consonants', you may like to think of some other examples in today's English.

Now for vowels:

(f) There are some examples in the passage where ME long vowels have become diphthongs in RP:

Table 10.3 ME vowels to RP diphthongs

ME	RP
ɑː	eɪ
ɑː	əʊ
uː	aʊ

This may seem like a small change, but – as we shall see in Chapter 12 – some processes of **diphthongization** were a feature of what is known as the **Great Vowel Shift**, a major change in vowel pronunciation that took place between ME and today. You will find CW10.1 useful if you are unsure as to what a diphthong is.

(g) But not all the movement from ME to RP is diphthongization. The passage also shows a few changes in the opposite direction: **monophthongization**, where ME diphthongs become RP long vowels:

Table 10.4 ME diphthongs to RP vowels

ME	RP
eɪ	iː
aʊ	ɔː

(h) Notice that in some (but not all) ME words, a final 'e' is pronounced as [ə]. This occurs in *entente* and *mente* (at the end of lines) but not in *wikke*. We have already discussed this 'schwa' vowel [ə] in section 10.2.2, and how it came to replace other vowels in unstressed positions. You may have noticed in your comparison of our ME and RP transcriptions that it is more common in RP than in ME. This shows that the process of weakening unstressed vowels continued after the ME period.

If you want to listen to more Chaucer read aloud, there are several internet sites which provide samples, most often of the *General Prologue* to *The Canterbury Tales*.

Activity section

10A   Verbs, strong and weak

Take a look at these examples of various ME verb forms. All these verbs were strong in OE. Are they strong or weak in ME? What is going on here?

Think too about these verbs in PDE. Are they strong (irregular) or weak (regular)? The dates of the Chaucer works mentioned are all in the late 1300s.

(i) helpen (to help)

- *The erthe helpide the womman.*
- *That hem hath holpen, whan that they were seeke.*

[From Wycliffe's Bible (the Book of Revelations). dated *c.*1382, and from Chaucer's *Prologue* to *The Canterbury Tales*.]

(ii) climben (to climb)

- *And shortly, up they clomben alle thre.*
- *and in this thought he climbed vpon the mountein.*

[Chaucer's *Miller's Tale*, and *Merlin: or, the early history of King Arthur: a prose romance*, dated 1450s.]

(iii) walken (to walk)

- *Til that I herde, as that I welk alone.*
- *He walked in the feeldes for to prye.*

[From Chaucer's *Troilus and Criseyde*, and his *Miller's Tale*.]

(iv) laugh3en (to laugh)

- *But for the moore part they loughe and pleyde.*
- *For had he lawghed, had he loured.*

[Again, both from Chaucer: the *Prologue* to the *Reeve's Tale*, the *House of Fame*, and *The Romaunt of the Rose*.]

(v) shinen (to shine)

- *His heed was balled, that shoon as any glas.*
- *Ne ruby noon, that shynede by nighte.*

[Both examples from Chaucer: the *Prologue* to *The Canterbury Tales*, describing the Monk, and the *Legend of Dido*.]

10B   Word order and Chaunticleer

Look back to the 'Chaunticleer passage' in 8.5 and find examples of the following word-order patterns, all of which were found in ME:

- an SVO order
- an SOV order
- a modal or auxiliary verb, with the main verb at the end of the clause
- a subordinate clause where the verb is at the end of the clause
- a pronoun object (or indirect object) coming before the verb
- inversion of S and V after the negative word *ne* (i.e. VS rather than SV)
- inversion of S and V in a question
- inversion of S and V after an adverb or adverbial phrase.

10C   Chaunticleer tricks Russell

These tasks involve comparing the ME and RP transcriptions of the Chaunticleer passage:

(a) Here are some ME words in which consonants are pronounced that would not be pronounced in RP. Identify the consonants and how they are pronounced in ME: *answerde, Chaunticleer, sire, heighe, fleigh, saugh*.
(b) Find some words where there is a long vowel in ME which has become a diphthong in RP.
(c) Now the contrary: identify words where there is a diphthong in ME which has become a long vowel in RP.
(d) Look at the way ME *əntentə* and *mentə* are pronounced. The words share a difference with the RP equivalents. What is it?
(e) [ə] is more common in RP than it was in ME. Find some words in the transcriptions where RP has [ə] and ME does not. What does ME have instead?

Further reading

Horobin and Smith (2002) offers a succinct and readable account of ME.

Burrow and Turville-Petre (2004) combines a description of the language with an anthology of prose and verse texts.

Fischer (1992) gives a detailed linguistic survey focusing on ME syntax. As with all the *Cambridge History of the English Language* volumes, the book as a whole offers an excellent reference guide to the area.

Horobin (2013) is a useful book overall. It has a chapter partly devoted to pronunciation, which includes discussion of the types of evidence that give us information about how ME was pronounced.

Notes

1 The phrase is taken from Caxton's 1490 *Prologue* to his translation of Virgil's *Eneydos* (Aeneid). He is probably not talking about grammar, but the phrase does capture just what happened to grammar during the ME period.
2 The estimate is from Baugh & Cable (2013: 158). They also suggest the role of the lower classes in this process.

ME literature

Inside and outside the 'field full of folk'

Middle English literature – the topic of this chapter – encompasses a wide variety of genres and styles. We begin by looking at an early work, *The Owl and the Nightingale*. One way in which this poem, and much else written during the ME period, differs from OE poetry is that it uses rhyme rather than alliteration as a major stylistic principle. But the alliterative tradition was far from being dead, and we look next at what is known as the 'Alliterative Revival'. Then comes a section on the period's most celebrated writer, Geoffrey Chaucer, and the chapter also contains one example of ME prose. But nowhere near all types of ME literature are covered, and for this reason there is more on the companion website for this chapter than for most others. It includes some activities, as well as additional information.

Before reading, think about what you already know about ME literature in general. And what about Geoffrey Chaucer? Do you know anything about his main works and what they were about?

11.1 An early work

One of the best-known ME poems, *Piers Plowman,* describes a vision in which the writer sees heaven, hell, and between the two, a 'field full of folk'. There are various ways of interpreting what this field is. On one level it is the human world in all its diversity, with all social levels represented. Some of the literature of the period vividly portrays this diversity, particularly the period's best-known work, Chaucer's *Canterbury Tales*. This is a book full of realism, but other popular genres and works of the day inhabit worlds of dreams and of romance. Some do not portray people so much as ideas – and, in some cases, animals and birds. We have already come across Chaunticleer and Russell. We start this chapter with one of the earliest of the noteworthy ME poems, and it is a poem about birds: *The Owl and the Nightingale*. Here is a 'Rough Guide' to it:

The Owl and the Nightingale

- **background**: A debate between an owl and a nightingale over their own prospective worth. The genre, known as 'verse contest' had its roots in Latin and French literature. The poem was written after 1189, and is 1,794 lines long. It exists in two manuscripts, one in the British Library and one in Jesus College, Oxford.

- **authorship**: Unknown, but quite possibly Nicholas of Guildford, a parish priest in the village of Portesham, Dorset. The winner of the birds' debate is not mentioned, but we do know that 'Maister Nichole of Guleforde' is to be the judge, and the text says nice things about him on more than one occasion. Indeed, at the end Nicholas is described as undervalued in his present job and should be promoted. Almost as if he wrote the poem...
- **content**: The debate covers a variety of subjects, including marriage, religion ... and even toilet cleanliness. The two birds argue their own value and trade insults with each other. The owl makes mention of valuable skills like ridding churches of rats. The nightingale's riposte is that she at least has a decent singing voice; the owl's only value is, according to the nightingale, that when it dies its corpse will be useful as a scarecrow.
- **value**: A lively debate – mostly amusing, though serious topics like the transience of life are touched upon.
- **quotation**: Here is what the nightingale says about the owl's voice:

> 'Hule,' ho sede, 'seie me soþ,
> Wi dostu þat unwiȝtis doþ?
> Þu singist aniȝt and noȝt adai,
> And al þi song is wailawai.
> Þu miȝt mid þine songe afere
> Alle þat ihereþ þine ibere.
> Þu schrichest and ȝollest to þine fere
> Þat hit is grislich to ihere:
> Hit þincheþ boþe wise and snepe
> Noȝt þat þu singe, ac þat þu wepe.
> ...'

> 'Owl,' she said, 'tell me the truth, why do you do what monsters do? You sing by night and not by day, and your whole song is "woe and alas". You could frighten with your song all those who hear your cries. You screech and scream to your companions, which is horrible to hear; to the wise and the foolish it seems that you are weeping, not singing...'

The owl does not take this lying down. Her answer:

> 'Ich singe bet þan þu dest:/ Þu chaterest so doþ on Irish prost'

> 'I sing better than you; you gabble like an Irish priest'.

Activity 11A (*Quotation questions*) focuses on selected words and language points in the quotations given in this chapter. Look at part (a) now. There is another quotation, giving a further illustration of avian rudeness in part (a) of CW11.1 (*Three more quotations*).

Given the early date of the poem, it is not surprising if it has an OE feel to it. But there are respects in which it is very different from OE poetry. Go back to 7.3 to remind yourself of the main characteristics of this. Then ask yourself these questions, basing your evidence on the 'Rough Guide's' quotations above:

- Is there any alliteration (7.3 talked about this) in the verse?
- What about rhyme?

The answer to the first question is 'no'. There is no alliteration, and this makes the poem very different from OE poetry. The answer to the second question is 'yes'. There is rhyme. The rhymed lines are in pairs – they are **couplets**. Because the lines have eight syllables, the scheme is called **octosyllabic couplets**. Incidentally, letters can be used to show rhyme schemes. 'aabb' indicates rhyming couplets. A scheme in which alternate lines rhymed would be shown as 'abab'.

In 7.3, the point was made that word-initial alliteration suited OE because it mirrored the language's word stress pattern, with the stress commonly falling on the initial syllable. But this did not happen so much in French, where the stress was often (though not nearly always) word final. Hence rhyme based on the 'ends' of words was more natural to French than alliteration, and it was partly as a result of the French influence that rhyme came into English. Indeed, the octosyllabic couplet was the rhyme scheme commonly used by twelfth-century French poets. The movement from alliteration to rhyme – from 'front' to 'back', if you will – was an

important feature of some ME verse, though not all of it, as we are about to see.

CW11.2 (*The Ormulum*) and CW11.3 (*Havelok the Dane*) give you two more 'Rough Guides' (with some associated language questions) to poems written relatively early in the ME period. They illustrate genres common at the time. You will notice that the second, *Havelok the Dane*, uses the same octosyllabic couplet form as *The Owl and the Nightingale*.

11.2 The Alliterative Revival

But not all poetry of the time was rhyming rather than alliterative. Indeed, some of the period's best poems were part of what is known as the **Alliterative Revival**. Exactly what inspired this revival is unclear. Were the poets, by using alliteration, making a conscious effort to return to OE traditions? Or was the movement not really a revival at all, but a continuation of a tradition that had not really died out? One characteristic of the poems written as part of this 'movement' is that they tended to be socially committed, dealing with the problems of society. They also tended to be written in the provinces (areas where sometimes traditions die hardest). They were a far cry from the new, fashionable, rhyming poetry of Chaucer and the London court.

One of the Alliterative Revival's best poems is *Piers Plowman*, written in about 1386. The author was one William Langland, of whom little is known, except that he had connections with the Malvern Hills area (in the West Midlands), where the poem is set. It tells of a series of visions. In the first, the poet is wandering in the hills, becomes drowsy and falls asleep by a stream. He dreams of a tower in which Truth lives, and a dungeon, the home of the Devil. Between the two is that 'field full of folk' mentioned in this chapter's title. Subsequent visions recount the poet's searches for Truth and for some allegorical characters named 'Do-well', 'Do-better' and 'Do-best'.

The poem is rather digressive and difficult to follow. But it is a highly imaginative work, containing much satire of corrupt modern ways. Here is a quotation from the poem's *Prologue*. The poet has just fallen asleep ... In the last lines of the passage you can see a hint of the poem's moral indignation.

> Thanne gan I meten a merveillous swevene
> That I was in a wildernesse, wiste I nevere where.
> Ac as I biheeld into the eest an heigh to the sonne,
> I seigh a tour on a toft trieliche ymaked,
> A deep dale bynethe, a dongeon therinne,
> With depe diches and derke and dredfulle of sighte.
> A fair feeld ful of folk fond I ther bitwene–
> Of alle manere of men, the meene and the riche,
> Werchynge and wandrynge as the world asketh.
> Somme putten hem to the plough, pleiden ful selde,
> In settynge and sowynge swonken ful harde,
> And wonnen that thise wastours with glotonye destruyeth

> Then I had a marvelous dream, That I was in a wilderness – I don't know exactly where. But as I looked eastwards, right into the sun, I saw a tower on a hillock, worthily built. There was a deep dale beneath with a dungeon in it. It had deep, dark moats, and was a dreadful sight. Between the two was a fair field full of folk. There were all kinds of men – rich and poor, some working, some wandering as was their lot. Some of them were ploughing, rarely resting. They toiled hard as they planted and sowed, to bring forth what wasters destroy through gluttony.

Part (b) of Activity 11A is about this quotation. If you would like to see another example of the poet's moral indignation at work (this time aimed at hypocritical churchmen), there is another quotation in part (b) of CW11.1. Also take a look at CW11.4 (*Sir Gawain and the Green Knight*), which gives information about another important work in the Alliterative Revival.

11.3 Geoffrey Chaucer

Fourteenth-century English literature was dominated by the figure of Geoffrey Chaucer, who lived from about 1343 till 1400. As well as being a prolific writer, he was also a courtier and diplomat. As you will have gathered from the number of times we have already mentioned it, *The Canterbury Tales* is his best-known work. Here is a 'Rough Guide' to it:

- **background**: The book takes the form of a 'frame tale', setting up a context within which a number of stories can be told. A similar frame tale is found in Boccaccio's *Decameron*, completed in 1353, where a group of characters fleeing Florence to escape the Plague tell stories to amuse themselves. Chaucer's book was very popular, and appeared in some eighty-three manuscripts. The best known of these is probably the illuminated Ellesmere manuscript, now in California. Many of the tales are written in ten-syllable ('decasyllabic') rhyming couplets, though other rhyme schemes are also used, and some of the stories are in prose.
- **authorship**: Chaucer started work on the *Tales* in about 1387. The plan was highly ambitious, and the work is unfinished; the completed part is some 17,000 lines long.
- **content**: The book tells of a storytelling contest. A group of around thirty pilgrims are travelling from London to the shrine of St Thomas Becket in Canterbury Cathedral, a popular destination for pilgrimages. The host of the Tabard Inn in Southward, their starting-point, is one Harry Bailly. He proposes that each pilgrim should tell four stories, two on the way to Canterbury and two on the way back. The prize for the best story will be a free supper at the Tabard on their return. In fact, only twenty-four stories are told. The book starts with a *General Prologue* containing pen portraits of twenty-one characters.
- **value**: The book is a pageant of fourteenth-century society, with the characters coming from all walks of life: the nobility (a Knight), professional men (a Doctor, a Lawyer), the religious (a Friar, a Parson), members of the lower classes (a Miller, a Cook) – and more besides.

Baugh (1948: 262) calls the book 'a miniature five-foot shelf of medieval literature', because it contains so many examples of contemporary literary genres. There is a courtly romance (*The Knight's Tale*); a popular romance (*The Tale of Sir Thopas*, one of two tales told by Chaucer himself), a Breton lay in *The Franklyn's Tale*, a sermon in *The Parson's Tale*. Coarser stories are told by the Miller and the Reeve (we met another 'reeve' in 3.2, you will recall). We have also come across an example of the 'beast fable' in the Nun's Priest's story about Chaunticleer (back in 8.5).

There are certain recurrent themes running through some stories. One is marriage, leading some scholars to talk in terms of a 'marriage group' of tales. But in general, the stories are 'character-led', rather than being thematically linked, and this is evident in the way they are ordered. For example: the Knight starts off with a tale of chivalry. The Monk is set to tell the next tale, but the Miller, who is drunk, insists on doing so. His story is about a carpenter. It is bawdy, and in stark contrast to the Knight's sophisticated contribution.

The Carpenter in the company takes umbrage at what the Miller says, and responds with an indecent tale about a miller.

Though writers before Chaucer had used English for their work, part of the value of *The Tales* is that they helped to promote the use of English as a vernacular.

- **quotation**: These are the celebrated opening lines of the book's *General Prologue*:

> Whan that Aprille with his shoures sote
> The droghte of Marche hath perced to the rote,
> And bathed every veyne in swich licour,
> Of which vertu engendred is the flour;
> Whan Zephirus eek with his swete breeth
> Inspired hath in every holt and heeth
> The tendre croppes, and the yonge sonne
> Hath in the Ram his halfe cours y-ronne,
> And smale fowles maken melodye,
> That slepen al the night with open yë,
> (So priketh hem nature in hir corages):
> Than longen folk to goon on pilgrimages

> When April with its sweet showers has pierced the drought of March down to the root, and bathed every vein in that liquid through whose power the flower is created; when the West Wind too with its sweet breath has breathed life into the tender shoots in every wood and field, and the young sun has run its half course through Aries, and small birds make melody – they who sleep all night with open eyes (so nature incites them in their heart): then people long to start out on pilgrimages.

Part (c) of Activity 11A asks questions about this quotation. CW11.1 gives a second excerpt from the *General Prologue*, part of Chaucer's description of the Prioresse.

There are some who regard another of Chaucer's works as his greatest achievement, the poem *Troilus and Criseyde*, written in the second half of the 1380s. There is a 'Rough Guide' to this poem (with associated language questions) at CW11.5 (*Troilus and Criseyde*).

11.4 A piece of prose

So far, all the works that have been mentioned are poetry. The ME period also produced prose works of value. Here is a 'Rough Guide' for one of the best known:

Morte D'Arthur

- **background**: A lengthy prose cycle of Arthurian legends, finished in 1470 and printed by Caxton in 1485. It is based on a number of French sources, and was used by the poet Tennyson (1809–92) for his cycle of twelve narrative poems called *Idylls of the King*.
- **authorship**: Sir Thomas Malory, who died in 1471. Little is known about him for certain. He was probably born in Warwickshire, was knighted before 1442 and served in parliament. He then turned to a life of crime, including rape, attempted murder, extortion and poaching. He spent about twenty years in prison, where he wrote *Morte D'Arthur*, and where he also died.
- **content**: A large collection of Arthurian stories, including the story of the search for the Holy Grail. Launcelot and Guinevere, as well as Tristan and Isolde, also make appearances. As the title suggests, the death of Arthur is also covered.
- **value**: A long and rambling work, but one which shows a love of chivalry. The book is most admired for its simple, terse style.
- **quotation**: In Book 1, Chapter 25, Malory tells how Arthur and Merlin went on a journey. Arthur was without a sword:

Soo they rode tyl they came to a lake the whiche was a fayr water / and brood / And in the myddes of the lake Arthur was ware of an arme clothed in whyte samyte / that held a fayr swerd in that hand / loo said Merlyn yonder is that swerd that I spak of / with that they sawe a damoysel goyng vpon the lake / what damoysel is that said Arthur / that is the lady of the lake said Merlyn / And within that lake is a roche / and theryn is as fayr a place as ony on erthe and rychely besene / and this damoysell wylle come to yow anone / and thenne speke ye fayre to her that she will gyue yow that swerd / Anone with all came the damoysel vnto Arthur / and salewed hym / and he her ageyne / Damoysel said Arthur / what swerd is that / that yonder the arme holdeth aboue the water / I wold it were myne / for I haue no swerd / Syr Arthur kynge said the damoysell / that swerd is myn / And yf ye will gyue me a yefte whan I aske it yow / ye shal haue it by my feyth said Arthur / I will yeue yow what yefte ye will aske / wel said the damoisel go ye into yonder barge / & rowe your self to the swerd / and take it / and scaubart with yow / & I will aske my yefte whan I see my tyme.

Glossary

samyte, samite (a rich silk fabric)	*damoisel*, maiden	*roche*, rock
besene, appointed, situated	*salewed*, saluted, greeted	*yefte*, gift
scaubart, scabbard		

Part (d) of Activity 11A asks questions about this quotation.

11.5 Looking at more ME literature

If you would like to explore more ME literature, you could write some 'Rough Guides' of your own. Activity 11B (*More ME 'Rough Guides'*) invites you to do this.

You could also read some of the works mentioned in this chapter. The story of *Sir Gawain* is a compelling one, and is available in various modern translations, including Armitage (2009). There is no doubt that Chaucer is the period's towering figure. *Troilus and Criseyde* is lengthy. But it is one of the great love poems of English literature, and you will be astonished at how 'modern' Criseyde's deliberations about love are. It is (of course!) best to read it in the original, but a good second best would be in modern translation – Windeatt (2008), for example.

You may also like to look at one of *The Canterbury Tales*. Since you have already seen some of *The Nun's Priest's Tale*, you could choose that one. Another interesting tale, of treachery and death, is *The Pardoner's Tale*. The comments above about 'best and second best' (original and translation) apply here too. Ackroyd (2010) is described as a 'retelling', in lively modern prose.

Activity section

11A Quotation questions

Here are some questions/comments based on each of the quotations in the text. They draw attention to interesting words and language points. Some answers are given in the *Answer section*.

(a) **The Owl and the Nightingale**
   (i) What is the word for 'she'? It is rather dramatically different from the PDE word; also from the word found in our Chaucer quotations (in CW11.5 for example).
   (ii) Find the word for 'truth'. A word from the same root occurs in 4.3's 'lettuce story'. Go back and look this up.
   (iii) Find the words for 'by night' and 'by day'. You may have come across the prefix *a-* being used in PDE for 'at' or 'on'. Can you think of any examples? (AS)
   (iv) Look at the ME word translated as 'horrible'. There is a PDE word with roughly the same meaning. What is it? Does it have different connotations from 'horrible'?
   (v) Look at how 'it seems that' is expressed. Try translating the phrase literally. (AS)
(b) **Piers Plowman**
   (i) Find the word translated as 'dream'. It is obsolete today (the last *OED* citation is 1840).

(ii) The word translated as 'but' made an appearance in the 'Rough Guide' to the *Anglo-Saxon Chronicle* in 7.2. Find this.

(iii) Find the word translated as 'poor'. This word has come into PDE with a different sense. What is this sense? Can you see how the change in meaning was possible?

(iv) Find the word translated as 'resting'. Maybe you can work out its connection with a PDE word. (AS)

(v) *Swonken* is translated as 'toiled'. What might the infinitive of the ME verb be? (AS)

(c) **The Canterbury Tales**

(i) 10.2.6 mentioned that there are several examples of the perfect aspect in this quotation. Find these.

(ii) Find the word translated as 'power'. This word has a different meaning in PDE. Say what the difference is. (You might like to explore the connection between this word and our word 'virile'). (AS)

(iii) Find the word for 'wood'. The word is archaic now, but you may have come across it in pre-twentieth-century literature.

(iv) There are two variants of the word for 'sweet' in the quotation. Find these. Why does this adjective come after the noun in one case, and before it in the other? (AS)

(v) 10.2.1 discusses the plural of the word for 'eye'. What is it here?

(d) **Morte D'Arthur**

(i) The symbol (/) is often used to indicate the end of a line of poetry. But this is not how it is used here. What do you think its use might be? Is it followed by a capital letter? (AS)

(ii) The lack of inverted commas makes the passage a little difficult for us today to read. Go through the passage adding these.

(iii) There is not much spelling variation in the passage, but there is one word which is spelled in different ways (hint: one of the spellings adds a letter at the end). The passage also contains two spelling versions of the PDE verb 'give'. Find these. (AS)

(iv) There are two words for PDE 'you'. What are they? When is one used, when the other? (AS)

(v) The glossary contains a few words with French origins. Which ones do you suspect they might be? (AS)

11B More ME 'Rough Guides'

Use the internet or other sources to write your own 'Rough Guide' to some or all of the works below. Use the same headings as in the text: background/ authorship/content/value/quotations – though for some entries you may not find something to say under every heading. If you can work together with others, you could share the load, doing one 'Rough Guide' each, and ending up with several which together give a more detailed picture of the period's literature. The works are:

Ancrene Wisse or *Ancrene Riwle* ('Guidance or Rules for Anchoresses'): like much of the poetry surviving from the mid twelfth to mid thirteenth century, this work (together with *The Ormulum*) is religious and didactic;

King Horn: like *Havelok the Dane*, an example of the romance genre, very popular at the time;

Pearl: thought to have been written by the author of *Sir Gawain*. Bishop (1968) calls it 'the most highly wrought and intricately constructed poem in Middle English'. It is a 'dream vision' poem, like *Piers Plowman*. The poet mourns the loss of his 'pearl' (possibly his daughter) and encounters her in a vision.

Answer section

Activity 11A

(a) (iii) *anight*, *aday*, and phrases like *aMonday* sometimes occur in English, though they are rather archaic.

   (v) Literally 'both wise and foolish it think...'.

(b) (iv) The PDE word is *play*.

   (v) The infinitive is *swinken*.

(c) (ii) Virile comes from the Latin root *vir*, meaning 'man'.

   (iv) Chaucer needs to end line 5 with a word to rhyme with *heeth*. Hence the order Adj + N.

(d) (i) The symbol (/) is known as a **virgule**, and it is a punctuation mark which indicates a pause. Sometimes it acts like today's comma, though notice that sometimes it is followed by a capital letter; perhaps in these cases it has the value of a full stop.

   (iii) *damoysel* is twice spelled with double 'l' at the end. 'Give' appears as *yeue* and *gyue*.

   (iv) 'You' is sometimes *ye*, sometimes *yow*. Ye is the nominative form, and *yow* is used for other cases. Take a look at 16.5, which discusses this.

   (v) *samyte*, *damoisel*, *roche*, *scaubart* (*salewed* has Latin roots).

Further reading

There are a number of anthologies of Middle English literature available, including Sisam and Tolkien (2009).

Another, which contains a longer description of the language, is Burrow and Turville-Petre (2004).

Two studies providing background information (including about language) are Turville-Petre (2006) and Burrow (2008).

Part IV

Interlude

12 A short interlude about long vowels

The Great Vowel Shift

This chapter is about major changes in the pronunciation of English which took place in the Middle English and Early Modern English periods. The changes were caused by what is known as the Great Vowel Shift. One of the issues that gets to be discussed in this short chapter is the fact that English spelling does not well represent the way English is pronounced. Think about this issue before you read the chapter. Give examples of where spelling and pronunciation are at odds in Present Day English. What might have caused mismatches to occur? Might it be remedied, and if so, how? If possible, think too about the relationship between pronunciation and spelling in another language you know.

CW10.1 (*Making sounds, and writing them down*) contains important basic information you need in order to understand what happened in the Great Vowel Shift. It really is worth taking another look at this before you read on.

12.1 The Great Vowel Shift

The Great Vowel Shift lasted from 1350 till 1700, and therefore spanned the Middle English (ME) and Early Modern English (EModE) periods. For this reason, it deserves a special 'interlude chapter' between our coverage of these. It was called the Great Vowel Shift, or GVS; generations of students, as Culpeper (2015) accurately and amusingly points out, sometimes like to refer to it as the 'Great Bowel Shift'.

To understand the GVS, we need to take a close look at vowels – how they are produced, and how categorized. We will be looking at diphthongs too. This is why it is important for you to be familiar with what is said in CW10.1, which discusses these issues. Also, if you are not very familiar with the phonetic symbols used for vowels and diphthongs, it is worth keeping one finger on the list at the beginning of this book (pp. xv–xvi), which gives these symbols and the associated sounds.

CW10.1 contains a diagram which shows some PDE vowels. Figure 12.1 shows another one for the vowels that we will be looking at in this chapter – the ME long vowels.

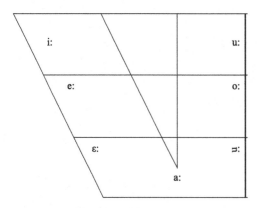

Figure 12.1 The ME long vowels

Not all the sounds here will be familiar to you from PDE. One example is [ɛ:]. If you have your finger on the list on pp. xv–xvi, you will notice that the example given for that vowel is not an English word. It is a French word, *même*. But the vowel did occur in ME. For example, the ME *clene* (meaning 'clean') was pronounced [klɛ:nə]. Another example is [a:], which is a long central vowel (between RP's front [æ] and back [ɑ:] – CW10.1 explains the terminology). It is found in the Australian pronunciation of *bath*.

There were two types of changes that affected these long vowels in the GVS. The first was **diphthongization,** a process in which **monophthong** vowels became diphthongs. The vowels in question were the most closed ones – those in the top third of Figure 12.1 – [i:] and [u:]. The sound [ə] came to be pronounced before these vowels. So monophthong [i:] became diphthong [əɪ], and [u:] became [əʊ].[1] Figure 12.2 shows this change, with arrows showing the direction of movement.

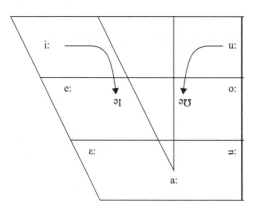

Figure 12.2 Diphthongization of [i:] and [u:]

If we use the symbol '→' to signify 'became', we can say that [i:] → [əɪ] and [u:] → [əʊ]. And because [ə] is a central vowel, we can also say that the two ME monophthongs moved before the end of the EModE period from their close front and close back positions towards the centre.

To show these changes in action, consider the ME words [tiːdə], meaning 'tide', and [huːs] meaning 'house'. With [iː] becoming [əɪ], and [uː] changing to [əʊ], we end up with [təɪd] and [həʊs]. When we come to look at EModE pronunciation, in 14.3, we shall find plenty of examples of these diphthongs. Just so that you can familiarize yourself with this part of the GVS, fill in the blanks in Table 12.1 to show what the pre- and post- GVS sounds would have been (answers in the *Answer section* AS). The first two examples are those we have just seen.

Table 12.1 Some examples of GVS diphthongization

Pre-GVS	PDE meaning	Post-GVS
[tiːdə]	*tide*	[təɪd]
[huːs]	*house*	[həʊs]
[riːd]	*ride*	
[fuːl]	*foul*	
	life	[ləɪf]
[striːf]	*strife, discord*	
	how	[həʊ]

The GVS took place over a long time span, and it is possible to work out the stages by which it happened, though the exact chronology of the stages is often unclear. It may be that this diphthongization was in fact the first stage.

What happened next is described in the following paragraph. If you want to try and work out for yourself the underlying principle behind the changes, take a look at Activity 12A (*Vowels shifting*) before reading on.

The GVS was first studied (and was indeed given its name) by the Danish linguist Otto Jespersen (1860–1943); we mentioned him in 9.2.1. It consists, he said, 'in a general raising of all long vowels'.[2] This 'raising' was the second, more major, direction of change. It was a movement upwards, with vowel pronunciations moving towards the top of Figure 12.1's diagram (you really do need to keep looking at this figure as you read the description below). One way of conceptualizing what happened is to say that the shifting vowels left 'empty spaces' and these were filled with the vowels immediately 'below' them on the Figure 12.1 chart. So, after the diphthongization we have just described, the highest closed positions previously filled by [iː] and [uː] became 'empty spaces'. The two more open vowels, [eː] and [oː], moved up to occupy these spaces. This meant that [eː] became [iː] and [oː] became [uː]. So we have [eː] → [iː] and [oː] → [uː]. Figure 12.3 illustrates the changes we have so far discussed: [iː] and [uː] becoming diphthongs and moving towards the centre; together with [eː] and [iː] sounds moving upwards to become [oː] and [uː].

As a result of these second changes, [feːt] in Chaucer's time (meaning 'feet'), became [fiːt], while [boːt] ('boat') became [buːt].

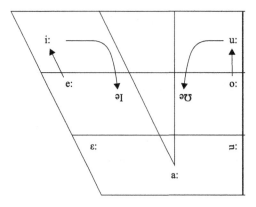

Figure 12.3 [e:] and [o:] move up

This upward movement continued for the other ME long vowels. The changes are shown below. Add arrows to Figure 12.3 to indicate them.

[ɛ:] → [e:]
[ɔ:] → [o:]
[a:] → [ɛ:]

Then, to check you have mastered all these changes, complete Table 12.2. The first three rows have already been filled in, using examples we have already seen.

Table 12.2 GVS sound changes

ME	EModE	Change involved	PDE meaning
[stri:f]	[strɔɪf]	[i:] →[ɔɪ]	*strife*
[fe:t]	[fi:t]	[e:] →[i:]	*feet*
[bo:t]	[bu:t]	[o:]→[u:]	*boat*
[ta:k]	[tɛ:k]		*take*
[mɛ:t]	[me:t]		*meat*
[fɔ:l]	[fo:l]		*foal*

These are the major components of the GVS. If you would like to work through the changes with a few more examples, look now at Activity 12B (*The GVS at work*).

Now give a thought to pronunciation today. Some of the examples we have looked at show that there are vowels which have not changed since the end of the GVS. So once ME [fe:t] had changed to [fi:t], no other change occurred, and [fi:t] is exactly how we pronounce *feet* today; the GVS accounts for changes that have persisted into PDE. But in some cases there have been other additional changes since then, that lead us to today's pronunciations. In the case of the diphthong [əɪ], for example – which we do not have in RP – we often find an [ai] today. So the EModE [təɪd] changed after the GVS to become today's [taid].

12.2   The GVS, sounds and spellings

Speakers of other languages who are learning English complain regularly about the considerable mismatch between English spellings and sounds. In a perfect linguistic world, each letter of the alphabet would have just one pronunciation, and each sound would be represented by just one alphabet letter. That way, you could look at a word on the page and know how it was pronounced. But alas, English is not like that at all. Think, for example, how the RP sound [ɪ] can be written in PDE. It may be an 'i', as in *sit*. But it can also be written 'e' (as in the first syllable of *became*), as 'ui' (in *build*), as 'u' (in *busy*), and even as 'o' (in *women*). In the same way, an alphabet letter like 'o' has various pronunciations. In RP it is [ɒ] in *moth*, [ʌ] in *mother*, as well as [ɪ] in *women*. Something of a mess. How did it happen?

Historical pronunciation changes are a major reason for these mismatches. The way a language is pronounced does of course change over time. Chapter 1 (1.2) made this point, and if you need more convincing, think about how your own language (whether it be English or some other) was pronounced fifty or more years ago – you will certainly have heard old films or recordings of pronunciation at that time. Think how it is different from today's pronunciation; there are certain to be differences. At some historical point, a word may be spelled in a way that reflects its pronunciation. Then the pronunciation changes, but not the spelling – writing is often more conservative than pronunciation in this respect. So the word is pronounced in one way and written in another. The GVS had its part to play in this. An example is the word *fool*. It was pronounced [foːl] in ME, and in fact 'oo' is a sensible enough way of representing the sound [oː]. Then the GVS changed the vowel to [uː], which is how it remains today. But the spelling was already fixed as 'oo'. Another example is the word *he*, pronounced [heː] in ME. Again, 'e' is a perfectly reasonable way of writing [eː], so the spelling made sense. But the GVS changed the vowel to [iː] and the spelling did not change to reflect this pronunciation shift.

As we will see in Chapter 14, there have been regular attempts to 'reform' English spelling to make it more rational. But the spoken language is always on the move, shifting pronunciations irrespective of how words are written. This is one reason why spelling reforms rarely succeed, alas.

12.3   The GVS: why?

Why did the GVS happen? One possible motivation was social. Görlach (1991: 67) describes a theory which relates the GVS to the upper classes abandoning French and turning to English, a process mentioned in 8.2. Perhaps they sought a distinctive way of pronouncing words to distinguish themselves from the *hoi polloi*. One way of 'sounding different' would be to use different vowels – they are much more subject to change than consonants. Perhaps this is what initiated the GVS. Socially motivated phonetic changes like this are very common. People like to distinguish themselves, to use the way they speak to announce where they come from, what their status is, what social group they belong to. They will eagerly pick up distinguishing linguistic features to mark their social identity. You may be able to think of examples of this in relation to your own language.

And why did vowels shift into the positions previously occupied by others? It is said that piranha fish, famed for their voracious appetites and sharp teeth, wisely keep their distance from each other. If one fish in the shoal moves slightly closer to its neighbour, that neighbour will move away to maintain distance. In no time, a chain reaction occurs, and every fish in the shoal has moved to maintain a safe distance from neighbouring sharp teeth. Sound shifts can be a bit like this. There is a **chain shift** involved. Perhaps it was the diphthongization of [iː] and [uː] which started the GVS chain in motion. Once it had started, and in order to maintain the overall oral cavity pattern, the other vowels shifted position. Like piranha fish.

Activity section

12A   Vowels shifting

(a) The text describes how the process of diphthongization changed [iː] into [əɪ], and [uː] into [əu]. Here is how the other ME long vowels (on the left) changed in the GVS. These changes follow a pattern. Make an attempt to work out what it is – you may not be successful, but it will be worth the effort. You will certainly need to refer constantly to Figure 12.1 in the text.

   [eː] became [iː]
   [oː] became [uː]
   [ɛː] became [eː]
   [ɔː] became [oː]
   [aː] became [ɛː]

(b) Now try to give the pattern in the form of a written statement which describes the process. Writing it down will help you make it as clear and accurate as possible.

12B   The GVS at work   AS

Here are some more words exemplifying the GVS changes. Use what you have read to fill in the blanks in the first two columns. Then fill in the third column. This will give you a complete picture of the changes we have discussed.

ME	EModE	Change involved	PDE meaning
[liːke]		[iː] → [əɪ]	like
	[goːt]		goat
[naːmə]			name
[muːs]			mouse
	[miːd]		mead
[grɛːt]			great
	[buːt]		boot

Answer section

Table 12.1

Pre-GVS [riːd] became [rəɪd]; [fuːl] became [fəʊl]; post-GVS [ləɪf] was [liːf]; [striːf] became [strəɪf]; and [həʊ] was [huː].

Activity 12B

Here is the completed table:

ME	EModE	Change involved	PDE meaning
[liːke]	[ləɪk]	[iː] → [əɪ]	*like*
[gɔːt]	[goːt]	[ɔː] → [oː]	*goat*
[naːmə]	[nɛːm]	[aː] → [ɛː]	*name*
[muːs]	[məʊs]	[uː] → [əʊ]	*mouse*
[meːdə]	[miːd]	[eː] → [iː]	*mead*
[grɛːt]	[greːt]	[ɛː] → [eː]	*great*
[boːtə]	[buːt]	[oː] → [uː]	*boot*

Further reading

For a detailed academic account of the GVS, see Wolfe (1972). The topic is also covered in detail in section 3.3 of Lass (1999a).

Shorter descriptions of the GVS can be found in most histories of English, including in Chapter 4 of Görlach (1991).

On the *OED* site there is a very short and useful summary of the GVS's effects. This is at http://public.oed.com/aspects-of-english/english-in-time/early-modern-english-pronunciation-and-spelling/.

Notes

1 Some accounts have the first element of the diphthong as [ɛ] or [a].
2 The quotation is from Jespersen (1909: 231).

Part V
Early Modern English

13

'Manie matters of singular discourse'

Some English Renaissance history

We now move from ME to EModE – the Early Modern English period, and this will take us up to the beginning of the eighteenth century. Chapters 13 to 18 deal with the English Renaissance, and there is a final chapter about the seventeenth century. This first EModE chapter focuses on the Tudor period, a particularly interesting time historically. After some general history, section 13.2 looks at the language situation of the time. The invention of printing was a major event, and it coincided with a growth of learning and a concerted effort to elevate English into a position where it could take over some of the roles traditionally associated with Latin. There is a section too (13.3) on the growing linguistic consciousness of the age, and the huge fascination that developed towards words and their effects.

Some things to do before you read:

- If you are not sure what the term 'Renaissance' means, and why it is applied to this period, find this out.
- The invention of printing is regarded by many as one of the most influential in human history. Why so important? Give some thought to what the consequences of the invention have been for mankind.
- Another issue discussed is the translation of the Bible into English. Some at the time thought a translation should be made, while others argued that the book should continue to be used in Latin. Think in general terms about what the arguments for and against an English Bible might have been.
- Some people to find out about: Henry VIII's six wives – who were they, how did they die? Why were some of them executed? Then there is William Caxton: it would be useful to know something about his life. Richard III is also mentioned; find out something about him.

13.1   A happy breed of men

Raphael Holinshed was a sixteenth-century English historian, best known to posterity because his *Chronicles of England, Scotland and Ireland* were often used by Shakespeare as sources for his plays. It is a book – the title page tells us – 'wherein ... are contained manie matters of singular discourse and rare observation'. This chapter will look at some of these 'manie matters', and will give a general historical background to the sixteenth century, an important part of the Early Modern English (EModE) period.

If you look at them in detail, all periods of history can appear full of fascination and interest. But English history of the period we are looking at here is particularly captivating. You have a king (Richard III), sometimes regarded as a wicked hunchback, implicated in the murder of two young princes in the Tower of London. Then there is another king (Henry VIII), who had six wives, and a queen (Elizabeth I), who announced: 'though I have the body of a weak and feeble woman, I have the heart and stomach of a king, yea and a king of England too'.

Our period begins with Henry VI, who was king from 1422 to 1461. Here is what Holinshed's *Chronicles* have to say about him: 'thus farre touching the tragicall state of this land vnder the rent [torn] regiment of king Henrie, who (besides the bare title of roialtie and naked name of king) had little appertaining to the port of a prince'. The nobles, Holinshed said, spent time 'seeking either to suppresse, or to exile, or to obscure, or to make him awaie'. Henry, who was a member of the House of Lancaster, was weak and mentally unstable, and this encouraged others to claim the throne, particularly Richard, Duke of York, who came from another branch of the same Plantagenet dynasty. Conflicting claims to the throne by the two families – York and Lancaster – led to the 'Wars of the Roses', which lasted for some thirty years, from 1455 till 1487. The 'roses' were the heraldic badges of the two parties involved, the white rose of York and the red rose of Lancaster. After a complex series of events, Yorkist Richard III became king. Both Holinshed and Shakespeare portray him as a wicked hunchback, though in real life he was apparently not quite so wicked, nor so hunchbacked. Richard was killed in battle at Bosworth (near the city of Leicester) in 1485. Henry Tudor, a Lancastrian and the first of the new Tudor dynasty, was victorious and became king. He, a red rose, reconciled the warring sides by marrying a white rose, Elizabeth of York. Tudor history is complicated. Table 13.1 gives some basic facts about the Tudor monarchs.

When Henry VII died, his son Arthur was married to Catherine of Aragon. When Arthur died young, his brother Henry promptly married Catherine himself, even though marrying the wife of a brother was not really permitted. She was the first of Henry VIII's six wives. Their fates are recorded in the rhyme: *King Henry the Eighth, / to six wives he was wedded. / One died, one survived, / two divorced, two beheaded.* Part of Henry's problem with wives was that most were unable to present him with a son and heir. The process of divorcing the first, Catherine of Aragon, and marrying the second – Anne Boleyn – caused a rift with the Pope and the Church in Rome, and led Henry to declare himself head of the English church, thus establishing his right to act without seeking the Pope's consent. This took place against a backdrop of growing religious conflict between Catholics and Protestants – a conflict that is reflected in the religious affiliations of Henry's queens. Catherine of Aragon, daughter of Queen Isabella

Table 13.1 Tudor monarchs

Monarch	Reign	Some basic information
Henry VII	1485–1509	Restored stability to the monarchy. His oldest son, Arthur, was heir-apparent, but died young.
Henry VIII	1509–1547	Henry VII's second son, he had six wives; broke with the Church of Rome.
Edward VI	1547–1553	Son of Henry VIII and his third wife, Jane Seymour. Died aged 15.
Mary I	1553–1558	Daughter of Henry VIII and his first wife, Catherine of Aragon. Like her mother, a Catholic; she became known as 'bloody Mary' because of her cruelty towards Protestants during her reign.
Elizabeth I	1558–1603	Daughter of Henry VIII and Anne Boleyn. An impressive and educated queen who never married, and left no heirs.

of Castile and King Ferdinand of Aragon, was a Catholic, and several other of Henry's wives were brought up as Catholics. Catherine Parr (his last wife), on the other side, was firmly Protestant. Henry himself was responsible for the dissolution of the Catholic monasteries, stripping them of the luxury to which they had become accustomed, and thus acquiring land and riches for himself. At the same time, he took steps to curb the more excessive expressions of Protestantism.

Anne Boleyn failed to give the king a son, but she did give birth, before she became queen, in fact. The daughter was named Elizabeth. A daughter was not what Henry wanted, and Anne (who was accused of adultery) became one of the beheaded wives. Immediately after her death, the king married Jane Seymour. But daughter Elizabeth eventually became queen, and ruled during what many regard as England's 'golden age'. Under her rule, the country's cultural life flourished. There were writers like Spenser, Sidney and Shakespeare (all of whom are discussed in Chapter 18). There were adventurers like Drake, the first Englishman to circumnavigate the globe. The spirit of the age was for exploration and discovery. It was a time when, according to the Victorian poet Francis Thompson, 'a man got up in the morning and said "I have an idea. If you have nothing better to do, let us go continent-hunting"'. It was also a time of huge English self-confidence. As the Spanish fleet – known as the Armada – came into sight, intent on conquering England, Drake (according to one, possibly apocryphal, story at least) declared he would finish his game of bowls before tackling the enemy. The fleet was formed in 1588 by Philip of Spain, who viewed some of England's actions as anti-Catholic and decided to teach the English a lesson. The fate of the Armada is as well known as that of Henry's wives. The ships were too cumbersome to react quickly to the nimble manoeuvrings of the British fleet and this, together with poor weather, led to the ignominious destruction of the 'invincible' Armada. England's self-confidence increased even more. In Shakespeare's play *Richard II*, there is a well-known passage about England and the English. It was not written about the Elizabethan Age, but it no doubt captures the patriotic feeling of that time:

> This royal throne of kings, this sceptred isle,
> This earth of majesty, this seat of Mars,
> This other Eden – demi-paradise –
> ...
> This happy breed of men, this little world,
> This precious stone set in the silver sea,
> ...
> This blessed plot, this earth, this realm, this England,
> ...
> This land of such dear souls, this dear dear land,
>
> (2 2.1.41)

If you would like to see some short descriptions of events described in this section, Activity 13A (*From the Chronicles*) gives extracts from Holinshed and invites you to identify what is being described.

13.2   A happy convergence

In 1471, a middle-aged Englishman by the name of William Caxton was living in the German city of Cologne. He was finishing off an English translation of the *History of Troy*, written by the French author, Raoul Le Fèvre. He was working very hard, translating a thousand words a day, and was exhausted. 'My pen is worn', he wrote, 'mine hand weary and not steadfast, mine eyes dimmed with overmuch looking on the white paper, and ... age creepeth on me daily and feebleth all the body'. He decided to master a new invention which was just making its appearance in the city. He goes on: 'therefore I have practised and learned at my great charge and dispense to ordain this said book in print after the manner and form as ye may here see'. The new invention – printing – was to save many future authors and copyists from weary hands and dimmed eyes.

The printing press was invented in 1439 by the German Johannes Gutenberg. Having learned the craft, Caxton eventually returned to England in 1476, where he opened a printing 'shop' in the precincts of Westminster Abbey. His shop saw the production of over a hundred printed works, including Chaucer's *Canterbury Tales* and Malory's romance *Le Morte d'Arthur*. Caxton himself made twenty-six translations, including the first in English of Ovid's *Metamorphosis*. It is hard to exaggerate the effect of printing on society. Perhaps the nearest modern-day equivalent is the introduction of the internet. In both these cases, written communication suddenly became possible to a previously unimaginable degree. In a moment, information and knowledge could be made available to a massive audience. Before Gutenberg's invention, producing a book was a long, expensive task, involving scribes laboriously copying texts out by hand. It was hugely time-consuming to produce even one copy, let alone huge numbers of a book, like the Bible, which was in heavy demand. After Gutenberg it was all very much simpler. A typeset form of the book was fed into the press, and in a very short time out would come as many copies as you wanted, all of them absolutely identical. The cost was comparatively low too.

This new technology that sprang into being so suddenly was part of a happy convergence of events. It coincided with a moment in history when there was much to write about. The Renaissance was a time of discovery in very many areas – not just geographical exploration, but science, mathematics, the arts and a huge range of skills including practical ones like – as we shall see in 15.1 – horse riding. There were literally hundreds of books just waiting to be translated from the classics, while new writers were anxious to make their own thoughts known in their subject specializations. There was also, just like today with the internet, a large audience ready to devour what was written. Though there are no exact statistics for literacy rates during the period, possibly 20 per cent of men were literate in the 1530s, increasing to 30 per cent by the end of Elizabeth's reign. In London (where Shakespeare and others had their audiences) the figures were doubtless higher, perhaps reaching 50 per cent. All in all, it really was a 'happy convergence': plenty of new subject matter to write about, plenty of new of readers to read it, and new technology able to produce what was required quickly.

But in what language was all this going to happen? Latin was traditionally the language of scholastic communication. But it was not a language much known by the population, many of whom were what was quaintly called 'unlatined'. To reach the required audience, communication had to be in English. And that was the rub, because according to the general view held in the first half of the sixteenth century, English was simply not up to it. A characteristic opinion of the time was expressed by one Richard Taverner. He translated a collection of psalms and prayers from Latin, and dedicated it to Henry VIII. 'My translation', the dedication reads, 'is rude, base, unpleasant, gross and barbarous'. He fears 'lest of good Latin I have made evil English, lest I have turned wine into water'. Of course, his tone is modest, as appropriate in a dedication to one's king (especially one celebrated for lopping off the heads of those who crossed him). But behind Taverner's words is a view of Latin common at the time. It is an eloquent, expressive, 'wine-like' language. And his view of English is equally common. It is rude, barbarous and 'watery'.

Such complaints about English may have been common but, as time went on, confidence in the new language grew. It had its defenders, none so strong as the pedagogue Richard Mulcaster, whose 1582 book *The Elementarie*, was a spirited defence of the use of English: 'I love Rome', he says, 'but London better, I favor Italie, but England more, I honor the Latin, but I worship the English'. These attitudes towards English – despair at the language's inadequacies followed by spirited defence of its value, were also found in relation to other European tongues. The **vernaculars**, as they were called, were seeking to gain recognition over and above Latin. Thus in 1542, we find an Italian humanist scholar, Sperone Speroni, writing a polemical defence of the vernaculars against Latin, called *Dialogo delle lingue*. In France, a movement known as La Pléiade was set up with the aim of enriching the French language. The movement's 'manifesto' was a book written by Du Bellay and appearing in 1549. It was called *Deffence et Illustration de la Languge Françoyse*. The movement to dislodge Latin from its privileged position was Europe-wide.

Nowhere was Latin's position more privileged than in religion. Latin was the language of Christianity and of the Church. If Latin could be dislodged from that particular position... The struggle is recorded in CW13.1 (*Translating the Bible*).

What was so inadequate about English that made it difficult for it to meet the challenges that the new 'happy convergence' required? A major one was the lack of vocabulary. There were simply not enough words in English to cope with the expanding mental and physical worlds of the Renaissance. Another was the lack of standard norms. There was too much variation in the language – too many dialects, too many ways in which the language could be spoken, written and spelled. Take a look at CW13.2 (*Eggs* or *eyren?*). It contains a story Caxton tells to illustrate this linguistic variation. Caxton, of course, helped to solve this problem. As you can imagine, the introduction of printing played a major part in bringing about standardization of the language.

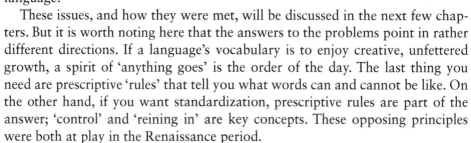

These issues, and how they were met, will be discussed in the next few chapters. But it is worth noting here that the answers to the problems point in rather different directions. If a language's vocabulary is to enjoy creative, unfettered growth, a spirit of 'anything goes' is the order of the day. The last thing you need are prescriptive 'rules' that tell you what words can and cannot be like. On the other hand, if you want standardization, prescriptive rules are part of the answer; 'control' and 'reining in' are key concepts. These opposing principles were both at play in the Renaissance period.

13.3 Fine volleys of words

Issues like the lack of linguistic standardization were identified and discussed at length in the Renaissance. Thus John Palsgrave, a priest in Henry VIII's court (who, like Richard Taverner, managed to die with his head on), wrote a Latin translation which he dedicated to the king. He hoped that his book would help to make English 'uniforme throughe out all your graces domynions'. This was all part of a new awareness of 'matters linguistic'. Language was the subject of debate – it was something that people talked about. The number of scholars who wrote on linguistic topics shows this. One of these was William Bullokar. He wrote a grammar of English, and, in 1580, a *Booke at large, for the Amendment of Orthographie for English speech*. This was one of a number of attempts in the period to develop a more 'phonetic' way of writing. Another was Richard Mulcaster's *The Elementarie*, which deals with the teaching of English and is full of linguistic advice. Seven years later comes George Puttenham's *The Arte of English Poesie*, a handbook on poetry and rhetoric.

This new linguistic awareness also made people particularly conscious of how they – and others – spoke. The comedies of Shakespeare and Ben Jonson are full of speakers who attract ridicule because they misuse words ('malapropisms' are discussed at length in 15.3). There are also plenty of judgemental comments on 'poor' linguistic practices. Here is one Richard Stanihurst describing, in his 1577 *Description of Ireland*, how people spoke in 'Weisforde' (the town of Wexford is in today's Ireland): 'they haue so aquainted themselues with the Irishe, as they have made a mingle mangle, or gallamaulfrey of both the languages, ... so crabbedly iumbled them both togyther [that they] speake neyther good English nor good Irishe'. A *mingle mangle* is a 'mishmash', and a *gallamaufrey* (or 'galli-maufry') is a 'confused jumble'.

But this self-consciousness about language also had a more positive side. There is a scene in Shakespeare's early comedy *The Two Gentlemen of Verona* where two characters, both courting the same lady (Silvia), enter into a complex play of words, both trying to impress Silvia, who is present, and both poking fun at each other. The jokes and puns come thick and fast, so much so that today's reader can only really follow by constant reference to an editor's commentary. It is a little piece of linguistic theatre, and at the end Silvia shows her appreciation by saying: 'A fine volley of words, gentlemen, and quickly shot off.' In the BBC DVD production of the play, the audience is enlarged to include a group of onlookers, who clap when particularly witty remarks are made – rather as today one would applaud a particularly funny joke of a stand-up comedian, or even (as one meaning of the word 'volley' suggests) an exceptional 'volley' in a tennis match. You can find this passage at CW13.3 (*The word-volley*). It shows that in Renaissance England, linguistic sophistication – 'fine volleys of words' – were much admired.

What this passage captures (and there are very many similar ones in Shakespeare) is that language was seen as something to be played with. This spirit accounts for Shakespeare's love of puns. According to Samuel Johnson, they were for the poet 'the fatal Cleopatra for whom he lost the world'. As a further Shakespearean example of word-play, take his Sonnet 135, which plays on the shortened version of his name: Will. Here are the first two lines (the word *overplus* means 'excess', and *to boot* means 'in addition'):

> Whoever hath her wish, thou hast thy Will,
> And Will to boot, and Will in overplus;

There are at least seven meanings of the word *will* played with in the poem. For a detailed look at the Renaissance in full 'pun', look at Activity 13B (*Where there's a Will*), which contains the sonnet and explores its uses of the word *will*.

13.4   The rogues in buckrom

For Old English we had the 'lettuce story' to help us approach the language, and for Middle English the 'Chaunticleer passage'. We need an EModE passage as a starting-point for exploring this stage of the language. Here is one. We shall call it the 'buckrom story'; *buckrom* or *buckram* was a coarse cloth used to make cheap clothes. The passage is taken from Act 2, Scene 4 of Shakespeare's play *Henry IV, Part 1*. The first to speak in the extract is Prince Hal, the king's son, who at the end of *Henry IV, Part 2* becomes Henry V. He is at this point busy misspending his youth, wasting away his hours with disreputable characters. Chief among these is Shakespeare's comic masterpiece, Jack Falstaff, a feckless mountain of a man who, though a knight, lives a life of debauchery. Falstaff and his companion Gadshill have attempted to rob some travellers on the highway, and have failed miserably. Prince Hal, with his friend Poins, question Falstaff and Gadshill on what happened. Falstaff's story is a pack of lies, invented to make him sound brave. The main joke is that he constantly tries to make his story more impressive by adding to the number of adversaries they encountered, like a fisherman exaggerating the number of fish caught. There is a glossary below the passage, which is given here using the spelling and orthography of the 1623 version:[1]

Rogues in buckrom

Prince: Speake firs, how was it?

Gad: We foure fet vpon fome dozen.

Falft: Sixteene, at leaft, my Lord.

Gad: And bound them.

Peto: No, no, they were not bound.

Falft: You Rogue, they were bound, euery man of them, or I am a Iew elfe, an Ebrew Iew.

Gad: As we were fharing, fome fix or feuen frefh men fet vpon vs.

Falft: And vnbound the reft, and then come in the other.

Prince: What, fought yee with them all?

Falft: All? I know not what yee call all: but if I fought not with fiftie of them, I am a bunch of Radifh: if there were not two or three and fiftie vpon poore olde *Iack*, then I am no two-legg'd Creature.

Poin: Pray Heauen, you haue not murthered fome of them.

Falft: Nay, that's paft praying for, I haue pepper'd two of them: Two I am fure I haue payed, two Rogues in Buckrom Sutes. I tell thee what, *Hal*, if I tell thee a Lye, fpit in my face, call me Horfe: thou knoweft my olde word: here I lay, and thus I bore my point: foure Rogues in Buckrom let driue at me.

Prince: What, foure? thou fayd'ft but two, euen now.

Falſs: Foure, *Hal,* I told thee foure.

Poin: I, I, he ſaid foure.

Falſt: Theſe foure came all a-front, and mainely thruſt at me; I made no more adoe, but tooke all their ſeuen points in my Targuet, thus.

Prince: Seuen? Why there were but foure, euen now.

Falſt: In Buckrom.

Poin: I, foure, in Buckrom Sutes.

Falſt: Seuen, by theſe Hilts, or I am a Villaine elſe.

Prin: Prethee let him alone, we ſhall haue more anon.

Falſt: Doeſt thou heare me, *Hal*?

Prin: I, and marke thee too, *Iack.*

Falſt: Doe ſo, for it is worth the liſtning too: theſe nine in Buckrom, that I told thee of.

Pron: So, two more alreadie.

Falſt: Their Points being broken.

Poin: Downe fell his Hoſe.

Falſt: Began to giue me ground: but I followed me cloſe, came in foot and hand; and with a thought, ſeuen of theeleuen I pay'd.

Prin: O monſtrous! eleuen Buckrom men growne out of two?

Falſt: But as the Deuill would haue it, three miſ-begotten Knaues, in Kendall Greene, came at my Back, and let driue at me; for it was ſo darke, *Hal,* that thou could'ſt not ſee thy Hand.

Prin: Theſe Lyes are like the Father that begets them, groſſe as a Mountaine, open, palpable. Why thou Clay-brayn'd Guts, thou Knotty-pated Foole, thou Horſon obſeene greaſie Tallow Catch.

Iew, Jew	*Ebrew,* Hebrew
sharing, sharing out the money that had been stolen	*bunch of Radish,* radishes symbolized leanness (and Falstaff was a very fat man)
murther, murder	*pepper,* trounce
horse, ass	*word,* (*ward*) posture of defence
point, sword	*I,* aye, yes
a-front, abreast	*targuet,* shield
sute, suite	*point,* sword point, but also the laces holding up stockings
hose, stockings	*pay,* kill
Kendall greene, a coarse type of cloth	*clay-brayned,* stupid
guts, fat person	*knotty-pated,* block-headed
horson, whoreson	*tallow catch,* dripping pan (to collect fat from cooking meat)

We will start looking at the 'buckrom story' in the next chapter. But here, in preparation, are some points to ponder:

(a) The passage contains the letter ſ. It is sometimes called **long s**, to distinguish it from the **short s** ('s') we use today. The two letters do not represent different sounds, but they are used in different contexts. Try to work out from the story when the two are used.

(b) The difference between 'u' and 'v' is also interesting. In PDE they represent different sounds, and there were two sounds in EModE as well. But both 'u' and 'v' could be used for each sound. Again, the use of the letters depends on context. Try to work out when they are used.

(c) The story is full of words that look like PDE words, but with slight spelling differences. Make a note of these. Are there any differences which occur sufficiently often for you to work out any general principles?

(d) Find examples of apostrophes in the story. What function do they serve? Compare what you find with how we use apostrophes in PDE.

(e) The use of capital letters in the story is at odds with PDE usage. When do we use word-initial capitals in PDE? Can you find any logic to how they are used in the story?

(f) What about the use of italics? When are they used?

(g) Look at the punctuation marks used in the story and note any differences from PDE usage.

The next chapter (14.2), takes up these issues. To finish the present chapter on a rude note: notice at the end of the 'buckrom story' the glorious barrage of insults the Prince looses on Falstaff. Shakespeare was a master in the art of the insult. Here is Falstaff, a few lines later, giving back to the Prince as good as he got. You do not have to understand all the words to savour the delights of these insults:

> Away you Starueling, you Elfe-skin, you dried Neats tongue, Bulles-piſſell, you ſtocke-fiſh... You Tailors yard, you ſheath you Bow-caſe, you vile ſtanding tucke.

Literary critics from outside Britain have sometimes wondered how we can have a national writer capable of such rudeness!

Activity section

13A   From the Chronicles   AS

Here are some passages from Volume 3 of Holinshed's *Chronicles of England, Scotland and Ireland*. They describe characters mentioned in the text. Identify these characters.[2]

(a) From the 1531 entry. Who is the lady referred to here?

> While the parlement sat, on the thirtieth day of March at afternoone, there came into the common house the lord chauncellor and diuerse lords of the spiritualitie and temporalitie, to the number of twelue, and there the lord

chancellor said: 'you of this worpshipfull house (I am sure) be not so ignorant, but you know well, that the king our souereigne hath married his brothers wife, for she was both wedded and bedded with his brother prince Arthur, and therefore you may suerlie saie that he hath married his brothers wife'. (766)

(b) Who is being described here?

As he was small and little of stature, so was he of bodie greatlie deformed; the one shoulder higher than the other; his face was small, but his countenace cruell, and such that at the first aspect a man would iudge it to sauour and smell of malice, fraud, and deceit. When he stood musing, he would bite and chaw busily his nether lip; as who said, that his fierce nature in his cruell bodie always chafed, stirred and was euer unquiet. (447)

(c) The date is 1533. Who is the wife, and who the child?

After that the king perceiued his new wife to be with child, he caused all officers necessarie to be appointed to hir, and so on Easter euen she went to hir closet openlie as queene; and then the king appointed the daie of hir coronation to be kept on Whitsundaie next following. (778)

(d) The year is 1536. Who are X and Y?

On the nineteenth of Maie queene X was on a scaffold (made for that purpose) vpon the greene within the tower of London, beheaded with the sword of Calis [Calais], by the hands of the hangman of that towne: hir body with the head was buried in the queere of the chappell in the tower ... Immediatelie after hir death, in the weeke before Whitsuntide, the king married the ladie Y ... which at Whitsuntide was openlie shewed as queene. (797)

13B Where there's a Will

(a) Here is the whole of Shakespeare's Sonnet 135. It is full of play around the word *will*. Like many of Shakespeare's sonnets, it is not always easy to understand his meaning fully; but read it a few times to gain the general sense. Then concentrate on the word *will*. Distinguish as many different senses of the word as you can in the poem. Do not look at (b) below before you have done this.

> Whoever hath her wish, thou hast thy Will,
> And Will to boot, and Will in overplus;
> More than enough am I that vex thee still,
> To thy sweet will making addition thus.
> Wilt thou whose will is large and spacious
> Not once vouchsafe to hide my will in thine?
> Shall will in others seem right gracious,
> And in my will no fair acceptance shine?

> The sea all water, yet receives rain still,
> And in abundance addeth to his store;
> So thou, being rich in Will, add to thy Will,
> One will of mine to make thy large Will more.
> Let no unkind, no fair beseechers kill;
> Think all but one, and me in that one Will.

(b) Here are seven EModE meanings of the word *will*, some of which you will have identified in (a). Try to find points in the sonnet where these might be intended. If modesty demands, focus on just some of them…

a desire	sexual lust	determination	a modal verb indicating futurity
William	vagina	penis	

Answer section

Activity 13A

(a) Catherine of Aragon; (b) Richard III; (c) Anne Boleyn and Elizabeth; (d) Anne Boleyn and Jane Seymour.

Further reading

There is no shortage of historical accounts of this fascinating period of English history. Fraser (1992) announces its focus in the title: *The Six Wives of Henry VIII.*

Mantel's trilogy of novels (2010, 2013, and forthcoming) also focus on Henry VIII's reign.

Weir (2009) is a very readable account of Elizabeth I's reign. There are many others.

An excellent book about the rise of English is Jones (1953).

Chapter 2 of Bailey (1991) deals usefully with the period in question.

Notes

1 1623 is the date of Shakespeare's First Folio. The passage is taken from *Mr William Shakespeare's Comedies, Histories, and Tragedies (1623). The Bodleian First Folio,* URL: http://firstfolio.bodleian.ox.ac.uk/. Date accessed: December 2015.
2 The page references are given in brackets after the quotations. They have been taken from Ellis (1965).

14

'Wryting treu' and 'soundying cleare'

EModE graphology, spelling and pronunciation

'Variation' is one of the keywords of this chapter, which focuses on graphology, spelling and pronunciation. As we look in detail at how Renaissance English was written, we will find much variation, with words often being spelled in more than one way. At the same time, spelling reform was in the air, with attempts being made to bring some order to the rather chaotic practices. In our look at pronunciation we concentrate on differences between Shakespeare's time and today. Despite all the variation, one conclusion of the chapter is that the language during the EModE period was gradually 'settling down' into the English that we now use.[1]

Some things to think about before you read:

- Think about spelling reform. If you wanted to reform a language's spelling, what principles could you follow? How could it be done?
- The chapter mentions modern attempts to perform Shakespeare's plays using the pronunciation of his time. Is there any value in doing this? What might it be?
- Some aspects of pronouncing PDE are frowned upon socially. The one mentioned in the chapter is not pronouncing 'h' at the beginning of some words (saying 'ouse instead of house, for example). Think of some pronunciations frowned upon in the version of English that you are familiar with, or in some other language.

14.1 What's in a name?

A major event in Shakespeare's play *Henry VI, Part 2* is a popular rebellion against the crown and government. It took place in 1450, and its leader was one Jack Cade. In this scene, Cade is on the lookout for class enemies – people showing signs of privilege and education. Here is how he tries to identify the educated:

Cade: Dost thou use to write thy name? Or hast thou a mark to thyself, like a honest plain-dealing man?
Clerk: Sir, I thank God I have been so well brought up that I can write my name.

That is enough evidence for Cade. The clerk can write his name. Cade's verdict: 'Away with him, I say; hang him with his pen and inkhorn [inkwell] about his neck.'

Writing your name may have been a sign of education in the fifteenth century, when Cade lived. More people could read in Shakespeare's century, the sixteenth, but there was plenty of spelling variation. Just how many different ways could there be of spelling a name? According to Bryson (2007), there were more than eighty ways that Shakespeare's own name could be spelt. Here are some of them:

Shackspeare	Shakspeare	Shaxpeare
Shakspeyr	Shackesper	Shagspere
Shaxspere	Shakysper	Shackspere
Shackespeare	Shakespear	Shakespere
Shaxper	Shakspere	Shackespere
Shexpere	Shakespeare	Shacksper
Shaksper	Shaxpere	Shakyspere

The list above is not in any kind of order. You may like to look through it and establish at what points in the word the variations can lie, tabulating the various possibilities at each point. For example, all spellings have the initial 'sh' – there is no variation. But one point where there *is* variation is in the following vowel, sometimes written 'a', sometimes 'e', and sometimes in other ways.

Spelling variations were very common indeed, not just in relation to names. The exclamation *marry*, in fact comes from a name (Mary, Christ's mother), but it entered common use as an expression of surprise. There seem to have been at least ten spellings of it, not counting dialect ones. Along with *marry*, you find *mary, marie, marye, marrie, mare, mari, mayry, marrye, marra*.[2] As it happens, the 'buckrom story' does not contain any real spelling variation, and so does not make the point well. The only minor piece of variation is that sometimes when the Prince speaks he is called *Prince*, and sometimes *Prin*. It would be tempting to suggest that the shorter form is used to save space, when the longer word might take a speech over onto another line – Renaissance scribes did use such space-saving ruses – though if you look through the story you will find that this does not really apply there. But you do not have to go far beyond the story text – before or after – to find spelling variation. Thus while the story above has *he*, the First Folio's next page has *hee*. And while the story has *mee*, on the page before you find *me*. The same is true for *yee* (in the passage) and *ye* (a few lines before). In the story, the Prince calls Falstaff *Iack* (Jack), and on the Folio's next page this becomes *Iacke*. There is variation all around.

All in all, it is no wonder that the English educator John Hart, in his 1569 book called *An Orthographie*, talks about 'confusion and disorder' in English spelling. The newness of the accepted use of English for writing is enough to explain the degree of variation, but there are other reasons. As we saw in Chapter 12, the GVS had caused problems regarding spelling–pronunciation relationships, and, as we shall see in 15.3, there was another huge influx of foreign words during the period. This added to the confusion, with many people unsure how to spell foreign-sounding words. There is no doubt that the introduction of printing helped standardization, although when Caxton set up his printing press in London, he had to use foreign compositors, and they brought with them their own spelling conventions; they were also quite prepared to waive rules when convenient.

John Hart's comment about 'confusion and disorder' in spelling shows that there was indeed much discontent with the situation, and the period saw various attempts at standardization. Early efforts included a 1530 spelling manual, which now exists only in fragments. It gave directions on how 'one may lerne to spel & to rede & how one shud wryte englysh treu'.[3] But how might this be done? How do you reform spelling?

The most obvious possibility is to base the system on how words are pronounced, trying to use a different writing symbol for each distinct sound. As we saw in 12.2, 'one sound, one symbol' is not at all what happens in PDE. Nor was it in EModE. Here is how William Bullokar puts it in his 1580 *Booke at Large for the Amendment of English Orthographie*:

[the letters of the alphabet] are not fufficient to picture Inglifh fpeech: for in Inglifh fpeech, are mo diftinctions and diuifions in voice [speech] … By reafon whereof, we were driuen, to vfe to fomme letters, two foundes, to fome three foundes…

In *An Orthographie*, John Hart tried to introduce a new 'phonetic' alphabet for writing, with each distinct sound (what we call a **phoneme** in linguistics today) represented by a different written symbol. He was by no means the last in history to try introducing 'one sound, one symbol'. Most failed partly because they generally ended up having to use many symbols unfamiliar to readers, making the spelling system difficult to learn. Difficulty for the learner is a sure recipe for failure, and this was the fate met by Hart's system. So too the system developed by Bullokar. He tried to keep to existing letters, but used diacritics – accents like ['] which could be put above a letter (as in á) to indicate a specific sound. This did not go down well with readers either. More successful were the efforts of two schoolmasters. Richard Mulcaster's *The Elementarie* (1582) contained a list of no fewer than 8,500 spellings. But the length of the list made the book expensive to buy. Most popular of all was Edmund Coote's *The English School-Maister* (1596), which was much shorter than Mulcaster's work. It contains a brief dictionary at the end. Just how rare dictionary use was in those days is suggested by CW14.1 ('*Directions for the unskilfull*'), which contains an extract from Coote's work.

14.2 Writing in the 'buckrom story'

14.2.1 Graphology

At the end of Chapter 13 (13.4) you were asked questions about various graphological points that came up in the 'buckrom story'. As likely as not, the first point you noticed came in the first two words. *Speake firs*, Prince Hal says, giving us two examples of the 'short s' (the one we use today), and one of the 'long s' (ſ), which we no longer use. The two do not differ in terms of pronunciation. But as you may have worked out, the 'short s' is used in word-final positions (as in *firs*), and word-initially when the word has a capital letter. The long 'ſ' is used in all other circumstances.

The difference between 'u' and 'v' also relates to where the letter comes in the word. In PDE these two letters represent different sounds, one a vowel and the other a consonant. But the story does not differentiate the letters in this way. Both can stand for either vowel or consonant. The letter 'v' is used at the beginning of words, for both lower and upper case, while 'u' occurs within or at the end of words. The first example of the modern-day vowel/consonant distinction for 'u/v' was noted in a book published in 1634, eleven years after Shakespeare's First Folio appeared.

There is one letter which we now have but which was not much found in EModE: 'j'. In the passage, there are two words which today we would write with an initial 'j': *Iew* and *Iack*. As it happens, these letters are capitals in the passage, but it would be the same if they were in lower case – 'i' would be used rather than 'j'. The latter started to be used around 1630, and in fact Shakespeare's Third Folio (dated 1664) has *Jew* and *Jack*.

14.2.2 Spelling

The story has two examples of **consonant doubling**, where a consonant is repeated at the end of a word. There is one you may not have come across because it involves the name of a place – Kendal (a town in today's English county of Cumbria). In the text it is *Kendall*. The other example is *Deuill*. This common practice was lamented by reformers like Mulcaster (1582), who complains about 'the dubling of consonants at the end of a word ... and a thousand such ignorant superfluities'. Mulcaster's theory as to why this happens is rather quaint. It was 'the swiftness of the pen sure, which can hardly stay upon the single ending *l*, that causeth this doubling'. The pen just cannot stop. Lass (1999a: 11) suggests the doublings were often just 'typographical decorations'.

Another of Mulcaster's 'superfluities' is the final 'e'. You will have found plenty of examples in the story of words ending in 'e' which would have no final 'e' in modern English – words like *foure*, *olde*, *adoe* and *heare*. Why are they there? Sometimes it is a remnant from an earlier form of the language. The ME verb *walken* ('to travel'), for example, over time became *walke*. The final 'e' was pronounced until about 1400, then it disappeared from speech but stayed on in the spelling. This is just the kind of process we discussed in relation to the GVS, in 12.2, where pronunciation changed and spelling stayed the same – a very common reason, we noted, why English spelling can be so bothersome. Though the 'e's we have been considering may be superfluous, they are not always so, and 'final e' can play an important role in spelling. This is described in CW14.2 (*The 'magic e'*).

You may have noticed some words in the story where the spelling 'ie' is used. One is *Iew* for *Jew*, which we have already discussed. There are another three: *fif-tie, alreadie* and *greasie*. In PDE we have a final 'y'. Using 'ie' for our final 'y' was very common in EModE, and once again Mulcaster has something to say about it: 'When … *i* is it self the last letter … it is qualified by the *e*, as *manie, merie* … where the verie pen, will rather end in the e, then in the naked *i*'.[4] But, Mulcaster goes on to note, 'y' is used when the stress falls on the final syllable – so we have *deny, cry*, not *denie, crie*. Incidentally, there are occasions in modern English when we add a suffix to a word ending in 'y', which then becomes 'ie'. So we 'change' 'y' to 'ie' when we add an 's' to it. This happens when we form a plural noun. For example, *history* becomes *histories*. We do the same when a verb takes a final 's': we write *I deny*, but *he denies*.

There are several examples in the story of words where a letter is missing, replaced by an apostrophe. In most cases, the missing letter is the 'e' of the *-ed* suffix; so *legg'd* stands for *legged*, and *pay'd* for *payed*. But an apostrophe can also replace the 'i' in *is* and the 'e' of the *-est* suffix. Find examples of both of these in 13.4's 'buckrom story'. The apostrophe often has a similar effect to the schwa vowel (discussed in 10.2.2), standing in unstressed syllables for weakened vowels. Activity 14A (*Standing in*) looks at a few more examples in a non-Shakespearean context.

14.2.3 Punctuation

You probably noticed that the passage uses capital letters in a way that is different from today. Think first about modern uses of the capital. When do we use it? Perhaps you have come across another modern language where the usage is different from PDE. One is mentioned at the end of the next paragraph, which also provides information about capitals in the 'buckrom story'. Before reading on, look at Activity 14B (*Upper and lower case*), which asks questions about this.

As in PDE, the letter following a full stop in EModE is always a capital, and so it is in the story. Notice, though, that after the exclamation mark in *O monſtrous!* there is a small letter – the exclamation mark is clearly not here regarded as signalling a sentence end. The colon, however, seems to be being regarded as a full-stop equivalent in *I haue pepper'd two of them: Two….* You find the same at one point in CW14.1. But the big point is that in the story there are also many words which start with a capital even though not at the beginning of a sentence. Sometimes in EModE they are adjectives. In the story *Clay* and *Knotty* might be regarded as examples, though in the case of the first it could be the first noun element of a compound noun. But mostly the capital-ized words are nouns. Yet not all nouns have capital letters – in the story there are many that do not: *man*, *bunch*, *foot*, among others. Some linguists suggest that capitals are used to mark out certain types of words. 'Important' nouns, for example; but why should *foot* be less important than *Hose*? The truth of the matter is that it is often difficult to find any rhyme or reason in the EModE use of capitals. Salmon (1986) argues that there was movement at this period towards the eighteenth-century situation when capitals were used for nearly all nouns. A language you may have come across where all nouns begin with a capital letter is German.

Italics in the story are used for the names of people. They are also used in drama for stage directions, and for place names (though perhaps 'Kendall' is regarded as an adjective rather than principally as a place name, so is not in ital-ics). You might like to ponder how we use italics today. And while pondering, it is worth thinking a little bit about the use of punctuation today, particularly the common marks '!', '?', '.', ';', ':' and ','. Do this, then take a look at CW14.3 (*Punctuation, body parts and lunch breaks*), which looks at the functions of punctuation in the Renaissance and today.

 If you would like to see how spelling became standardized, you might like to look at CW14.4 (*Comparing folios*), which contains two versions of part of the 'buckrom story' in facsimile ('exact copy') form. One is as it appears in the First Folio, and this gives you some sense of what the actual text looked like. The second is from a facsimile of the Fourth Folio, dated 1685. Compare the two versions in relation to the points about graphology that have been made in this section.

14.3 Pronunciation

Thomas Wilson was a diplomat and scholar, and his *Arte of Rhetorique* was published in 1553. Its last part is about elocution. Good pronunciation, Wilson says, is not just a question of having 'a cleare soundying voice'. It involves the 'apt ordering ... [of] ... the whole bodye' in the service of the words being uttered. But what did the Renaissance 'cleare soundying voice' sound like? Just how different from today's pronunciation was Shakespeare's? Perhaps not so much. Kökeritz (1953) – a major study of Shakespearean pronunciation – argues that today we 'would be able to understand Shakespeare ... with little effort'. Crystal agrees: 'people generally expect [Shakespearean pronunciation] to be much more different from Modern English than in fact it is, and it comes as a bit of a surprise to realize that it is in many respects identical' (2005: 36).

Of course, we have to approach the question of how words were pronounced more than 400 years ago with caution. In 4.2.4, we looked at some of the evidence for what we know about how OE was pronounced. We shall do the same for EModE later in this chapter (14.5). Though some types of evidence are quite reliable, it is important to realize that pronunciation is, of its very nature, a variable thing. People today pronounce words differently from each other, not just according to where they come from, but also following their own personal styles and idiosyncrasies. It was like that in the sixteenth century too. Also, at that time, there did not exist any strong sense of what we now call RP, regarded by many as a statusful way of speaking – it was mentioned in 10.3. Thus, in the huge social mix of sixteenth-century London, you would have been likely to meet a great variety of pronunciations, and much more of course if you take the country as a whole. In this chapter, we will be comparing aspects of sixteenth-century pronunciation with RP. If the version of English you use is not RP, you need to be alert to the fact that some of these comparisons may not hold in exactly the same form, given your version of English pronunciation.

There have been a number of studies of EModE pronunciation, including Dobson's (1957) lengthy and very detailed *English Pronunciation: 1500–1700*. But in recent years the focus of interest has been on Shakespeare in particular, and there have been productions of Shakespeare plays delivered in what is called **Original Pronunciation** (OP). A major experiment was undertaken by London's Globe Theatre in 2004 when for three days *Romeo and Juliet* was performed using OP. The guiding linguistic spirit behind this project (and indeed behind OP in general) is David Crystal, and his book, Crystal (2005), describes in detail how the project was conceived and realized. A number of other OP performances have followed, and there are two websites – http://originalpronunciation.com/ and www.pronouncingshakespeare.com/ – which discuss OP and provide examples.

By far the best way of approaching Shakespearean pronunciation is to start by listening to an example of OP. CW14.5 (*Star-crossed lovers*) focuses on the Prologue to Shakespeare's *Romeo and Juliet* (1.1.1), spoken by the Chorus figure. It is read twice, the first time following the principles of OP, and the second time in my normal RP accent. The written text of the passage is also given. In a moment, we will look at distinct areas of difference between EModE and RP. But first, listen to the recording to form an impressionistic view of the differences between then and now. Are there many? More, or fewer, than you expected?

To help you do a more detailed comparison, here are phonetic transcriptions of my readings – the OP version on the left, the RP on the right. Incidentally, you will notice that the OP transcription contains the sound [ɤ]. This is the sound that became [ʌ] in PDE, and is described on the list of 'Phonetic symbols used' (p. xv):

Take a moment to compare the two transcriptions. In the next section, differences between EModE and RP are discussed. If you would like to work out some of the differences for yourself, look at Activity 14C (*Pronunciations compared*). Also, if you are a non-RP speaker, you may like to identify differences between your pronunciation and the RP version above.

Figure 14.1 OP and RP version of the Prologue to *Romeo and Juliet*

	OP version	RP version
1	tuː əʊsoːldz, boːθ ələɪk ɪn dɪgnɪtəɪ,	tuː haʊshəʊldz, bəʊθ əlaɪk ɪn dɪgnɪti,
2	ɪn fɛːr vəroːnə, hweːr wɪ leː əʊr seːn,	ɪn feə vərəʊnə, weə wɪ leɪ aʊə siːn,
3	frəm eːnʃənt grɤʤ breːk tə njuː mjuːtnəɪ,	frəm eɪnʃənt grʌʤ breɪk tə njuː mjuːtəni,
4	hweːr sɪvɪl blɤd meːks sɪvɪl andz ənkleːn.	weə sɪvɪl blʌd meɪks sɪvɪl hændz ənkliːn.
5	frəm foːrθ ðə feːtl ləɪnz əv ðeːz tuː foːz	frəm foːrθ ðə feɪtl lɔɪnz əv ðiːz tuː fəʊz
6	ə peːr əv staːr krɒst lɤvrz teːk ðɛːr ləɪf;	ə peə əv staː krɒst lʌvəz teɪk ðeə laɪf;
7	huːz mɪsədventərd pɪtjəs oːvərθroːz	huːz mɪsədventʃəd pɪtɪəs əʊvəθrəʊz
8	dɤθ wɪð ðɛːr deθ berəɪ ðɛːr peːrənts strəɪf.	dʌθ wɪð ðeə deθ berɪ ðeə peərənts straɪf.
9	ðə fɪərfəl pæsɪʤ əv ðɛːr deθ maːrkt lɤv	ðə fɪəfəl pæsɪʤ əv ðeə deθ maːkt lʌv
10	ənd ðə kəntɪnjʊəns əv ðɛːr peːrənts reːʤ,	ənd ðə kəntɪnʊəns əv ðeə peərənts reɪʤ,
11	hwɪtʃ, bɤt ðɛːr tʃɪldrənz end, naːt kʊd rəmɤv,	wɪtʃ, bət ðeə tʃɪldrənz end, nɔːt kʊd rəmuːv,
12	ɪz naʊ ðə tuː əʊrz træfɪk əv əʊr steːʤ;	ɪz naʊ ðə tuː aʊəz træfɪk əv aʊə steɪʤ;
13	ðə hwɪtʃ ɪf juː wɪð peːʃənt iːrz ətend,	ðə wɪtʃ ɪf juː wɪð peɪʃənt ɪəz ətend,
14	hwɒt iːr ʃəl mɪs, əʊr təɪl ʃəl strəɪv tə mend.	wɒt hɪə ʃəl mɪs, aʊə tɔɪl ʃəl straɪv tə mend.

14.4 Some sound differences between then and now

14.4.1 Some consonants

(a) [r]

One of the first things you may have noticed is the pronunciation of the sound [r]. This is an interesting sound in a number of languages, and we have adjectives, like 'rolled' and 'trilled', which describe different ways of pronouncing it. There is even a noun, 'rhotacism', which the *OED* defines as the 'unusual pronunciation or pronounced production' of [r]. You might like to think (in an informal way) of different kinds of 'r' pronunciation you have come across in your life. Then look at Activity 14D (*Being rhotic*), which asks you to think specifically about today's British RP and Australian versions of 'r' (an issue we touched on briefly in 10.3).

What the activity shows is that in RP today the letter is sometimes pronounced and sometimes not. Where it occurs at the beginning of a word (word-initially) or before a vowel, it is pronounced, as in *run, recent, enroll, acronym, arrive*. But it is not pronounced inside a word (word-medially) before a consonant, or at the end of a word (word-finally) – except for sometimes when the next word begins with a vowel (in *far away*, for example). The words in Activity 14D like this are *teacher, arm, cart, fair* and *fewer*. Languages or dialects which do not pronounce the 'r' before a consonant or in word-final position are called **non-rhotic**. But not all 'Englishes' are non-rhotic. In American and Scots, for example, the 'r' is pronounced almost wherever it is written. Another such language is EModE, which is why you find so many 'r' sounds in the OP recording you have heard. Consequently, it is easy to know when to pronounce the 'r' in EModE. The general rule of thumb is 'if there is an "r" in the spelling, pronounce it'.

But how exactly was the EModE 'r' pronounced? One of Shakespeare's contemporaries, Ben Jonson, was best known as a playwright but he also wrote a book entitled *English Grammar* in which he describes 'r' as the 'dog's letter' (*littera canina* in Latin), because it sounds like a growl. Jonson provides a detailed description of how to make the sound, with 'the tongue striking the inner palate, with a trembling about the teeth. It is sounded firme in the beginning of words, and more liquid in the middle, and ends; as in *rare* and *riper*'. From this description, it sounds as if initial [r] may have been a little 'trilled' as, for example, in the Italian word *terra*.

(b) [h]

People can be very particular about the way [r] is pronounced, and the same is true about [h]. In RP, it is frequently dropped when in an unstressed position, so a sentence like *Hand him his hat* is likely to be pronounced as if it were *Hand im iz hat* where the initial [h] of the unstressed words *him* and *his* is dropped.[5] But in EModE it was common for [h] to be omitted at the beginning of a stressed syllable, which is not normal today. Some today consider 'dropping your aitches' (saying *'ouse* instead of *house*, for example) a mark of lack of education. But this view only began in the nineteenth century, and in Shakespeare's day there was no such derogatory association. As Kökeritz puts it (1953: 308), 'the correct use of *h* had not yet become a shibboleth of gentility'.

(c) [hw]

The pronunciation of 'wh', when it comes at the beginning of a word, is interesting. In many (though not all) versions of RP, initial 'wh' in words like *what* and *which* (but not *who* and *whose*) is pronounced [w]. So *witch* and *which* are **homophones** – the term used to describe different words pronounced in the same way. But in EModE, 'wh' could be pronounced [hw]. So these words were not homophones, because the second would start with [hw]. This sound comes from OE, where it was reflected in the spelling; you may recall the word *hwæt* from the 'dead reeve passage' in 3.2. The OE 'hw' spelling became reversed in the twelfth century, to give 'wh'.

14.4.2 Some vowels and diphthongs

(a) 'Monophthongs then, diphthongs, now'

EModE [ɛ:] for RP [eə]. You will have noticed in the *Romeo and Juliet Prologue* (or whatever passage of Shakespeare you have been considering) that some sounds which are today diphthongs were then monophthongs. One example is the word *fair* (line 2 of the transcription). In RP this is pronounced with the sound [eə], while in EModE it was [ɛ:]. 'Monophthongs then, diphthongs, now' is indeed a common phenomenon in many versions of English today. As Kökeritz (1953: 161) says: 'one of the major differences between [RP] and late 16th-century pronunciation is the absence in the latter of certain diphthongs and diphthonging tendencies which characterize our speech today'.

EModE [e:] for RP [eɪ]. Another example of 'monophthong then, diphthong now' is modern [eɪ] being pronounced [e:]. This happens in the word *fatal* (line 5 of the transcription). Today, in RP, we would pronounce the word with a diphthong: [feɪtl]. But in EModE it was a monophthong ([fe:tl]). Again you are invited to find the other eight examples in the passage – careful, though, because there are in addition a further three words having the [e:] sound which would not be pronounced [eɪ] today. The *Answer section* lists these eight examples. Incidentally, RP is full of diphthongs, but there are some present-day British English accents where you find monophthongs instead. For example, many speakers of Yorkshire dialects pronounce words like *mate* with the monophthong [e:]. My RP pronunciation is [meɪt] (AS).

EModE [o:] for RP [əʊ]. A third case of 'monophthong then, diphthong now' is the RP word *foes*, which today's RP speakers pronounce with the diphthong [əʊ] – [fəʊz]. You will see from the transcription that it was pronounced with [o:] (line 5). Find the other four examples of this in the passage (again bearing in mind that there are other instances where the RP sound would not be [əʊ]). The four examples are given in the *Answer section* (AS).

(b) Centralized diphthongs

Despite the 'monophthongs then, diphthongs, now' tendency, EModE was far from being diphthong-free. Take a look through the *Romeo and Juliet* transcription and make a list of all the diphthongs. You may notice something about their first element. In nearly every case, the diphthong's first element is the central vowel [ə] – the first element, you will recall from 12.1, of diphthongs that came about in the GVS. So the RP [aɪ] in *die* is [əɪ]; the RP [aʊ] in *how* is [əʊ], and the RP [ɔi] in *joy* is [əɪ]. Go through your list of EModE diphthongs and note in each case what they are in RP. You will see that EModE [ə] stands for a number of RP first elements. You will also incidentally find one case of 'diphthong then, monophthong now'. This is the RP sound [ɪ], which in EModE was sometimes pronounced as the diphthong [əɪ]. There are three occurrences in the *Romeo and Juliet* transcription where in RP we would find the monophthong [ɪ] – at the end of the words *dignity* (line 1), *mutiny* (line 3) and *bury* (line 8).[6]

14.5   Historical pronunciation: some more about how we know

We have already touched on the kind of evidence which leads to knowledge about pronunciation. That was in 4.2.4, which was concerned with the pronunciation of OE. One type of evidence, we saw there, was spelling. It is true that a word's spelling gives nothing like entirely accurate information about pronunciation. But the way people have chosen to represent a word on the page does give us some indication of the sounds it contains. This is one reason why spelling reformers are often interested in sounds, and (as we saw in 14.1) frequently concentrate their efforts on trying to make spelling reflect pronunciation. Several spelling reformers were mentioned in 14.1. CW14.6 (*Caned for Greek pronunciation?*) tells the fascinating story of another person, John Cheke, also interested in pronunciation matters.

Cheke, along with others mentioned earlier in this chapter – Hart, Bullokar, Mulcaster, Coote and Wilson – shows just how much interest there was in matters linguistic during this period. Some of these writers give us very precise information about pronunciation. Here, for example, is John Hart describing the pronunciation of [t] and [d]. You make the sounds, he says, 'bei leing ov iur tung full in ðe palet ov iur mouθ, and tučing hardest of iur for- tiθ' (by laying of your tongue full in the palate of your mouth, and touching hardest of your fore-teeth'). It has been said that the best of Hart's phonetic descriptions are as 'good as anything modern' – that is, in modern phonetics.[7]

The rhymes that poets use can be another useful source of phonetic information. In his Sonnet 62, Shakespeare has the lines: 'Sin of self-love possesseth all mine eye,/And all my soul, and all my every part;/And for this sin there is no remedy.' He is rhyming *eye* and *remedy*, words which do not rhyme in RP today. We need to be cautious what we conclude from this. Sometimes poets are not very careful with the words they rhyme, being content with rhyming sounds that are only vaguely similar; so perhaps the two words did not exactly rhyme at all. Or perhaps *remedy* was pronounced as today, and *eye* was pronounced [iː]. Or was *eye* pronounced as it is today, and *remedy* with a final [aɪ]? In theory, there is yet another alternative, that neither word was pronounced as today, and that there is some other word-final sound to make the rhyme. By looking at enough rhymes of the same sort, we may be able to work out which possibility is most likely. In the case of this particular example, it seems that *remedy* was pronounced like *eye* today, rather than *eye* like *remedy* today.

Puns are yet another source of information. These often depend on words being pronounced in the same (or very similar) ways – they are homophones (the word was used in 14.4.1). Examples of homophonic pairs in RP are *told* and *tolled*, *morning* and *mourning*, *soul* and *sole*. Shakespeare is full of homophonic pairs like these being used for puns. At the beginning of *Julius Caesar*, for example, a citizen is stopped in the street and asked what his job is. He is, he replies, a 'mender of bad soles'. This is taken to mean that he is a churchman ('mending souls'), but in fact he is a cobbler ('mending soles'). The fact that the two words *soul* and *sole* can be used in a pun indicates that they were pronounced (then, as now) in the same way. But because pronunciation changes over time, some words which were homophones in Shakespeare's day are today pronounced differently. In other words, they could have been puns then, but are not now. One example comes in Shakespeare's play *As You Like It*. The court jester, Touchstone, is philosophizing about life and the passing of time. He says: 'And so from hour to hour we ripe, and ripe,/ And then from hour to hour we rot, and rot.' The comment causes mirth. The reason is, as Kökeritz observes, that the word *hour* would have been pronounced like our present-day *oar*, which would also be the way the word *whore* would have been pronounced. If you read the passage again, replacing *hour* with *whore*, it takes on a quite different, and humorous, air. It is an example of a pun telling us something about pronunciation of the day.

14.6   'Settling down': a key phrase

It is over four hundred years since Elizabeth I died. Given this length of time, it is noteworthy how little the language has changed. Certainly, as far as graphology and spelling are concerned, there was, we have seen, a lot of instability and variation. But processes of standardization were at work, and when it comes to pronunciation, we have seen that the Elizabethans did not speak that differently from how we do today. All in all, 'settling down' is a key phrase for this chapter. So too, we shall find, when we come to look at grammar in Chapter 16.

Activity section

14A   Standing in

As a general rule, letters in unstressed syllables which are pronounced very lightly are the ones that tend to get replaced by an apostrophe in EModE. Here are some of the common occasions when this happens. Below the list are some examples, all taken from the early scenes of Ben Jonson's play, *Volpone*. Match the examples with the listed occasions.

- the vowel sound in an *-ed* verb ending;
- some lightly pronounced medial vowel ('medial', recall, means occurring inside a word);
- letters in a preposition, a pronoun or the definite article;

- parts of common verb sequences, particularly using the auxiliary verbs *do*, *be* or *have* – either part of the pronoun or part of the verb goes.

the long'd for sun	*shewd'st like a flame*	*God that giv'st*	*threat'ning*
ne'er	*would'st*	*'tis*	*e'en*
'twas	*i'the galley*	*the vulture's gone*	*fall'n asleep*
you're			

14B Upper and lower case

Look at the 'buckrom story', concentrating solely on capitals and lower case letters at the beginning of words. Here are some statements about the use of capitals in this version. Which of the statements are true, which false? In all statements except for the first, do not consider capitals at the beginning of sentences.

(i) The letter following a full stop is always a capital.
(ii) The full stop is the only punctuation mark followed by a capital letter.
(iii) All nouns have capital letters.
(iv) Only nouns have capital letters.
(v) Only 'important' nouns have capital letters.
(vi) Only nouns describing animate objects have capital letters.

The 'answers' are given in the text of 14.2.3.

14C Pronunciations compared

(a) Here are some points to notice about sounds in RP and EModE. Use the two transcriptions given in Figure 14.1 to identify the differences.
  (i) [r] Note down when a written 'r' is pronounced in RP, and when not. Do not worry at this stage if you cannot see the principle behind the usage you find; there is an activity in a moment which will enable you to work this out. What about in EModE? Can you see any differences?
  (ii) [h] Notice when it is pronounced in RP, and when in EModE.
  (iii) There is a difference between EModE and RP in the pronunciation of word-initial 'wh'. What is it?
  (iv) How is the RP diphthong [eə] pronounced in EModE?
  (v) What about the RP diphthong [eɪ]?
  (vi) And the RP diphthong [əʊ]?
  (vii) How is RP's word-final [ɪ] pronounced in EModE?
  (viii) The first element of some RP diphthongs is different in EModE. Take a look at RP [aɪ], [aʊ] and [ɔɪ].
(b) Although pronouncing EModE words is perhaps not a life-skill you consider of crucial importance, saying some words may help fix some pronunciation points in your mind. For your 'EModE pronunciation practice', try saying

the words below. They have been chosen to illustrate the points above; so in (i) the focus is on [r], in (ii) it is on [h], and so on:

(i)	conjecture	third	morning	danger	umbered
(ii)	hum	hammers	horrid	host	head
(iii)	when	where	which	when	what
(iv)	where	care	despair	chair	rare
(v)	lake	cage	pay	obey	age
(vi)	go	slow	odour	though	show
(vii)	army	paly	drowsy	tediously	patiently
(viii)	wide	fire	foul	hour	toy
	destroy	sounds	night	foils	time
	drowsy	royal			

14D Being rhotic

In British RP and Australian PDE, a written 'r' is sometimes pronounced, sometimes not. Here are some words containing the letter 'r':

(i) run	(ii) teacher	(iii) arm	(iv) recent	(v) enrol
(vi) cart	(vii) acronym	(viii) fair	(ix) arrive	(x) fewer

If you speak one of these versions of PDE, look at (a). If not, look at (b).

(a) Use the examples to try and work out the 'rule' which controls whether an 'r' is pronounced in RP/Australian (hint: the relevant factors are the position of the letter in the word, and the surrounding sounds).

(b) In example (i) above, a British RP or an Australian speaker would pronounce the 'r', but in example (ii) not. In the other examples: (iii) not pronounced (NP); (iv) pronounced (P); (v) P; (vi) NP; (vii) P; (viii) NP; (ix) P; (x) NP. Use this information to work out the 'rule' which controls when the 'r' is pronounced (hint: the relevant factors are the position of the letter in the word, and the surrounding sounds).

Answer section

14.4.2

EModE [eː] for RP [eɪ]

Apart from *fatal*, the other words are: *take* (line 6), *rage* (line 10), *stage* (line 12), *patient* (line 13), *lay* (line 1), *break* (line 3), *make* (line 4), *ancient* (line 3). The three words with EModE [eː], but RP pronunciation other than [eɪ] are *scene* (line 2), *unclean* (line 4) and *these* (line 5).

▨ EModE [oː] for RP [əʊ]

Apart from *foes*, the other examples are *both* (line 1), *Verona* (line 2), ***overthrows***, and *overthrows* (line 7).

Further reading

Wells and Taylor (1986) is an 'original-spelling' edition of Shakespeare's complete works.

The Wells and Taylor book contains an introductory section, Salmon (1986), on spelling and punctuation of Shakespeare's time.

For a fascinating general account of spelling take a look at Crystal (2013).

Two books mentioned in the text provide academic and very detailed accounts of Renaissance pronunciation: Kökeritz (1953) and Dobson (1957).

Crystal (2005) gives a more accessible and briefer coverage of Shakespearean pronunciation.

For an even shorter account, look at the *OED*'s website: http://public.oed.com/aspects-of-english/english-in-time/early-modern-english-pronunciation-and-spelling/.

Notes

1 In this and following chapters, parts of the coverage are based on Johnson (2013).
2 The information is taken from Lutzky (2012).
3 These attempts at standardization are described in Salmon (1986).
4 This quotation is cited in Salmon (1986), whose discussion is used as the basis for what is said about 'final *e*' in this section.
5 The example is from MacCarthy (1950).
6 There are a number of other examples and discussions of OP online, including: http://originalpronunciation.com/ and www.youtube.com/watch?v=dWe1b9mjjkM, a recording based on an OP performance of *A Midsummer Night's Dream*, also involving David Crystal, given at the University of Kansas in 2010. Kökeritz (1953) contains phonetic transcriptions of no fewer than twenty passages.
7 In these paragraphs, the examples and the quotations (plus the rendition of Hart into RP) are taken from Lass (1999a).

15

Turning water into wine

Renaissance words

This chapter focuses on lexis and looks at how EModE dramatically expanded its word stock, partly by borrowing and partly by using 'native resources', including affixation and compounding.

Some societies, and some people in them, have strong views about taking words from other languages. Think of what arguments might be put forward *for* and *against* the heavy borrowing of words from foreign languages. What effects will the introduction of many loanwords have on the borrowing language? EModE views on this will be discussed in 15.2.

Section 15.4.1 looks at how affixes can develop new words. Suffixes can be used to form words of various parts of speech. Think of a few PDE suffixes which are used to form: adjectives, nouns, verbs, adverbs. If possible (which it may not always be) consider the 'meanings' which your suffixes convey.

Among the authors mentioned in this chapter are Christopher Marlowe, Ben Jonson and Edmund Spenser. Find out something about them and their works. Another person mentioned is Richard Mulcaster (he also came up in 13.2 and 14.1). Find out something about him.

15.1 'Curvets' and 'two-like' triangles

The picture of English painted in Chapter 13 was of a language struggling for recognition. Latin, you will recall from 13.2, was described by Richard Taverner as a 'wine-like' language, while English was seen as barbarous and 'water-like'. The inadequacies of English, we saw, were twofold. One was the lack of standardization, and Chapter 14 showed how that was being addressed. The second was an impoverished vocabulary. This chapter is about what steps were taken to develop the lexis so that it was adequate for the new demands that were being made on it – steps to help change English from 'water-like' to 'wine-like'. In this section we will look at two types of solution. We have already come across both of them in relation to OE and ME lexical development. Now we see them put to work in the context of EModE.

Thomas Bedingfield was born in Norfolk, probably in the early 1540s. As a young man he went to London and became a translator of books from

Italian into English. His specialization was a genre popular at the time, called 'courtesy literature' – books which taught skills and good manners to courtiers: self-improvement books for Renaissance gentlemen. In 1584 he translated a book about horse riding, written by a famous Italian equestrian, Claudio Corte. Bedingfield's translation met with a problem. Many of the specialist horse-riding terms used in Italian did not have English equivalents. Bedingfield comes clean about this a number of times. For example, here is the heading for his Chapter 15: 'Of that motion which the Italians call Corvette or Pesate, whereof in our language there is not (for aught I know) any proper term yet devised'. And here is Chapter 3's heading: 'How to teach your horse in the figure like unto a snail, which Master Claudio calleth Caragolo or Lumaca'. What the Italian words *caragolo* and *lumaca* express is a half-turn to the left or right. But what to call these things in English?

The problem was a very common one at the time. It was also faced by the Welsh mathematician Robert Recorde. His claim to fame, incidentally, was that he introduced the mathematical symbols '=' and '+'. In 1551 he wrote *The Pathway of Knowledge*, a translation of part of Euclid's book on geometry called *Elements*. Recorde claimed that his was the first geometry book written in English. It was not surprising, then, that he had to decide how to refer to various concepts which had names in Greek and Latin but not necessarily in English. For example, he needed to talk about triangles where 'two sides be equal and the third unequal, which the Greekes call *Isosceles*'. How to say this in English? Similarly with 'rectangle', and 'tangent' (a straight line touching a curve). Of course, today we use the Greek- and Latin-based words, *isosceles*, *rectangle* and *tangent*. But these words were not in use before Recorde's time.

Bedingfield and Recorde explored different solutions to their lexical problems. Bedingfield's approach was to bring the Italian terms into English. Throughout his book, he speaks about *corvettes* (the leaping, frisking movements that a horse makes). He even makes an English verb out of the Italian word, talking on one occasion of *to corvette* and on another of *corvetting*. He also gives an explanation of the word, to help readers understand it – a very useful thing to do when introducing a foreign word: '*Corvetta* is that motion, which the crow maketh, when … she leapeth and jumpeth upon the ground: for *Corvo* in the *Italian* tongue signifieth a crow, and a leap in that sort is called *Corvetta*'. His solution works, and the word does in fact enter the English language, though the form changes to *curvet*. Shakespeare uses the word a few times, and it remained in use until the nineteenth century. Bedingfield's *caragollo* lasted even longer. By the mid seventeenth century it had become *caracol*, and it is still used today in dressage.

Bedingfield borrows, but Recorde has another solution. He mentions the Greek word *isosceles*. But then he goes on to say of the triangles that 'in English *tweyleke* may they be called'. *Twe* means 'two', and *leke* (*like*) signifies that the triangle has two equal sides. It is a 'two-like' triangle. For 'rectangle' he invents the term *long square*, and his word for 'tangent 'is *touch line*. So rather than borrowing Latin or Greek words, he creates new phrases or compounds. Though new, they are based on already-existing English words.

As we saw in 9.2, Bedingfield's type of solution was very common in ME, while using native resources (like Recorde) was favoured in OE times. EModE used both solutions in profusion, and, as we are about to see, there was much debate for and against both of these vocabulary enlargement strategies.

15.2   To borrow or not to borrow: the inkhorn controversy

Elizabethan England was an outward-looking society, very open to the innovation which exploration brought. There were linguistic consequences. Raleigh came back to Elizabeth's court laden with potatoes and tobacco, with new words for these, from the Spanish *patata* and *tabaco*. The English travelling in France returned with words like *bigot*, *bizarre* and *entrance*. When they came back from Italy, they imported *balcony* and *violin*. But by far the largest number of loanwords in the period came from Latin, a language with high status and authority. According to one estimate, as many as 13,000 Latin-based words entered English between 1575 and 1675.[1]

For many, the borrowing was out of control, and satirists of the age lost no time in making fun of the excesses. Ben Jonson does this in a particularly vivid way. His play *The Poetaster* (first performed in 1601) has a character named Crispinus. He is given an emetic by Horace which makes him vomit words – most of which have Latin roots. Here they are (in order of vomiting):

retrograde, reciprocall, incubus, glibbery, lubricall, defunct, magnificate, spurious, snotteries, chilblaind, clumsie, barmy, froth, puffy, inflate, turgidous, ventosity, oblatrant, obcaecate, furibund, fatuate, strenuous, conscious, prorumped, clutch, tropologicall, anagogical, loquacious, pinnosity, obstupefact.

Nearly all these words are in the *OED*, though a few of them have Jonson's play as their only citation. If you have access to the *OED*, you might like to look some of them up. What is particularly interesting is how many of these words are still in use today. To some extent, our language still 'vomits Latin', or, to put it in a more positive and genteel fashion, still benefits from a rich vein of Latin words.

Then there is the character of Don Adriano de Armado in Shakespeare's play *Love's Labour's Lost*. He is a boastful Spanish knight who wants to impress everyone by showing how well he knows the king, and what the king gets up to. Here is what he says:

Sir, it is the King's most sweet pleasure and affection to congratulate the Princess at her pavilion in the posteriors of this day, which the rude multitude call the afternoon.

Armado's *congratulate* is from the Latin *congratulari*, and is being used here to mean 'pay respects to'. But what particularly delights Armado's listeners is his bizarre way of describing the afternoon as the *posteriors of the day*, and it still seems bizarre to us today. *Posterior* came from Latin into English early in the sixteenth century. Armado is using it to mean 'later part', but then, as now, it could refer to the 'later part' of the body: the buttocks. Little wonder that Armado's pageboy should say about his master and friends: 'They have been at a great feast of languages and stolen the scraps.' 'Posteriors of this day' is one such scrap.

Excessive borrowings of this sort led to a debate that goes under the name of the 'Inkhorn Controversy'. An 'inkhorn' is an inkwell, and 'inkhorn terms' were strange and obscure words, often used by scholars (the 'inkhorn' connection), and generally borrowed into English from foreign tongues. On one side of the controversy were those who regarded foreign borrowings as useful additions to the language. Those against thought that imports made, as we saw in 13.3, what the clergyman Ralph Lever rather colourfully calls 'a mingle mangle' of English. For Lever and many others, the alternative to a mingle mangle was to 'devise understandable terms, compounded of true and ancient English words'.[2] Before reading the next paragraph, take a look at CW15.1 (*To borrow, or not to borrow*). It contains some quotations from writers on both sides of the Inkhorn Controversy, and allows you to see for yourself the kinds of arguments put forward. It also contains one voice from a later age – George Orwell, the twentieth-century novelist and essayist. He is there to show that the borrowing issue lived on. His point of view is that bad writers use foreign words in an effort to sound 'grand'. Even into recent times, there are some cultures with national organizations (like the French Academy in France, discussed in 19.2.1), which encourage the avoidance of loanwords from other languages. Many ages and many countries have their own version of the Inkhorn Controversy.

If you would like to see another example of 'inkhorn language', look at CW15.2 (*A sacerdotal dignitee*). It shows a letter so full of 'inkhorn' that it is extremely difficult to understand.

15.3 Borrowed words

It must have been extremely unsettling for the Elizabethans to find their language suddenly flooded with masses of new words. Perhaps it is something like – only on a much larger scale – the invasion of new words and expressions that technology, computers and the internet have brought into today's English: gigabytes and apps, lists that are 'populated', screens that are 'touch-enabled', https, ISPs, tweets and Twitter. Things could be made to feel a little less unsettling for the EModE public if the new words were 'anglicized' a little. Activity 15A (*Anglicizing Latin words*) explores ways in which this was done. Take a look before reading on.

There were, it is true, a few Latin words which stayed as they were when imported. Shakespeare, for example, uses the noun *augur* (from the Latin *augur*) in the sense of 'soothsayer', and Jonson uses it as a verb. The activity includes several other examples of words imported without change. But normally some modification was made. Often the original Latin ending would be dropped. The verb *expunge*, for example, is the Latin verb *expungere* without the Latin ending, and *imitate* is from Latin *imitatus*, meaning 'copied'. In the same way, the adjective *immature* is Latin *immaturus* without the adjective ending, and the noun *invitation* is from *invitationem*.

Instead of being dropped, some Latin suffixes developed English equivalents. So the *-ence* at the end of *transcendence* is the *-entia* of Latin *transcendentia*. Another example is the Latin ending *-abilis* which became *-able* in English. So Latin *inviolabilis* became English *inviolable*. And Latin *-ia* (from Greek) could become *-y*. *Parodia* and *anarchia* are examples in the activity. *Commentary* comes from Latin *commentarius*, with *-ius* changed to *-y*. To digress for a moment: a few minutes exploration in the *OED*, or some other dictionary giving etymologies, will reveal what interesting histories many words have. Elyot (one of the 'pro-borrowing' supporters mentioned in CW15.1) uses *commentary* to mean 'notebook' or 'collection of notes'. It is originally associated with the Latin word *commentum* which meant 'invention' or 'interpretation', and gives us our word *comment*.

An odd occurrence that sometimes happens is that you find two different versions of the same word, both coming from the same Latin source. For example, in Shakespeare's *Troilus and Cressida*, a character talks about actions which *conduce* ('lead to') hot passions. But in another Shakespeare play, *All's Well That Ends Well*, someone is *conducted* to a lodging. Both verbs come from the Latin *conducere*, which means 'to lead'. *Conduce* is *conducere* without the *-re*, and *conduct* is *conductus* ('led') without the *-us*. Both *conduct* and *conduce* remain in PDE.

It is common for Latin loanwords to change not just their form but also their grammar or their meaning. For example, the noun *dislocation* (when a bone is displaced, possibly from Latin *dislocationem*) had been in use since 1400, but the verb *dislocate* is used perhaps for the first time in Shakespeare's *King Lear*. In a violent argument with his wife, one character in the play talks about his hands being able to 'dislocate and tear [her] flesh and bones'. We will talk much more, in 15.4.2, about another change, whereby verbs become nouns. As for changing meaning, here is another Shakespearean example. When Othello asks that his wife Desdemona should be allowed to come with him on a military expedition to Cyprus, he insists that she should have 'such accommodation ... as levels with her breeding'. She must, in other words, be given somewhere suitable to lodge. We use the word *accommodation* in the same sense today. The word had come into the language earlier in the sixteenth century, but it meant 'the process of adaptation'.

Attempts to 'anglicize' foreign loans will have helped the population to come to terms with the greatly expanding vocabulary. Another source of help were the 'dictionaries of hard words' that came into existence. One example was Robert Cawdrey's 1604 *Table Alphabeticall of Hard Usual English Words*. You can find this online at www.library.utoronto.ca/utel/ret/cawdrey/cawdrey0.html. You may like to amuse yourself by looking up these words on Cawdrey's list and finding out what they meant: *adustion, cibaries, domicelles, to pese, thwite*. It is informative to look through Cawdrey and see the large number of words that are in normal use today but which clearly caused Renaissance readers problems. Cawdrey's dictionary, and others like it, are discussed later in 19.2.2.

But in spite of efforts to help, many people were left struggling with the influx of strange words. 'Strange' is what they truly were. As we will see in the next section, EModE had many new coinages based on already-existing words. Although such words were new, people had some chance of understanding them, because they contained familiar elements. But foreign words could be totally strange, unlike any other words people had ever seen before. A person who only knew English would have nothing to 'latch onto' when coming across these words. Take a look at CW15.3 (*Speaking 'eloquente englysshe'*). It contains a story that shows just this, about a student who wanted his shoes mended.

No wonder people made mistakes. John Hart, a spelling reformer who died in 1574, puts it like this: borrowing, he says, 'causeth many of the countrymen to speak chalk for cheese, and so nickname [misname] such strange terms as it pleaseth many well to hear them'. The examples he gives of the kinds of mistakes people make with words of Romance origin include *dispense* for *suspense*, *defend* for *offend*, or *stature* for *statute*.

Dramatists were quick to pick up on the comic potentiality of characters who 'speak chalk for cheese'. What we now call malapropisms ('the mistaken use of a word in place of a similar-sounding one' is part of the *Shorter Oxford English Dictionary*'s definition) are a common form of wit, especially in Shakespeare. The word comes from the character of Mrs Malaprop in Richard Sheridan's play *The Rivals*, first performed in 1775. So when she says a character is 'as headstrong as an allegory on the banks of the Nile', she means *alligator*, not *allegory*. Another term for malapropisms is 'dogberryisms' after the name of Constable Dogberry, in Shakespeare's *Much Ado about Nothing*. Here is how Dogberry tells the Governor about the capture of two shady individuals by his night watch patrol:

> our watch, sir, have indeed comprehended two aspicious persons, and we would have them this morning examined before your worship.

He means *apprehended*, not *comprehended*, and *suspicious*, not *auspicious* (or *aspicious* as he says it). Schlauch (1965) classified malapropisms according to which part of the word has been 'misplaced'. Activity 15B (*Indited to dinner*) asks you to think about her classification, and also gives you the chance to explore some more malapropisms. If you are going to look at this, now is the time to do so, since the following paragraph includes the 'answers'.

Schlauch identifies three main types of malapropism. Sometimes a mistake is made with the prefix, as when (in ii) Slender says *decrease* instead of *increase*.

The second type is when a suffix is mistaken, as when Mistress Quickly says *infinitive* for *infinite* (example iii). In the third type, the roots of words are confused. Elbow's use of *cardinally* for *carnally* is like this (in iv), and so is Mistress Quickly's *indite* for *invite* (in i). The use of *deflowered* for *devoured* (in v) is the same. If you find working out malapropisms fun, there are five more in CW15.4 (A *honeysuckle villain*).

Malapropisms are alive and kicking today. Here are two from George Bush, US president from 2001 to 2009. On one occasion he said: 'I am mindful not only of preserving executive powers for myself, but for predecessors as well'. And on another: 'We cannot let terrorists and rogue nations hold this nation hostile or hold our allies hostile'. Perhaps he meant *reserving* instead of *preserving*. Certainly, for *predecessors* read 'successors', and for *hostile*, 'hostage'.

15.4 Native resources

A way to increase the vocabulary without creating a 'mingle mangle', and avoiding the risk of 'speaking chalk for cheese', was to follow the OE procedure of using 'native resources' to develop new words. The resources we looked at in 5.2 were affixation and compounding. We will look at these two processes again here, and will add a third.

15.4.1 Affixes

Affixation, a common means of word formation in both OE and EModE, remains popular today. Take the prefix *un-* as an example. If you approve of something you see on the popular social medium, Facebook, there is a 'like' button to press. Then, if you change your mind, you can press the 'unlike' button – to *unlike* it. The social networking sites have created other *un-* verbs. As we saw in 5.1, if you go off a Facebook friend, you *unfriend* them, and there is even a new noun to go with the new verb: you can describe someone as *an unfriend*. Then there is *unfollow*, and even *unfan*.

The *un-* prefix was also popular in EModE. One of Shakespeare's examples comes when Lady Macbeth is steeling herself for the murder of King Duncan. She asks the spirits to fill her with cruelty:

> Come, you spirits
> That tend on mortal thoughts, unsex me here
> And fill me from the crown to the toe top-full
> Of direst cruelty.
>
> (1.5.38)

'Take away my female qualities' is what she means. There are several other striking new *un-* words in Shakespeare. In *Richard II*, Gaunt hopes that his 'death's sad tale may yet undeaf the king's ear'. Then there is the character in *The Merry Wives of Windsor* who has made a fool of himself, and asks whether there is any way to *unfool* himself, while in *Macbeth*, the Porter's piece of wisdom is that, when it comes to lechery, alcohol both *provokes and unprovokes* – it 'provokes / the desire but it takes away the performance'. According to one estimate, Shakespeare uses 314 new *un-* words, and that is just one affix in just one writer's work. Activity 15C (*Un-*) looks at some more EModE words, this time from sources other than Shakespeare. Take a look also at CW15.5 (*Out-Heroding Herod*), which is about another of Shakespeare's favourite prefixes: *out-*.

You may remember from 5.2.2 that while prefixes change meaning, they do not change a word's part of speech. It is true that suffixes do not always change the part of speech: they can be used, for example, to make a new noun out of an already-existing one. But they can also change the part of speech. Before reading on, do Activity 15D (*Some popular suffixes*), which looks at a few of the suffixes common in EModE.

Two of the suffixes in the activity – -*ness* and -*itude* – are used to form nouns. The -*ness* in *filthyness* changes the adjective *filthy* into an abstract noun. The suffix -*itude* is also used to form abstract nouns, often expressing a state or quality. The activity's example is *servitude*: a word which may have been first used by Caxton in the fifteenth century, with the suffix coming ultimately from the Latin -*itudo*.

The activity also has two examples of suffixes used to form adjectives. Shakespeare's *vasty* means the same as 'vast', and the -*y* may have been added to give the word an extra syllable to help the rhythm of the poetry. We do of course use the suffix today, often changing a noun into an adjective and often meaning 'having the quality of' or 'full of' – as in *snowy*. A suffix we came across in CW5.2 is -*ly*, which was described as a 'prolific formative'. It is the only suffix in Activity 15D used to form an adverb (*palely*). This is an 'adverb of manner'; CW5.2 is again the place to look to be reminded what that is.

Sentence (iv) in the activity has two examples of the suffix -*ize* (*ciuillize* and *aguize*, meaning 'adorn'), also very common in PDE. It can mean to 'make' or 'turn into' – so a rough paraphrase of *civilize* might be 'to make civil'. Here, -*ize* is added to an adjective. If you would like to see more EModE suffixes at work, CW15.6 (*More EModE suffixes*) is the place to go.

In 5.2.2 our example of how useful affixes can be in extending the language showed the OE verb *habban* and the various OE words created from it by affixation. Affixes proved similarly useful in EModE, and many examples could be given showing large numbers of new words developing out of some noun or verb. As a modest example, take the word *direful*, mentioned in CW15.6. It comes from the adjective *dire*, which has an *OED* first citation in 1567. If you have access to the *OED* online, look up *dire*, and use the box on the right-hand side of the screen to find other words with this root. There are at least four appearing within fifty years of *dire*, and the number increases if you look up these four words and find some of their own derivatives. All these words have disappeared from the language, except as archaisms. If you do not have access to the *OED* online, you can find these words in the *Answer section* (AS).

15.4.2   Another use of native resources

This section starts with an activity. Before reading, look at Activity 15E (*Weirding language*).

In the 1980s and 90s, the American cartoonist Bill Watterson produced a cartoon strip about the adventures of Calvin, a six-year-old boy, and his stuffed tiger toy, Hobbes. In one cartoon, Calvin announces that he likes to 'verb words. I take nouns and adjectives and use them as verbs. Remember when "access" was a thing? Now it's something you do. It got verbed'. He concludes by introducing his own new verb: 'verbing weirds language', he says. But Tiger Hobbes gets quite irritated at Calvin's 'verbing'. In fact, irritation is a common reaction to this linguistic process. Quite recently some sports writers started using the noun *podium* as a verb. *To podium* means to win a medal at a games meeting. Here's the reaction of one blogger: 'these linguistic absurdities continue, aided and abetted by the network people. The latest is truly bizarre, from the Olympic coverage: "She was unable to podium." Arrrrgh. Grrrrr. Comment unnecessary'. Like many procedures that enrich the language, 'verbing' can cause many such reactions from those who feel that the result is a 'mingle mangle'.

EModE writers often take 'a thing' and 'verb it'. Example (i) in Activity15E shows this. *Lip* started life as a noun in OE, but Chapman – writing in 1605 – is using it as a verb. In fact, along with Shakespeare, he was possibly one of the first to do so. This process of changing one part of speech into another without adding a prefix or suffix (a noun to a verb in this case) is called **functional shift**, or **conversion**. It was a popular lexical development strategy in the sixteenth century, and there was a linguistic reason which partly explains this. As we saw at various points in Chapter 6, OE used suffixes to show what part of speech a word was. Thus the OE for 'lip' was *lippa*, with the *-a* suffix indicating that the word was a noun. If a verb 'to lip' had existed in Anglo-Saxon times, it might have been *lippan*, with a different suffix – the verbal *-an*. Different endings for different parts of speech tended to make functional shift difficult. But as grammatical suffixes began to disappear from the language, it became a little easier to 'convert' words from one part of speech to another.[3] The EModE *lip* carries no suffix to mark it as a noun or verb, so it could be used as both. In this case, the conversion was 'noun → verb'. Before reading on, go through all the examples in Activity 15E indicating the part of speech changes that are involved.

Example (i) in the activity (*lip*) involves one of the most common shifts, 'noun → verb'. (ii) (*whisper*) has the conversion working the other way round, with the verb *whisper* becoming a noun. In example (iii), the adjective *mellow* changes into a verb. An adjective – *grievous* – is also the starting-point in (iv), but here it changes into what is called an **intensifier** – a class of words like *very* and *really* which give additional force – to the adjective *sick* in the case of (iv). Example

(v) is particularly interesting. Here, the words *grace* and *uncle* are turned into verbs – very curious conversions indeed. We sometimes use similarly curious conversions in PDE, especially to indicate anger (which is what York is indicating in the Shakespeare sentence). Here is a recent example taken from an internet blog:

Child: Mum, PLEASE let me go to the cinema
Mum: Oooh! I'll cinema you in a minute

You may be able to think of some more PDE examples using this 'I'll X him (her, you)' formula. It is one found in EModE. In Shakespeare's play *The Merry Wives of Windsor*, a character named Ford comes face to face with an old woman, Mother Prat, whom he hates. 'I'll prat her', he says, and proceeds to beat her with a stick.

If you want more examples of EModE conversions, take a look at CW15.7 (*Coffining the corpse*), which gives five more. These shifts can have a startling effect. CW15.8 (*Shakespeare and electroencephalograms*) describes a fascinating neurological experiment which measured the effect of functional shifts on brain activity.

15.4.3 Compounds

By the time he reaches Act 5, Shakespeare's hero, Macbeth, is really sick at heart. 'I have lived long enough', he gloomily says. He has nothing to look forward to in his old age. People will hate him, and be superficially polite to him out of fear:

> that which should accompany old age,
> As honour, love, obedience, troops of friends,
> I must not look to have, but in their stead
> Curses, not loud but deep, mouth-honour, breath
> Which the poor heart would fain deny and dare not

Mouth-honour well captures the idea of people showing respect in words but not actions. The word is probably a Shakespearean creation. It is a compound noun, and compounds were as popular in EModE as they had been in OE (5.2.1 is where the OE ones were discussed). To give you some idea of how many compounds there are in Shakespeare: *mouth-honour* is in the 24th line of *Macbeth*, Act 5, Scene 3, and it is already the scene's fifth compound. You can use the internet to provide further evidence of their popularity. Find the text of a play or poem written in the period – it could be Shakespeare, Marlowe, Spenser, Jonson (if you want the titles of their works, look these authors up on the internet). Once you have found the online version of a work, use your computer's 'Find' facility to search for hyphens ('-'). Of course, not all the hits you get will be compounds, but many will be. If the work is lengthy, you will find dozens, even hundreds, of them. Incidentally, not all writers use a hyphen to mark a compound. It happens to be *mouth-honour*, but it might just as well have been *mouth honour*. You also find compounds made up of two words joined into one word without a hyphen. Marlowe has *fire-works*, but today we write *fireworks*.

Sometimes it is fairly obvious what a new compound means. Here are some 'heart-based' compounds, all with first OED citations in the sixteenth century: kind-hearted (1535), gentle-hearted (1595), heart-breaking (1591), heart-wounding (1599). Shakespeare has a little rash of -hearted compounds in his play Henry VI, Part 3: hard-hearted, gentle-hearted, soft-, sad- and proud-hearted. All easy to understand even if you have not come across them before. But in the hands of the right author, the compounds can be very imaginative and thought-provoking – comparable indeed to the OE kennings we discussed in 7.3. So in Shakespeare's Henry VI, Part 3, old age is described as chair-days (days spent largely sitting in a chair), and in his Measure for Measure, the blood of the cruel ruler is called snow-broth (a soup made of snow). Activity 15F (Belly-cheers and scrape-pennies) contains some compounds used by EModE writers, and invites you to think about how they might be categorized, the topic of the next few paragraphs. Look now at all parts of the activity.

In EModE, the most common new compounds were nouns or adjectives. One way of classifying these is in terms of the combination of the parts of speech involved. Many nouns were nouns joined to other nouns (N+N). Alongside Shakespeare's mouth-honour and snow-broth we have fire-works, companion-prince, and the activity's belly-cheer ('gratification of the stomach'), all used by Shakespeare's contemporary, Marlowe. Noun compounds can also have a verbal element ('V+N' or 'N+V'). Lack-love and scrape-penny ('miser') are examples from the activity. As for adjectives, the verb forms ending in -ing (the present participle suffix) and -ed (the past participle suffix) were particularly popular. A widow in Shakespeare's Richard III is described as a care-crazed mother in one line, and as beauty-waning in the next – she was losing her looks. Jonson used wool-gathering and double-tongued. Another popular combination (not shown in the activity) was 'N+Adj'. You find blood-raw in Marlowe and thread-bare in Spenser. In fact, compounds can involve almost any part of speech, and some EModE ones sound very odd today. In Shakespeare there is hence-departure, here-remain, back-return, and some longer ones like to-and-fro-conflicting and always-wind-changing. In Love's Labour's Lost, one character talks about making a world-without-end bargain.

There are many ways in which the two parts of a compound can relate to each other in terms of meaning. In Romeo and Juliet, the heroine's body is described as tempest-tossed – meaning a body tossed 'by a tempest'. But when someone in Macbeth is called trumpet-tongued, it is because his tongue 'is like (as loud as) a trumpet'. The 'milk-compounds' you saw in part (b) of Activity 15F show the variety of meaning relationships that can be involved. A milkmaid is 'a maid who milks cows'; the milksops are sops 'comprised of milk'; the milkpaps are breasts 'containing milk'. As for adjectives, milk-white refers to the colour of milk, but when a character in King Lear is described as milk-livered, it refers to the weak, benign quality of the liquid, not its colour. Incidentally, and just to suggest how common vivid compounds are throughout Shakespeare, nine lines before *milk-livered* in *King Lear*, a *head-lugged bear* has been mentioned. This is a bear that has been baited by being dragged by the head.

Activity 15F, part (c) gives some examples of how compounds were used. Description of nature is one such use. As well as *lazy-puffing* clouds, Shakespeare has *heaven-kissing* hills, *fearful-hanging* rocks, *fen-sucked* fogs. Spenser describes elms as *vine-prop* (an adjective meaning 'supporting vines'), and has his own version of Homer's 'rosy-fingered dawn' (it is *rosy-fingred Morning*). Sometimes word combinations are semantically unusual. Shakespeare describes one character as *dumb-discoursive*. *Discoursive* means 'communicative' – almost the opposite of *dumb*; what he means is 'silent and yet communicative'. Similarly, Spenser has *foole-happie*.

As we have seen with Shakespeare's *lack-love* and Lodge's *scrape-penny*, compounds are particularly useful as insults. Look back to the last lines of the 'buck-rom story' in 13.4 and you will find a string of abusive terms, many of which involve compounds. Then there is Falstaff's riposte – also given in 13.4. Abusive compounds galore.

Something which suggests the readiness of EModE writers to use compounds is their **nonce** use. A **nonce word** is one specially created for a particular occasion – 'nonce' means 'for then once'. Here is an example from Marlowe's play *Dr Faustus*, where a character says: 'Do ye see yonder tall fellow … he has killed the devil, so … should be called kill-devil all the parish over'. The compound *kill-devil* is invented to fit this one particular situation. And in Shakespeare's *Love's Labour's Lost*, a character tries to catch the attention of the ladies by talking about their *sun-beamed eyes*. There is no response, so someone suggests another compound, involving a *sun/son* pun. It would be better, they say, to call the ladies' eyes *daughter-beamed*. Very nonce.

Many of the compounds that came into use during the EModE period are still with us today. Shakespeare's plays contain many. There is *salad-days* (from *Antony and Cleopatra*), *star-crossed* (*Romeo and Juliet*), *sea-change* (*The Tempest*), *barefaced* (*A Midsummer Night's Dream*), and *bloodstained* (*Titus Andronicus*). But there are many that did not make it. To explore some of these, look at CW15.9 (*Some gone-away compounds*). If you have access to the *OED* online, take a look also at CW15.10 (*Looking for EModE compounds*), which suggests how to look for EModE compounds in the dictionary.

15.5 EModE vocabulary today

On more than one occasion in this chapter, we have come across EModE words that are still in use today. This is one reason why modern audiences can watch plays by Shakespeare or his contemporaries and understand a great deal. Although EModE is 'Early', it is clearly 'Modern English'.

But when thinking of vocabulary, we must not forget 'false friends'. These were described in 9.2.1 as words which 'may look familiar – just like PDE words – but may in fact have changed meaning over the centuries'. You need to beware of these in EModE literature. Go back one last time to 13.4's 'buckrom story' passage. Find some words which still exist today, but with changed meanings. You will find some listed in the *Answer section* (AS). If you want further proof of how common false friends are, open a copy of Shakespeare's (or some other Renaissance writer's) works at random and start reading. How long is it before you find a false friend?

Activity section

15A Anglicizing Latin words

Here are twenty Latin words (some of them previously Greek too) which gave rise to English words, mostly in the sixteenth century. Identify the English words and say what changes (if any) have been made to the Latin words to 'anglicize' them.

augur	colon	immaturus	confluentia
commentarius	anarchia	interim	vernacularus
consul	centenarius	transcententia	turgidus
invitationem	circus	impeccabilis	parodia
transmittere	imitatus	expungere	inviolabilis

15B Indited to dinner

Here are five examples of malapropisms, all taken from Shakespeare plays. The relevant words are in boldface.

(a) What word was intended for each?
   (i) Mistress Quickly, a character in several Shakespeare plays, often 'speaks chalk for cheese'. Here, she is trying to have Falstaff arrested because he owes her money. She knows where the officers can find him (*Henry IV, Part 2*):

   *he is **indited** to dinner to the Lubber's Head in Lumbert Street to Master Smooth's the silkman.*

   (ii) In *The Merry Wives of Windsor*, Slender talks about a possible marriage between himself and Mistress Anne Page:

   *I will marry her, sir, at your request. But if there be no great love in the beginning, yet heaven may **decrease** it upon better acquaintance when we are married.*

   (iii) Mistress Quickly is still trying to get Falstaff arrested. He never pays his bar bill (*score*) (*Henry IV, Part 2*):

   *I am undone by his going, I warrant you, he's an **infinitive** thing upon my score.*

(iv) In *Measure for Measure*, the Viennese authorities are on the lookout for brothels to close down. Constable Elbow knows of one:

Escalus: *How dost thou know that, constable?*

Elbow: *Marry, sir, by my wife, who, if she had been a woman **cardinally** given, might have been accused in fornication, adultery, and all uncleanliness there.*

(v) In *A Midsummer Night's Dream*, Bottom is playing the part of Pyramus in a drama. His love, Thisby, has been eaten by a lion. He laments:

O wherefore, nature, didst thou lions frame,
*Since lion vile hath here **deflowered** my dear?*

(b) The five passages contain examples of each of Schlauch's categories. For each passage, write the malapropism and the intended word down side by side. This will enable you to identify which part of the word has been mistaken. Then look for common elements in the parts of the words which are mistaken, in order to work out what Schlauch's three categories are.

15C *Un-* AS

These examples of '*un*-words' probably came into English during the sixteenth century. The examples are all taken from the *OED*. Work out what you think they all mean; most are quite easy, though you may need to use the *Answer section* for one or two of them.

(i) *The number of needlesse lawes **vnabolisht** doth weaken the force of them that are necessarie.* (Hooker, 1593)

(ii) *To bee **uncoated** out of that their masking garment of holynesse, whereof they vaunted themselves.* (Golding, 1571)

(iii) *Mr. Lock, whom these two days he hath looked for, and mervaileth not a little at his **uncoming**.* (Mathews, 1593)

(iv) *But now though many faultes perchaunce be yet left behind **vncastigat**, ... I trust your maiestie ... wyll pardon me.* (Bible, 1539)

(v) *Yet stands he stiffe **vndasht**, **vnterrified**.* (Daniel, 1595)

You might also like to try inventing a few of your own words using the prefix *un-*.

15D Some popular suffixes

(a) Here are five sentences with the boldface words showing examples of suffixes used in EModE. Write down the suffixes, the parts of speech of the root words, and of the ones they form. In some cases, but perhaps not all, you may be able to give some indication of how the suffixes 'function'. As an example: in the case of (i), *filthynes*, the suffix is *-nes* (PDE *-ness*). The root word (*filthy*) is an adjective, and the suffix forms a noun. The general function of the suffix is to form abstract nouns.

(i) The prieste washeth his handes, that no outward **filthynes** should seclude hym from the communion. (Watson, 1558)

(ii) I can cal spirits from the **vasty** deepe. (Shakespeare, 1598)

(iii) He hath constrayned such to yeelde to inforced obedience and **servitude**. (Fleming, 1576)

(iv) The plough-lob (irregular ploughing) I can **ciuillize**, The franticke man with grace **aguize**. (adorn) (Copley, 1595)

(v) Who **palely** shining gaue no perfect light, But each thing was obscurde by obscure night. (Trussel, 1595)

(b) All the suffixes shown above are used today. Think of a few PDE examples for each one.

15E   Weirding language

Here is some information about word usage. The second line in each case gives an example of an EModE usage (most of the dates given are *OED* first citations). What is going on here? Pay particular attention to the parts of speech involved.

(i) *Lip*: used as a noun in OE.
   1605: *Lip her, knave, lip her.* (Chapman)

(ii) *Whisper*: used as a verb in OE.
   1609: *The sea-mans whistle / Is as a whisper in the eares of death.* (Shakespeare)

(iii) *Mellow*: an adjective in ME.
   1575: *Those sunnes do mellowe men so fast As most that trauayle come home very ripe.* (Gascoigne)

(iv) *Grievous*: an adjective in the 1300s.
   1598: *He cannot come my lord, he is grieuous sicke.* (Shakespeare)

(v) *grace*: a noun in ME (as a title); *gracious*: an adjective in ME.

   1597: Bolingbroke: *My gracious uncle –*
   York: *Tut, tut, grace me no grace, nor uncle me no uncle!* (Shakespeare)

15F   Belly-cheers and scrape-pennies   AS

(a) Here are some compounds used by EModE writers. What might the boldface words mean? Try to paraphrase them: some are easy, but for some you may need the *Answer section*.

   (i) Marlowe is describing students enjoying themselves:
   ... the students...
   *Who are at supper with such **belly-cheer***

   (ii) Lodge is describing a *usuer* ('usurer'):
   *he is to think wel of his master **Scrape-peinie**, the usuer, who is willing ... to [lend him money]*

(iii) The lady Shakespeare is describing is an unhappy and ageing widow:

> A **care-crazed** mother to a many sons
> A **beauty-waning** and distressed widow

(iv) Shakespeare's King Lear is also not happy. He:

> Strives in his little world of man to out-storm
> The **to-and-fro conflicting** wind and rain.
> This night, wherein the **cub-drawn** bear would couch ('shelter'),
> The lion and the **belly-pinched** wolf
> Keep their fur dry

(v) Spenser is describing trees:

> The **vine-prop** Elme, the Poplar neuer dry,
> The builder Oake, sole king of forrests all

(vi) Shakespeare's Romeo describes the clouds:

> Of mortals that fall back to gaze on him
> When he bestrides the **lazy-puffing** clouds

(vii) Shakespeare's Troilus does not trust the Greeks:

> But I can tell that in each grace of these
> There lurks a still and **dumb-discoursive** devil
> That tempts most cunningly

(viii) In Shakespeare's *A Midsummer Night's Dream*, Puck is describing a man who is being discourteous to a woman who loves him:

> Pretty soul, she durst not lie
> Near this **lack-love**, this **kill-courtesy**

(b) Here are some compounds involving the word *milk*, all used by Shakespeare. Paraphrase them so that the 'meaning relation' between the parts is clear. For example, in the case of *milkmaid*, it refers to a 'maid who milks cows'.

milkmaid	*milksop*	*milkpaps*
milk-white	*milk-livered*	

(c) Find examples in the passages under (a) of:

- a description of nature
- an insult
- two adjectives with seemingly opposite meanings juxtaposed together.

Answer section

Dire-related words (section 15.4.1)

As well as *dire*, the *OED* has: *direful* (1583), *direly* (1583), *dirity* (1600), *diral* (1606).

■ False friends in the 'rogues in buckrom' passage (section 15.5)

Here are the EModE meanings: *targuet* (target): 'shield'; *word* or *ward*: 'guard', 'defensive stance'; *points*: 'laces to attach clothing'. The word *hose* meant a 'stocking-like clothing for the leg', a meaning that it can still carry today. The verb *mark* used in the sense of 'take note of' is rare today, though it is still found in phrases like 'mark my words'.

■ Activity 15C

unabolished ('not abolished'); *uncoated* ('with coat taken off'); *uncoming* ('failure to arrive'); *uncastigate* ('not castigated'); *undashed* ('not discouraged'); *unterrified* ('not terrified').

■ Activity 15F

belly-cheer: gratification of the stomach; *scrape-peinie*: miser; *care-crazed*: made frail by cares (the word *crazy* is discussed in 1.2); *beauty-waning*: becoming less beautiful; *to-and-fro conflicting*: battling backwards and forwards; *cub-drawn*: drained of milk by cubs; *belly-pinched*: with empty stomach; *vine-prop*: supporting vines; *lazy-puffing*: gently blowing; *dumb-discoursive*: dumb and yet communicative; *lack-love*: empty of love; *kill-courtesy*: destroyer of courtesy.

■ Further reading

Nevalainen (2006) has two chapters (4 and 5) dealing with vocabulary.

Nevalainen (1999) provides detailed and scholarly coverage of the area.

Durkin (2014) is another scholarly account. Part VI deals with the period covered in this chapter.

Kastovsky (2006) is a general consideration of the area, not related to just EModE, but providing lots of information about (among other things) word-formation processes.

■ Notes

1 The estimate is from Nevalainen (2006: 53).
2 As we shall see in 19.2.2, this is the strategy used by the French Academy to keep foreign words from coming into French.
3 A similar argument is made in 9.1 partly to explain the influx of borrowing in ME (as the grammatical suffixes of OE disappeared).

<table>
<tr><td>16</td><td>## 'True and well-speaking a language'
Renaissance grammar</td></tr>
</table>

The grammar of EModE does not pose many comprehension problems for us today. The differences between then and now are relatively subtle, as the language settled down into its PDE form. Some things to consider before you read this chapter:

- 16.3 is about 'do-support' – using the verb *do* to form questions and negatives in English. Find out about this grammatical feature in advance. Identify what kind of questions and negatives need and do not need do-support in PDE.
- 16.4 is about modal auxiliary verbs. Find out about these in advance too.
- CW16.2 (*An EModE corpus*) talks about the use of corpora in language research. It mentions the British National Corpus. If you have internet access, got to www.natcorp.ox.ac.uk/ and find out what this is. The page offers you the chance to look up a word and find fifty hits. Try doing this with a few words of your choice.
- There are some PDE grammatical uses that are frowned upon socially. One of the examples given in this chapter is the use of 'double negatives' – saying *I haven't got no money*'. Think of some other grammatical uses frowned upon in the version of English that you are familiar with, or in some other language.

16.1 'Grammatical oddities'

Ben Jonson, best known as a playwright, also wrote a book called *The English Grammar*. Here is its first sentence: 'Grammar is the art of true and well-speaking a language'. How much of the EModE art of 'true and well-speaking' is different from today's? Well, the English of the Early Modern English period really was modern English. When we read or hear the language (in the plays of Shakespeare, for example), we do not have major problems of comprehension at the level of grammar. There will of course be points at which we are aware of 'oddities' in the language, and we will sometimes have to think twice to understand what is being said. But the language is no longer quite so foreign for us, and we can usually cope quite well with it. The big changes of the ME period – the simplification of suffixes and the loss of inflections – are all now behind us. One of the key phrases for the period was mentioned at the end of Chapter 14 and can stand for grammar as well as other areas of the language. It is 'settling down'. Other key phrases might be 'half-way house' (between OE/ME and PDE), and 'gradual movement towards the forms of PDE'. And many of the oddities you may notice are 'on the way out' – yet another possible key phrase. To illustrate the point, take a look at Activity 16A (*Some oddities that writers uses*). It contains seven pieces of grammatical usage that you will find strange but will probably not have much trouble understanding. They are discussed briefly in the next few paragraphs.

Point (i) in Activity 16A is to do with the genitive. In EModE, as today, there were two main ways of expressing the genitive: a 'synthetic' way using the -'s inflection, and an 'analytic' way using the preposition *of* (the synthetic/analytic distinction is discussed in 10.2.5). The activity shows another two methods, though they were not commonly used, and were indeed 'on the way out'. One uses the word *his*. The activity's examples are *Sejanus his fall*, and *the count his galleys*. It is tempting to think that this *his* is associated with gender, since Sejanus and the Count are both masculine. But a non-Shakespeare example from 1607 suggests otherwise. The example is *Mrs Sands his maid* (meaning 'Mrs Sands's maid'), and here the **referent** – the person being referred to – is clearly feminine. The form is probably something to do with pronunciation. In some circumstances, the ME -'s genitive was pronounced /ɪz/, and written *is* or *ys*. *Count's* for example could be written *Countys*. So *Countys galleys* would look and sound rather like *Count his galleys*. People may have assumed that the two forms were the same and used one for the other.[1] The other form is sometimes called the 'split genitive'. *The king's daughter of England* is the activity's example. In fact, it contains two genitives – 'the king of England' and 'the king's daughter'. In PDE we would keep the phrase 'the king of England' together, and put the -'s genitive on the phrase's last word: *the king of England's daughter*. Once again, our key phrase 'on the way out' holds here. There are a few examples of split genitives in Shakespeare, but in general he follows what has come to be PDE practice. So you find *The Duke of Norfolk's signories*, and *My Lord of York's armour*. Think how these last two examples would be written using split genitives.

The activity's point (ii) is to do with the comparative and superlative forms of the adjective (mentioned in 6.1.1). As with the PDE genitive, we have both synthetic and analytic ways of expressing this. Sometimes we use the suffix -*er* (usually with shorter words: *warmer, colder*), and sometimes the word *more* (for longer adjectives: *more accurate, more understandable*). In PDE, using the two forms together – saying *more bigger*, for example – is often regarded as a sign of a lack of education. But in EModE, **double comparatives** like *more weaker* were acceptable. So too were **double superlatives**, where both the suffix -*est* and the word *most* were both used. When Brutus stabs Julius Caesar in Shakespeare's play, it is described as the *most unkindest cut of all*, a phrase which the eighteenth-century poet and Shakespeare editor Alexander Pope found vulgar. He changed it to *the unkindest cut of all*. But even then, these constructions were comparatively rare, and there are plenty of examples in the period of writers following our PDE rules.

Like double comparatives and superlatives, **double negatives** – as in *I haven't got no money*, for example – can also today be socially stigmatized. Example (iii) shows two examples of EModE sentences containing more than one negative. There are two in the first – *I cannot go no further* – while the second example has four (*no, nor, never* and *none*). There is no sense of grammatical bad practice here, and in fact the double negative was often used to give additional emphasis, as it is in many other languages.

In 10.2.1 we saw that, in ME, the *-en* noun plural suffix was in competition with the *-s* suffix which we use today. Point (iv) shows that *-en* lasted into EModE, though probably the activity's *shoon* and *skyen* had a dated feel about them even then; again, the label 'on the way out' is appropriate. 'Impersonal verbs' are shown in (v). In these, the subject is an 'impersonal' *it* (*it would like you*, and *it yearns me not*). You may have come across them in languages like Italian, where the way of saying 'I like' is (translated literally) 'to me it pleases' – *mi piace*. They were found in OE and ME and, in remnant form, in EModE. Today they are rarities, though you do find them in phrases like *it seems to me*, for example.

When you come across examples like those in (vi), you may think that they are Renaissance 'typos'. 'It should be *wake*, and *ache*', you might feel. In fact the *-s* was sometimes regarded as a plural verb ending. The force of analogy is a powerful one in language use (we saw the example in 10.2.3 of strong verbs becoming weak), and is arguably at work here. The *-s* is of course a third person singular verb ending (as in *he likes*). Perhaps people were just 'generalizing' this to other verb forms. Some PDE dialect speakers say *they likes* or even *I likes*.

The examples in (vii) contain relative clauses (they were mentioned in 10.2.4). In PDE, we use *who* (and *whom*) when a person is being referred to – in linguistic terminology, when the **antecedent** is animate (a person, normally). *Which* is used when the antecedent is inanimate; we also, of course, have the word *that* which can refer to either. The activity's examples (*John Mortimer, which ...* and *a vice ... who...*) show that this 'animacy rule' was not always respected in EModE – you have *which* with an animate in the first example, and *who* plus an inanimate in the second. The latter was more common that the former, and by the eighteenth century, our own animacy rules were in force. Notice, incidentally, that we still have difficulty today with inanimate genitives. The animate genitive is *whose*, and many people will use this even with an inanimate antecedent. We might say *The bank, whose director died ...* rather than the more clumsy (but perhaps more grammatically correct) *The bank, the director of which died....*

In relation to several of the 'oddities' discussed in this section, we have seen that more than one form was in use at the same time. So alongside those 'split genitives' we find plenty of 'unsplit genitives'. Variation like this was a characteristic of the time, and is worth a closer look...

16.2 -s and -eth: variation, language spread, and gender

In Shakespeare's play, *The Merchant of Venice*, Portia is trying to persuade Shylock to be merciful – he has the power of life and death over another character, Antonio. Her words are quite well known. Using these lines as evidence, ask yourself this question: in EModE what is the verb ending for the third person singular present tense?

> The quality of mercy is not strained,
> It droppeth as the gentle rain from heaven
> Upon the place beneath. It is twice blest,
> It blesseth him that gives and him that takes.
> 'Tis mightiest in the mightiest, it becomes
> The throned monarch better than his crown.
>
> (4.1.182)

The answer is that there are two forms. One is the *-s* that we use today, found here in *gives*, *takes* and *becomes*. But you also find *-eth for -eth* in *droppeth* and *blesseth*. This is a remnant of the OE and ME ending *-ð* (you can find examples of this in 6.2.2). As the passage shows, both were on the go in EModE times. If you were to look at the whole of this scene in Shakespeare, you would find that the *-s* form was in the ascendancy, being used twice as much as the *-eth* for *-th*, which was on the way out, moving towards the obsolete status that it has in PDE. So it is a question of 'movement towards the forms of PDE'.

But how do grammatical changes (from *-ð/-eth* to *-s*) occur? Variation plays an important role. The existence of two competing forms provides a necessary condition. A common process is for new forms to emerge, co-exist alongside old forms, and then replace them. One of the factors sometimes involved is geographical. Look at Figure 16.1 showing the regional distribution of *-s* in EModE. Concentrate on the London, North and East Anglia lines. What do they show? Activity 16B (*The spreading -s*) will help you decide. It has specific questions you can use Figure 16.1 to answer.

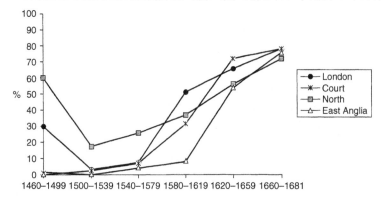

Figure 16.1 Replacement of *-eth for -th* by *-s* in verbs other than *have* and *do*. Regional distribution of *–s*. From Nevalainen and Raumolin-Brunberg (2003: 178)

The figure shows that the *-s* form started in the north and spread slowly over the country. We have come across such 'north to south' movement at various points before (in 10.2.1, for example). To illustrate this particular case: in the 1350s, the Archbishop of York wrote a catechism (a piece of religious writing with instructional aim) which appeared in both Northern and Midland dialect versions. One phrase in the catechism reads (in PDE) 'as Saint John says in his gospel'. In the Northern version this is *als seint Iohn saies in his godspel*, while the Midland version has *as seynt Ion sayeth in hys gospel*.[2] The *-s* form was on a slow march southward. **Supralocalization** is the name given to the process whereby a language form moves from one geographical location to another. Notice how relatively suddenly, during the 1540–1579 period, the form catches on in London – capital cities are always on the lookout for new linguistic 'fashions'. In rural East Anglia, with a more conservative attitude towards change, the adoption comes much later.

Here is another figure from Nevalainen and Raumolin-Brunberg (2003). What does this one show?

Figure 16.2 Replacement of *-eth for -th* by *-s* in verbs other than *have* and *do*. Gender distribution of *-s*. From Nevalainen and Raumolin-Brunberg (2003: 123)

The figure indicates that though at first men seem to use *-s* more than women, the situation very rapidly changes, and for most of the period covered by the figure, it is women who forge ahead in taking up the new form. Language change is often pushed forward by a group of individuals who adopt a linguistic form and make it dominant, and women are one group of people whose influence has been particularly studied from this point of view. Here is another example: as long ago as 1946, Auguste Brun, a specialist in the Provençal dialect, found that while men in the region spoke Provençal, the younger women tended to use French. Brun regarded this fact as contributing significantly to the disappearance of the dialect.[3] It may be that on occasions women are quicker to adopt new forms coming from elsewhere, while men have a tendency to stay with established forms.

16.3 The 'half-way house': do-support

Another example of EModE as a 'half-way house' involves what is called **do-support**. This relates to how we use the verb *do* to ask some questions and form some negative sentences in PDE. Examples are *do you like coffee?* and *I don't like coffee*. If you are not sure about how do-support works in PDE, why not take a look at CW16.1 (*Just do it*) before you read on? It includes an activity and an explanation. It also mentions the use of *do* to give emphasis in some contexts, as in *Oh, I do like coffee*.

English is rather 'odd' among the world's languages in forming interrogatives and negatives with do-support. Another, more common, way of asking questions, used by many languages, is by inverting subject and verb (inversion was discussed in 10.2.4). In German, for example, *Martin kennt Mary* ('Martin knows Mary') becomes *Kennt Martin Mary?* (literally 'Knows Martin Mary?').

In the case of negatives, a common strategy among world languages is simply to introduce a negative word (what is known as a **particle**). In German, the particle is *nicht*: *Martin kennt Mary nicht* – literally (but with more English word order) 'Martin knows not Mary'. OE was just like this. In 4.3's 'lettuce story', the devil says *Ic sæt on anum leahtrice*. The interrogative form would be *Sæt Ic on anum leahtrice?*[4] The negative particle in OE was *ne*, so the positive *Hē cōm* ('He came') would be *Ne cōm hē* – literally 'not came he'). But what about EModE? Take a look at Activity 16C (*EModE interrogatives and negatives*).

The examples in Activity 16C show that interrogatives and negatives could be formed as in PDE, using *do*. Hence Shakespeare's *does your business follow us?* in example (i), and *it does not please me* in (iv). But the other ways mentioned above are also used. Instead of *do'st thou think…?*, Marlowe has *think'st thou* (vi), and the negative *gaze not on it* (in v), would in PDE use *do*: *do not gaze on it*. This is the variation associated with transition, and again, it can be illustrated by a graph. The one below is taken from Ellegård (1953), adapted by Barber (1997), and it plots the use of *do* from 1500 to 1700. Look first at the three lines showing questions and negatives (three because negative and affirmative questions are treated separately). The lines are not straight because language change rarely happens in a straight line. But the direction of travel is very clear. Then look at the line showing affirmative declarative use of *do*. What does it show? Taking the graph as a whole, try to arrive at some statements about the use of *do* during the period.

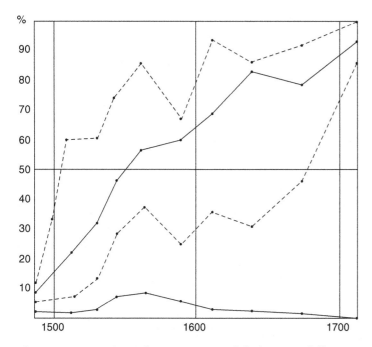

Figure 16.3 Auxiliary *do*. Percentages of *do* forms in different types of sentences, 1500–1700. Upper broken line: negative questions; upper solid line: affirmative questions; lower broken line: negative declarative sentences; lower solid line: affirmative declarative sentences. Adapted from Ellegård (1953).

The graph shows the use of *do* for questions and negatives gaining in strength over time. But for affirmative declaratives, the opposite is true. This use of *do* diminishes over the period, toward the position we see today, where affirmative declarative *do* is the exception rather than the rule. In other words, the norms that we have today were in the process of being established. But the existence of variation shows that the process is not yet complete – we are in the 'half-way house'. Variation exists because the language was in flux and more than one form was available for use.

16.4 Modal auxiliaries

Perhaps you noticed that at the beginning of the previous section we said that in PDE *some* questions and *some* negatives use do-support. We also mentioned alternative ways, sometimes found in EModE, of forming these two sentence types – using inversion of subject and verb (for questions), and the particle *not* (for negatives). In fact, there is a group of PDE verbs which regularly use these latter ways, and which do not (barring a few exceptions) use *do* at all. These are called **modal auxiliary verbs**, and include *must, can* and *may*. If they are followed by a **lexical verb** (a normal, non-auxiliary verb), then that is in the infinitive: *He must go, she can swim* – it is not grammatical to say **he must goes* or **she can swims*. The interrogative and negative forms of these example sentences are not **Do you must go?* or **You don't must go*, but *Must you go?*, and *You must not go*.

Many of these modal auxiliary verbs in EModE were as they are now, but there are some slight differences in meanings, just sufficient to lead to occasional comprehension problems. Activity 16D (*Some EModE modal auxiliaries*) invites you to speculate about the meanings of some EModE modals.

The PDE verb *can* may be used to express possibility, ability, or permission – *He can swim* may today mean 'it is possible for him to swim', 'he is able to swim' or 'he is permitted to swim'. Examples (i) and (ii) in the activity show *can* at work as a lexical verb meaning 'to know' or 'to have skill'. This sense of 'knowing' is present in the PDE words 'canny' and 'cunning'.

A modal that has an interesting semantic history is *may*. Its associated form *might* gives a clue to the original meaning. In PDE it can indicate permission or possibility: *He may come* could have either one of these meanings. But originally it was associated in meaning with the noun *might*, meaning 'power', 'strength'. *He may/might come* would have signified the capacity to come. EModE uses *may* to indicate permission or possibility as we do today, though the phrase *as I may remember* (example iii) sounds odd to modern ears, and carries a sense of power perhaps, meaning 'to the extent that my powers of memory suggest'.

In PDE, many speakers make no distinction between *shall* and *will*, saying either *I shall come* or *I will come*. PDE speakers do, however, distinguish the associated forms *should* and *would*. *He should brush his teeth every day* suggests a 'moral' obligation, while *He would brush his teeth every day* can suggest a habit. This difference is not always found in EModE, where the two forms tend to be indistinguishable. This is apparent in examples (iv) and (v), where *would* makes more sense to the modern reader.

Will is another modal which has a slightly different semantic coverage from PDE. It has a number of uses in PDE, and one is to make statements or predictions about the future, as when we say *It will rain tomorrow*. Its original sense, as a lexical verb, is 'wish' or 'want', and this sense is carried in the subtitle of Shakespeare's play *Twelfth Night*, which is *What You Will*. It is also found in the activity's examples (vi) and (vii). Is *will* used in EModE to make statements about the future, as it can be today? You might like to look at Shakespeare's instances of the word. This can be done on the 'Shakespeare's Words' website (www.shakespeareswords.com/) – an invaluable resource for exploring Shakespeare's language. Put the word *will* in the 'Search' box. You will find over 5,000 instances cited. Of course, this total includes examples of *will* used as a noun, and these are not relevant here. It will also exclude the shortened *'ll* form (as in *I'll*), which you would want to include (though in fact there are not so many of those in Shakespeare). So the search will not throw up everything that you want, but a glance through some of the instances it does provide will make it hard to resist the conclusion that making statements about the future is indeed a use. Incidentally, the change that *will* made from being a lexical verb to an auxiliary – part of the language's grammatical system – is an example of the process that is called **grammaticalization**.

Earlier, the forms *might* and *would* were described as 'related to' *may* and *will*. You might be tempted to think of them as the past-tense forms of these verbs. But the difference between *He may come* and *He might come* is not to do with tense but with degree of possibility. *Might* is more tentative than *may*. You can see that the difference is not to do with tense because both these sentences have their own separate past-tense forms – *He may have come* and *He might have come*. But there are two examples in the activity of a word which shows a proper past-tense form. It is not a word that is used today, but you will probably have no problem in understanding it: *durst*. This is the past tense of *dare*, and examples (viii) and (ix) show it being used in this sense. In PDE, of course, we have the past-tense form of *dared*. This form was coming into the language in the Renaissance period. A look on the 'Shakespeare's Words' website (just mentioned) will reveal nine uses of it in Shakespeare, in comparison with fifty-six uses of *durst*.

You may be wondering where linguists like Nevalainen and Raumolin-Brunberg get their data from. Appropriate data sources for linguistic studies is an important issue. CW16.2 (*An EModE corpus*) looks at one extremely important method of data collection, using language **corpora**.

16.5 *Ye, you* and *thou*: some basics

For many today, the word *ye* suggests a kind of romantic antiquity which you are invited to experience when you buy food from *Ye olde cake shoppe*. The *ye* here is in fact a version of *the*, where the 'y' is a modernized version of the OE letter thorn [þ] which stood for 'th' (4.1 will refresh your memory). The *ye* we will look at here is another one – the variant of *you* occasionally found today in expressions like the interjection *Ye Gods!* In 1500, the difference between *ye* and *you* was one of case. *Ye* was the nominative (subject) pronoun, *you* was for other cases – like the PDE difference between *I* (nominative) and *me* (other cases). The same distinction held between *thou* and *thee*. Here are a few lines from a letter Catherine of Aragon (the first of Henry VIII's six wives; you can read about her in 13.1) sent to Cardinal Wolsey, who at the time held the post of 'Almoner' (the official dispenser of alms). She is requesting him to keep in touch and to send news regularly, and promises to do the same (*mine* refers to the 'letters' she will send). The letter, signed 'Katherine the Qwene', was written in 1513. The *ye/you* distinction held then, and you are invited to put the appropriate forms in the spaces (AS):

> And so I pray ____, Mr Almoner, to continue as hitherto ____ have done; for I promise ____ that from henceforth ____ shall lack none of mine, and before this ____ should have had many more, but I think that your business scantily giveth ____ leisure to read by letters.[5]

By the end of the sixteenth century, things were different. Here are some lines from Shakespeare's play *The Tempest*, written in about 1610. What is happening here on the *ye/you* front?

> Caliban: As wicked dew as e'er my mother brushed
> With raven's feather from unwholesome fen
> Drop on you both! A south-west blow on ye
> And blister you all o'er!
>
> (1.2.321)

By that time, there was, in the words of Baugh and Cable (2013: 243), 'very little feeling any more for the different functions of the two words'.

We need say no more about *ye* (or *yee* as it is spelled in 13.4's 'rogues in buckrom' speech). Much more interesting – and problematic – is the difference between the *thou* and the *you* forms. Incidentally, we will use the word *thou* to refer to all the associated forms (including *thee*, *thy* and *thine*), while *you* will stand for all its associated forms. *Thou* is hardly used at all today, except in a few fixed phrases like *fare thee well* and *holier than thou*, as well as in some religious contexts and in a few British dialects. The next chapter starts by looking at the differences of usage in EModE. Some are quite subtle, but there is one obvious, highly unsubtle, one that we can deal with here. The secret lies in Caliban's words above: *Drop on you both*. If the referent is plural, it has to be *you*; *thou* cannot be used when you are talking to more than one person. The problems of usage occur because both forms can be used in the singular: if you are talking to one person, you could use either *thou* or *you*. When do you use one and when the other? That is the question. It is one to do not with 'rules of grammar' but with 'rules of use' (the term was introduced in 1.2). We need to leave the world of grammar and move into pragmatics … and Chapter 17.

Activity section

16A   Some oddities that writers uses

Here are seven points where EModE diverges grammatically from PDE. Two or three examples are given of each. Try and identify what the point is each time; some hints are given below if you need help. Describe as precisely as you can what is happening in these examples, and how PDE differs.

(i) *Sejanus his Fall* (the title of a play by Jonson about the Roman soldier Sejanus)
Once in a seafight 'gainst the Count his galleys
I did some service (Shakespeare)
The King's daughter of England (Malory)

(ii) *This was the most unkindest cut of all* (Shakespeare)
He grows more weaker still (Fletcher)

(iii) *I pray you, bear with me, I cannot go no further* (Shakespeare)
And that no woman has, nor never none
Shall mistress be of it, save I alone. (Shakespeare)

(iv) *Spare none but such as go in clouted shoon,* (Shakespeare; *shoon* = 'shoes')
And, rapt with whirling wheeles, inflames the skyen (Spenser; *skyen* – 'skies')

(v) *If it would like you to extend your schedules ...* (Wilson)
It yearns me not if men my garments wear (Shakespeare)

(vi) *troubled minds that wakes* (Shakespeare)
My old bones aches. (Shakespeare)

(vii) *John Mortimer, which now is dead....* (Shakespeare)
a vice very ugly and monstrous who under the pleasant habit of friend-
ship...infecteth the wits (Elyot from Barber)

Hints – the sentences are about: (i) expressing possession; (ii) adjectival comparatives and superlatives; (iii) negation; (iv) noun plurals; (v) what are called
'impersonal verbs'; (vi) verb plural forms; (vii) relative clauses.

16B The spreading -s

Use Figure 16.1 in the text to answer these questions:

- Where was the *-s* first used?
- Beginning in the period 1540 to 1579, one area adopted the form particularly
rapidly. Which?
- Which area was the slowest to adopt *-s*?
- By 1660 to 1681, roughly what proportion of users continued with the *-eth*
for -th form?
- Do you have any thoughts about why the graph excludes *have* and *do*?

16C EModE interrogatives and negatives

Below are some EModE interrogatives and negatives. Do they follow the same
PDE rules mentioned in the text and considered in detail in CW16.1? To work
this out systematically, begin by marking each sentence as interrogative or negative. If you find rules different from the present-day ones, state what they are,
and formulate how the negatives/interrogatives would be said in PDE:

(i) *Now, fair one, does your business follow us?* (Shakespeare)
(ii) *Affords this art no greater miracle?* (Marlowe)

(iii) *I lik'd but loved not* (Sidney)

(iv) *No, sir, it does not please me* (Shakespeare)

(v) *O, Faustus, lay that damned book aside,*
And gaze not on it (Marlowe)

(vi) *Think'st thou that I who saw the face of God ... Am not tormented?*
(Marlowe)

(vii) *One Signior Lorenzo di Pazzi; do you know any such, sir, I pray you?*
(Jonson)

(viii) *We do not stand much upon our gentility* (Jonson)

16D   Some EModE modal auxiliaries

Here are five examples of verbs which could be used as modal auxiliaries in
EModE (though sometimes they are being used as lexical verbs below). All of
them bar one are still used in PDE, but you will probably find the uses here a
little unfamiliar. Consider what the modal auxiliaries might mean in these sentences, and what they mean in PDE.

(i) *He coulde it by hart* (Paynell).

(ii) *... the French can well on horseback* (Shakespeare)

(iii) *You, cousin Nevil, as I* may *remember...*
Did speak these words, now proved a prophecy (Shakespeare)

(iv) *I should rather die with silence, than live with shame* (Jonson)

(v) *The rude son should strike the father dead* (Shakespeare)

(vi) *I will no reconcilement* (Shakespeare)

(vii) *I will not reason what is meant hereby, / Because I will be guiltless of the*
meaning (Shakespeare)

(viii) *That durst dissuade me from thy Lucifer* (Marlowe)

(ix) *What stately building durst so high extend / Her loftie towres vnto the*
starry sphere (Spenser)

Answer section

Passage in 16.5

And so I pray **you**, *Mr Almoner, to continue as hitherto ye have done; for I prom-*
ise **you** *that from henceforth ye shall lack none of mine, and before this ye should*
have had many more, but I think that your business scantily giveth **you** *leisure*
to read by letters.

Further reading

Barber (1997) covers many aspects of EModE, and has two chapters devoted to grammar.

D. Crystal (2008) focuses on Shakespeare's language and, like Barber, covers many linguistic areas, including grammar, in a highly accessible way.

Johnson (2013) also deals with Shakespeare. It has a chapter on grammar which includes activities for class or individual use.

Nevalainen and Raumolin-Brunberg (2003) is a study which looks at a number of EModE grammatical points from a sociolinguistic point of view.

There are two chapters in Lass (1999) which deal with grammar in a detailed and scholarly fashion. Lass (1999a) covers morphology, and Rissanen (1999) syntax.

Notes

1 The 'Mrs Sands' example is taken from Barber (1997: 146), and the suggested explanation comes from Baugh & Cable (2013: 241).
2 The example is from Freeborn (2006: 212). The 'thorn' has here been rendered by 'th'.
3 Brun's work is cited in Grégoire (2006).
4 The 'lettuce story' also has the example *Hwæt dyde Ic hire?* The verb *do* is here being used as a lexical verb. The PDE version would need two *do* verbs, one a lexical verb and one in do-support: *What did I do to her?*
5 The text, which has been modernized, is from the *Letters and Papers, Foreign and Domestic, of the Reign of Henry VIII: Preserved in the Public Record Office, the British Museum and Elsewhere, Volume 1*, Google eBook.

17 'I thou thee, thou traitor'

Some Renaissance pragmatics

As we saw in Chapter 1 (section 1.2), 'rules of use' are not universal. They vary from culture to culture, and from age to age. This chapter looks at some pragmatic differences between EModE and today. It starts where the previous chapter left off, considering the complex factors that govern the choice of *thou* versus *you* in EModE. Politeness is a pervading theme throughout most of this chapter, and a final section looks at 'pragmatic noise' – the use of words and phrases that appear insignificant but can be very meaningful in conversational interactions.

Before reading on, think about the word *thou*. Does it mean anything to you? What do you know about this word?

Section 17.2 is about politeness, particularly in relation to asking people favours, or to do things for you. Think about politeness in your culture. Imagine you are in a railway carriage and want a fellow passenger to open the window. Jot down some ways of asking, according to the identity of the person you are asking (they may be a stranger – adult or child – or a member of your family travelling with you). Choose ways showing different degrees of politeness. Identify what linguistic features make these ways more or less polite.

The last section of the chapter looks at the exclamation *ah*. Words like this can often convey multiple meanings, and it can be very difficult to pin down exactly what these are. Think of some circumstances when *ah* is used in PDE? What about *er*? Again, here you are likely to come across a variety of uses.

17.1 Much more on *you* and *thou*

Hunstonworth is a village in the Durham area of north-east England. In the 1560s there was a court case in which one Nicoll Dixson was accused of stealing sheep. Hope (1994) uses part of the court witness reports to illustrate a common usage of *thou* and *you*. The exchange here involves Masters Antony and Ratcliff, who are relatively high-class people, and the lower-class Roger Dunn. Note in passing the use of *will* (*woll*) to mean 'wish' (as discussed in 16.4). But particularly notice who uses *you*, who *thou* and to whom. Can you establish a possible 'rule of use'?[1]

Antony: Dyd not thou promess me that thou wold tell me and the
            parson of Hunstonworth who sold George Whitfield sheep?
Donn: I need not unless I woll.
Ratcliff: Thou breaks promess.
Donn: You will know yt soon enowgh, for your man, Nicoll Dixson,
            stole them, that ther stands, upon Thursday before Christenmas
            then last past.
            [Donn says Radcliffe will never be able to prove him a thief.]
Donn: For although ye be a gent., and I a poore man, my honestye
            shalbe as good as yours.
Ratcliff: What saith thou? liknes thou thy honestye to myn?

This exchange illustrates one of the determinants in the *thou/you* choice: status or class. If we divide the world into 'high' and 'low' status people, then conversational exchanges will involve one or more of these four:

- a high-status/class person speaking to another high-status/class person (high → high)
- a low-status person speaking to another low-status person (low → low)
- a high-status person speaking to a low-status person (high → low)
- a low-status person speaking to a high-status person (low → high)

Our sheep-stealing exchange illustrates two of these situations. We find high → low when Antony and Ratcliff address Roger Donn, and low → high when Roger Donn addresses them; *thou* is used high → low, and *you* low → high. What about the other two situations? Take a look at Activity 17A (*Thou and you, high and low*) before reading on.

Example (i) in the activity suggests that in high → high (Othello to Desdemona), the *you* form is used. In the case of (ii), the servant and the maid use low → low, and the pronoun is *thou*. But (iii) is low → low too. At the beginning of this dialogue, the brothers use *you* to each other, though you will notice that a *thou* form creeps in at the end.

The sheep-stealing exchange plus these activity examples suggest the following:

high → low: *thou*
low → high: *you*
high → high: *you*
low → low: *thou* or *you*

But status/class is just one of the determinants. A second important one is intimacy. It may be that the servants in activity example (ii) use *thou* to each other, not because of their class, but because they are friends. You may have come across some languages, like French and German, which have forms that seem similar to EModE *thou* and *you*. Examples are *tu* and *vous* in French, *du* and *Sie* in German. The *thou* (*tu*, *du*) forms can indicate intimacy, and indeed a change from *you* to *thou* forms can be a meaningful mark of growing intimacy. It is rather as changing from surname to first name used to be like in Anglo-Saxon societies, though nowadays first names have started being use more commonly, even on first meeting. In French there is a verb *tutoyer* which means 'to give the *tu* form', interpreted as a sign of becoming more friendly; there is one in German too: *duzen*, 'to give the *du* form'. As we shall see, there was also an EModE verb: *to thou*. It could be that the activity's example (iii) is showing a significant *you* → *thou* movement as Dromio of Syracuse, at the end of the extract, gives the *thou* to his long-lost brother. We have no way of knowing whether this shift to *thou* is permanent, since it occurs in almost the last line of the play: perhaps they are eternally *thou* to each other thereafter ... or not. We shall never know.

As you might expect, status and intimacy can pull in different directions – status might suggest a *you*, intimacy a *thou*. In such circumstances, status can often win. This is shown in the activity's example (i). Othello and Desdemona are a married couple (and the two Dromios are closely related to each other), yet the prince and his wife (like the Dromios) use statusful *you* rather than intimate *thou*. Lass (1999a) has an even more revealing example from the correspondence between Sir Thomas More (councillor to Henry VIII) and his daughter Margaret Roper. He uses *you*:

> Your doghterly louing letter ... was and is, I faithfully assure you ... inward confort vnto me...'

But Lass draws attention to one particularly interesting passage:

> Surely Megge a fainter hearte than thy fraile father hath, canst you not haue...

At this point, Thomas More uses *thy* rather than *your*. But notice the verb, *canst*. It is the form that goes with *thou*, yet the pronoun used is *you*. It is as if More wants to use *thou* with his daughter but cannot quite bring himself to do so.

It is a feature of languages like French and German – and many others with similar distinctions – that once intimacy has led *you* to become *thou*, the change is a relatively stable one. In EModE, it was more unstable – speakers could switch between *you* and *thou* and back again according to their current feelings.[2] In other words, a shift from one form to another could signal a relatively brief change in attitude. Shakespearean lovers, like Romeo and Juliet, or Petruchio and Katherine in *The Taming of the Shrew*, switch backwards and forwards in this way, sometimes according to the state of their amorous relationship. Here is an example. In *The Taming of the Shrew*, Petruchio marries the 'shrew-like' Kate, whom he succeeds in 'taming'. Towards the end of the play, there is a competition between the male friends to see who has the most obedient wife. The three husbands involved send for their wives, requiring them to stop what they are doing and come running to their husbands immediately. Kate shows how 'tame' she has become by being the only wife to obey. When she comes, Petruchio asks her where the wives of his friends, who failed to obey, are. Notice Petruchio's *your* here:

Kate: What is your will, sir, that you send for me?
Petruchio: Where is your sister, and Hortensio's wife?

But then, a few lines later, he asks Kate to tell her women friends to be more obedient to their husbands:

Petruchio: Katherine, I charge thee tell these headstrong women
What duty they do owe their lords and husbands.

Why the *thou* here? Perhaps he is feeling particularly affectionate towards her because she has obeyed him. Because the relationship between Kate and Petruchio is a particularly stormy one, there are plenty of interesting examples of changes from *you* to *thou* and back again; another one will be mentioned in a moment.

It is not just amorous feelings that can bring on a change to *thou*. There is an 'angry *thou*'. Barber (1981) is a study of *thou* and *you* use in Shakespeare's *Richard III*. One of his examples involves two murderers. As lower-class people, they use *thou* to each other, and *you* to their social superior, the Duke of Clarence. This usage follows the 'rules of use' about status, discussed earlier. But the murderers switch to *thou* when they get angry with Clarence. Another study of these pronouns is Brown and Gilman (1989), who focus on four of Shakespeare's tragedies. They find an example, in *Macbeth*, of the 'grateful *thou*'. Then there is a 'sardonic and contemptuous *thou*'. The title of this chapter gives an example. In 1603, Sir Walter Raleigh was on trial for being implicated in a plot against James I. The crown prosecutor, Sir Edward Coke, is said to have accused Raleigh: 'All that Lord Cobham [another person implicated in the plot] did was by thy instigation, thou viper; for I thou thee, thou Traitor!' This is an example of the verb *to thou*, like the French *tutoyer* and the German *duzen*, though here used to express contempt rather than intimacy.

But even with all these different kinds of *thou* in existence, it is often difficult, in Shakespeare for example, to explain changes from *you* to *thou* and back again in terms of shifting emotions. To explore this, take a look at CW17.1 (*Taming a Shrew*). It focuses on one speech from Shakespeare's play and invites you to speculate about what is controlling the use of the pronouns. A way of exploring this in a more general (though inevitably a more time-consuming) way would be to use the 'Shakespeare's Words' website (mentioned in 16.4), choose a Shakespeare play (preferably one you know), select two characters and plot their pronoun use to each other. In many cases, you may find shifts which are difficult to explain in terms of the factors we have discussed.

But what other factors could there be? Calvo (1990) suggests associations between *thou* and certain speech acts, and she mentions insults, promises, expressions of gratitude. There have also been studies investigating whether certain verbs attract *thou* forms more than others (Mulholland, 1967), and even that sometimes a shift in form of address may be associated with nothing more than a change of conversational topic. Lass (1999a: 153) suggests yet another distinction. He uses the word **distal** to describe when speakers feel emotionally 'distant' from one another, as opposed to **proximal**, when there are feelings of closeness. 'Among the factors', he says, 'that appear to trigger *you* for regular *thou* users are mothers-in-law ... business, social superiors and unreal conditions (verbs of guessing, conjecture etc.)'. Perhaps this distinction may go some of the way towards explaining what is happening in the *Taming of the Shrew* passage in CW17.1...

... or maybe not. In her article on *you/thou* usage, Wales (1983: 114) concludes that from the thirteenth century onward, shifts may 'occur within the same sentence, so that contextual changes are often hard to justify'. She warns that though on some occasions there may be credible explanations for the 'unstable', retractable use of *thou* in terms of affection, anger or some other emotion, it really is difficult to account for all uses in such terms. Another conclusion she reaches is that, overall, *you* is the **unmarked** form, and *thou* the **marked** one, which is the linguist's way of saying that *you* is normally used, unless there is a special reason for using *thou*. As Quirk (1959: 41) suggests: '*you* was the neutral form, of wide application; *thou* was the particularised form used in special contexts and for special effect'. It may, in other words, just be that *you* is used unless you have some special reason to deviate into *thou*. This is suggested by some interesting statistics Wales gives, related to the drama of the time, that:

- *thou* forms are far outnumbered by *you* forms;
- momentary shifts from *you* to *thou* are more frequent than shifts from *thou* to *you*.

Statistics like these show that once again it is a case of 'gradual movement towards the forms of PDE', where *you* is universally used except in a few specific contexts.

If you have not had enough of *thou* and *you*, take a look at CW17.2 (*Thou in love and hate*). It contains a lengthy activity focusing in detail on one scene from Shakespeare's *Richard III*, and bringing together a number of the points made in this section.

17.2 Being polite

In EModE there was, we have seen, a verb *to thou*. Here is another example of its use. In Shakespeare's play *Twelfth Night* (3.2.43), Sir Toby Belch is trying to goad Sir Andrew Aguecheek into having an argument with Cesario. The advice which Toby Belch gives is: 'If thou thou'st him some thrice, it shall not be amiss'; 'call him *thou* a few times', he is saying, 'and that should do the trick'. Using the wrong form of address is being recognized as a way of being impolite. Forms of address really did play an important role in polite behaviour. Our look at ME forms of address in 9.3.1 shows the same thing.

Addressing people properly is part of what is called **discernment politeness** – conforming to social conventions requiring use of the appropriate forms according to the status and standing of your **addressee** (the person you are talking to). This form of politeness was very important in OE, ME and EModE. It can of course be extremely important in PDE too. But today we place much emphasis on what is called **negative politeness**. This phrase needs some explanation. It refers to politeness that tries to mitigate any negative consequences of what is being asked. For example, when we ask someone a favour, we often like to de-emphasize the inconvenience it will cause them. We may also go out of our way to make it clear that we are not giving them an order, and that they are free to act without any pressure. Here are some PDE examples:[3]

(a) Perhaps you might like to investigate epilepsy in dogs and do an article on the subject.
(b) Perhaps you could open the door, could you?
(c) Would you like to read? (said by a teacher to a pupil in class)

In these three sentences, the verb forms (*might like to*, *could* and *would*) suggest to the addressee that they have some choice in the matter. The sentences are couched as suggestions or requests. In fact, they may well be disguised orders. (a), for example, might be said by a university tutor, telling his student what to do. And if a teacher said (c) to a pupil in class, it would be an instruction to take a turn at reading aloud. PDE is particularly fond of these indirect modes of negative politeness. Indeed, British society has been called a 'negative politeness culture', no less.[4] But not all societies are the same, and in fact example (c) is taken from Thomas's (1983) experiences when teaching English in the Soviet Union. It is an example of what she calls 'cross-cultural pragmatic failure'. She noticed that when she said 'Would you like to read?' in class, her pupils might reply 'No, I wouldn't'. They were not being cheeky, which is how that reply would have been interpreted in an English classroom. They were simply interpreting what looked like an invitation … as an invitation. They really thought they were being given a choice, which is – after all – exactly the impression that negative politeness tries to give. Jucker and Taavitsainen (2013) argue that while negative politeness is very common today, it is a recent phenomenon, not much found in OE, ME or EModE.

As with much EModE language study (until recently, at least), a great deal of attention to politeness has focused on Shakespeare. Brown and Gilman (1989), for example, look at the politeness strategies found in Shakespeare's *Othello*, *Hamlet*, *Macbeth* and *King Lear*. Another study, by Kopytko (1995), adds four comedies – *The Taming of the Shrew*, *A Midsummer Night's Dream*, *The Merchant of Venice* and *Twelfth Night*.

Brown and Gilman (1989) is based on the theory of politeness developed in Brown and Levinson (1987). A central part of this theory is that there are three factors which control degree of politeness – how polite a person will be in a given situation:

(a) The power relationship (P) holding between speaker and hearer. If the speaker is socially superior to the hearer, he or she is likely not to bother much with politeness, and might even go for the brusque imperative. But if the hearer is socially powerful and the speaker not, then a more polite approach will be required. This factor can be described as **vertical social distance**. It is to do with whether the speaker is higher up or lower down on a vertical axis.

(b) The distance relationship (D) between speaker and hearer. If they know each other well and are friends, then you might expect a more informal, less polite, interaction. But if the two are strangers, politeness may be required. This factor can be described as **horizontal social distance**. It is to do with whether speaker and hearer are close or distant on a horizontal axis.

(c) Ranked extremity (R). This is the 'size' of what is being considered. If you are just asking someone to lend you a pen for an hour, not much politeness is required. But if you are a young adult asking your parents to lend you several thousand pounds towards your first house purchase, then all your politeness skills will be brought into play.

Brown and Gilman's purpose is to find out whether these factors – (P), (D) and (R) – are important determiners of politeness in the plays they are considering. Their research method is interesting. They develop a method of giving utterances 'scores' for how polite they are. So the brusque imperative would score low, and a request using *Could you possibly...* would score high. Then they identify pairs of Shakespearean utterances which differ in terms of just one of the three factors. For example, in some pairs, both the distance between the interactants (D) and the (R) that is involved are roughly the same. The only difference is the (P). In other pairs, the difference will be between (D) but not (P) and (R), and so on. This enables them to see how degree of politeness (as measured by their 'scores') is related to (P), (D) and (R). Do the utterances of socially inferior speakers score more on the politeness scale than the utterances of a socially superior speaker? What about when the conversation is stranger → stranger as opposed to friend → friend? Or when the (R) is very high?

Their results: for the factors (P) and (R), these are generally as Brown and Levinson's theory predicts. Both factors are seen to be important. As regards (D), the theory predicts that more distant interactants will be more polite with each other. But in fact Brown and Gilman find that 'the more the speaker likes the hearer, the greater the concern with the hearer's face and so the more polite the speech; the less the liking, the less the concern and also the politeness' (p. 193). Sometimes people – in our world as well as Shakespeare's – are polite to people they like, irrespective of whether they are strangers.

One of the paper's other interesting observations concerns 'excessive politeness'. Sometimes, they note, a character uses more politeness than a situation seems to require. In such cases, there is sometimes a 'hidden agenda' – something more important is being suggested than is being stated. For example, Brown and Gilman note that 'one of the politest speeches' in *Macbeth* (according to their method of scoring) is when Macbeth suggests to Banquo that they need to talk about something relatively unimportant (the witches' prophesies). A small amount of (R) would be involved, you might think. But in fact Macbeth is really asking Banquo, indirectly, whether he will be a part of the conspiracy which will involve murder. Given this off-record intention, the degree of politeness is not excessive at all.

Although pragmatics is a relatively recent area of linguistic interest, a considerable amount of work has been done, including in 'historical pragmatics', which looks (as we are doing) at aspects of pragmatics over time. This chapter just dips one toe into the very large pragmatic lake. This is particularly true in the area of politeness, by now a well-studied area. But it is also true of all areas covered in this chapter, very much including the one we are about to consider.

17.3   Pragmatic noise

A fascinating feature of pragmatics is that it can 'get to parts of language that other areas do not get to'. A good example is the study of what Culpeper and Kytö (2010) call **pragmatic noise**. This involves words like *ah, ha, oh, um* and *fie*. They are undeniably an important part of conversation, yet linguistics has had little to say about them. It is true that 'traditional' grammar does recognize a part of speech called **interjections**, which may include such words, as well as expressions like *dear me* and *heavens*. An important characteristic of pragmatic noise words is that they are not 'normal' words being used in a special context (so *dear me* and *heavens* would not count). Also they do not 'behave grammatically' – taking inflections, or having fixed positions in sentences, for example. Often they act as **discourse markers**, expressing what the speaker's or writer's feeling or attitude is towards what they are saying.

Culpeper and Kytö (2010) is a large-scale study of historical pragmatics, using EModE dialogues as its data. A long section of the book deals with pragmatic noise. We will here focus on just one item – *ah*. It is in common use today, and before looking at EModE usage, you might like to think about some of the various occasions when it is used in PDE. Activity 17B (*Ah, so that's what it means*) will help with this.

When we are talking about words like *ah*, it is better to think in terms of 'areas of meaning' rather than actual hard-and-fast meanings. One PDE area of meaning for *ah* is to express a significant emotional response, such as surprise, discovery, solution or revelation. The activity's example (i) – *Ah, John. There you are* – suggests surprise or discovery. In (ii) the phrase *ah, wait a minute* may convey the notion of a problem being worked out; sometimes in PDE you will find *aha* used here too. The second area of meaning shown in the activity – examples (iii) and (iv) – is to express disagreement, or to correct someone. Both these uses were found in EModE. One of the *OED*'s examples of the 'discovery' sense comes from a 1591 drama by John Lyly called *Endimion – The Man in the Moone*. When Endimion is woken up by a kiss, one of the characters announces: 'Ah, I see his eyes almost open.' The first *OED* citation for the 'disagreement' sense is 1560: 'Here th' emperoure interruptynge, ah (sayeth he) what shulde that good man refourme?' – the speaker is interrupted by the Emperor, who expresses disagreement.

There are other EModE uses of *ah* that may sound a little odd today, though it is usually easy to find similar PDE equivalents. One is to express sorrow. So when Queen Elizabeth in Shakespeare's *Richard III* learns of her children's deaths, she says: 'Ah, my poor princes! Ah, my tender babes!' Perhaps today we would make a change in the vowel, preferring *oh* to *ah* here. But we do today use *aaah* to express sympathy, often with a mock seriousness. EModE *ah* is often used in cases of unrequited love, as in Shakespeare's *The Merry Wives of Windsor*, where Slender, who is rather hopelessly in love with one Anne Page, is moved to announce: 'Ah, sweet Anne Page!' Again, one might imagine today's unrequited lover preferring *oh*. The use of *ah* as a way of attracting attention is also a little odd today. It dates back to ME times, and an EModE example in the *OED* comes from John Redford's 1547 *Moral Play of Wit and Science* where one of the characters asks: 'Ah! syr, what tyme of day yst?'

If you have access to the internet, you might like to browse through Shakespeare's instances of *ah* as listed on the 'Shakespeare's Words' site (mentioned in 16.4). There are almost two hundred of them, though perhaps a good number of these have been added by later editors. You may find some that could be 'attention attractors', and the exercise will also give you a good idea of the variety of situations in which the word could be used. This in turn may lead you to suggest a few more areas of meaning to add to those we have discussed. Then take a look at Activity 17C (*A fico for Shakespeare's exclamations*). It discusses seven exclamations found in Shakespeare (though not all of them would qualify as 'pragmatic noise'). How many of them are still in use today? Where they are not found in PDE, how would their sense be conveyed nowadays?

It may seem like an anti-climax to end the chapter with the consideration of such 'non-words' as *ah*. But, in a sense, the recognition that such words are worthy of study is a climax that linguistics has reached – going deeper than before into the very matter of spoken interaction, into those apparently insignificant items that can carry so much information about what we are feeling and want to say. *Ah* is, you could argue, a very important word indeed.

Activity section

17A *Thou* and *you*, high and low

The sheep-stealing extract looks at low → high and high → low interactions. But what about high → high and low → low? Mark the following situations as high → high or low → low, and note whether *thee* or *you* is used.

(i) From Shakespeare's *Othello*. Othello (a high-ranking military man) is happy to see his (high-ranking) wife, Desdemona. He says: *It gives me wonder great as my content / To see you here before me. O my soul's joy!* Then, later in the play, here is Desdemona trying to persuade Othello to reinstate his lieutenant Cassio, whom she describes thus: *A man that all his time / Hath founded his good fortunes on your love, / Shared dangers with you.*

(ii) From an early comedy play, *Gammer Gurton's Needle* (*Gammer* means 'grandma'). The characters speaking are Hodge, Gammer Gurton's servant, and Tib, her maid:

Hodge: *I say, Tib, if thou be Tib, as I trow sure thou be, What devil make-ado is this, between our dame and thee?*

Tib: *Gog's bread, Hodge, thou had a good turn thou wert not here this while! It had been better for some of us to have been hence a mile;*

(iii) From Shakespeare's *The Comedy of Errors*. Dromio of Syracuse and Dromio of Ephesus are twin brothers, but have been apart for years, and have only just realized they are brothers:

Dromio of Syracuse: *There is a fat friend at your master's house That kitchened me for you today at dinner. She now shall be my sister, not my wife!*

Dromio of Ephesus: *Methinks you are my glass, and not my brother. I see by you I am a sweet-faced youth. Will you walk in to see their gossiping?*

Dromio of Syracuse: *Not I, sir. You are my elder.*

Dromio of Ephesus: *That's a question. How shall we try it?*

Dromio of Syracuse: *We'll draw cuts for the senior. Till then, lead thou first.*

17B   Ah, so that's what it means

(a) When do we use the word *ah* today? Before looking at the examples below, try to come up with some main uses.

(b) These sentences exemplify two common uses in PDE. Identify what these are. Think about the contexts in which these sentences might be said:
   (i) Ah, John. There you are. I was beginning to think you weren't coming.
   (ii) I can't work that out. Ah, wait a minute. Yes, now I understand it.
   (iii) Ah, but you're wrong. That's not why I did it.
   (iv) Ah yes, but on the other hand...

(c) If your first language is not English, consider what word your mother tongue would use in these sentences in the place of *ah*.

17C A fico for Shakespeare's exclamations AS

Here are examples, questions and explanations related to seven exclamations found in Shakespeare.[5] Sometimes you will certainly have to speculate a little when answering the questions; the purpose of asking them is to encourage you to think about the possible range of meanings of the exclamations. You can check your speculations in the *Answer section*:

(a) *Fico* (and *foh*)

> Pistol: 'Steal'? Foh,
> A fico for the phrase!
> (The Merry Wives of Windsor)

Fico is the Italian for a specific fruit. On one occasion, Pistol also uses the Spanish version of this word: *figo*. The word expresses contempt, and may often be accompanied by an obscene gesture. The English word for the same fruit is also used in PDE as an expression of contempt. What is the English name, and what is the expression? When is it used in PDE? The example above also contains another exclamation: *Foh*. It is a variant of *faugh* which is used even today to express disgust, especially of a smell (a 1700 example from the *OED* is: 'Faugh, the nauseous fellow! he stinks of poverty...').

(b) *Fie*

A common EModE interjection is *fie*. These two examples will suggest what emotion it expresses:

(i) In *Much Ado About Nothing*, Margaret makes a rather risqué comment. Hero replies: *Fie upon thee, art not ashamed?*

(ii) And here is Hamlet, at the beginning of one of his big soliloquies, using the word twice:

> How weary, stale, flat, and unprofitable
> Seem to me all the uses of this world!
> Fie on't, ah, fie, 'tis an unweeded garden
> That grows to seed.
>
> (Hamlet)

What might we say in PDE?

(c) *Go to*

Another common Shakespearean exclamation. What does it express, and how would we say it in PDE? Like a number of exclamations, is often said twice. In the first example, Ophelia tells her father Polonius that Hamlet has wooed her 'in honourable fashion'. Polonius is not pleased:

(i) *Ay, 'fashion' you may call it. Go to, go to.*

(Hamlet)

(ii) In this example from *All's Well That Ends Well*, the Countess is telling Helena not to be silly:

No more of this, Helena; go to, no more, lest it be rather thought you affect a sorrow than to have't.

(d) *Pish*

An expressive word, this, used in just two plays, *Othello* and *Henry V*. But what does it mean? The following two examples may help.

(i) Othello is in a bewildered state, thinking about how his wife Desdemona lost the precious handkerchief he gave her, and how she may have committed adultery with Cassio. He is about to have a fit:

It is not words that shakes me thus! Pish! Noses, ears, and lips. Is't possible? Confess? Handkerchief?

(ii) Nym and Pistol are always exchanging insults. Here they are in *Henry V* with swords drawn. An Iceland dog is a kind of sheepdog with pointed ears and a reputation for snapping:

Nym: Pish!
Pistol: *Pish for thee, Iceland dog! thou prick-eared cur of Iceland!*

(e) *Tush*

At the beginning of *Hamlet*, the two watchmen, Marcellus and Barnardo, tell Horatio about the ghost they have seen. Will it come again tonight? Horatio is sceptical. He says: *Tush, tush, 'twill not appear.*

This is another exclamation which is often said twice, as in the example above. What kind of emotion is being expressed here? How might one express it in Modern English?

(f) *Heigh-ho (hey-ho)*

In *Much Ado About Nothing*, Beatrice is lamenting that she does not have good looks (dark-skinned or *sunburnt* was not regarded as attractive) and would never find a husband:

Beatrice: *Good Lord, for alliance! Thus goes every one to the world but I, and I am sunburnt; I may sit in a corner and cry 'Heigh-ho for a husband'!*
Don Pedro: Lady Beatrice, I will get you one.

The words, sometimes spelt *hey-ho*, are also occasionally used in PDE in roughly the same sense. What is it?

(g) *Buzz, buzz*

The example below contains a strange exclamation, not used today at all. Perhaps the context provides a clue as to what it might mean?

Polonius (whom Hamlet regards as rather a tedious old fool) informs Hamlet that the actors have arrived. *The actors are come hither, my lord* he says (*Hamlet*). Hamlet's reply is: *Buzz, buzz*.

What might a twenty-first century Hamlet have said here?

Answer section

17C   A fico for Shakespeare's exclamations

(a) The fruit is the fig. In PDE it is still sometimes used in expressions like *He doesn't give a fig*, meaning 'He couldn't care less'.

(b) *Fie* (often followed by *on*) expresses disgust or indignation. There is no word in PDE that directly translates it. In (i) we might use *damn you*, and in (ii) *damn it*, or in both cases something stronger…

(c) *Go to* is often used to express impatience or disbelief. *Come come, come now, come off it* are ways of expressing it in PDE.

(d) *Pish* is used to expresses contempt, impatience or disgust. No PDE equivalent springs to mind. According to the *OED*, *pish* may be derived from *push*. The semantic idea is that when you disdain something, you push it off or away. The PDE phrase *get away with you* carries the same notion of 'pushing off', but in many contexts would not be a modern 'translation' of *pish*.

(e) *Tush* is used to express mild impatience, disbelief or disparagement. In PDE one might on occasions say *come off it*, or even *don't be silly*.

(f) *Heigh-ho* In PDE *hey-ho* is used to express resigned acceptance, with overtones of weariness or disappointment. This is close to what it means in the Shakespeare example.

(g) *Buzz, buzz*. The expression is used to express impatience, often at being told something already known. One (but not the only) use of the PDE phrase *So what's new?* expresses this sort of idea.

Further reading

Culpeper and Kytö (2010) is mentioned in the text in relation to pragmatic noise. In fact, the whole book is worth a look for what it has to say about EModE pragmatics.

Studies of historical pragmatics have been scarce up till now, but this is changing. Jucker and Taavitsainen (2013) does not deal solely with EModE but contains much that is relevant to that period.

Chapters 8 and 9 of D. Crystal (2008) deal with pragmatic issues, as does Chapter 5 of Johnson (2013).

Notes

1 From the deposition of *Christopher Egelston, of Hunstonworth, yoman, aged 40 years. Case no 61* Surtees Society 1845, 62–4.
2 McIntosh (1963) is one of those who points out this difference between EModE and languages like French and German.
3 Examples (a) and (b) are used by Jucker & Taavitsainen (2013), and are taken from the British National Corpus. Examples (c) is from Thomas (1983).
4 The phrase, which is also much applied to Japanese society, is Brown & Levinson's (1987: 230).
5 This activity is taken from Johnson (2013: 143).

18 'Well turned, and true filed lines'

Renaissance literature

This chapter is about EModE, especially Elizabethan, literature. Before reading, consider what you already know about the literature of the period. Think of the names of some authors and their works. What genres did they write in? Can you identify any preoccupations of the age that made appearance in the literature? And that man William Shakespeare? What do you know about his life and work?

In 1623, seven years after Shakespeare died, a collection of most of his plays appeared in what is called the First Folio; 'folio' was a paper size reserved for publications of some importance. Ben Jonson wrote a poem praising Shakespeare, which appeared at the front of the First Folio. At one point it speaks of his 'well turned, and true filed ['polished'] lines'.

Shakespeare was indeed the pinnacle of Elizabethan writing. But it was an age full of 'well turned, and true filed lines'. The EModE period had an interesting literature from beginning to end, and Elizabeth's reign yielded the richest.

18.1 Lyrical poetry

In the 1580s, the poet Philip Sidney wrote a sequence of love poems called *Astrophel and Stella*. In this one, the poet addresses the moon, alone and 'wan' in the sky, and wonders whether it is, like him, suffering from unhappy love:

His Lady's Cruelty

> With how sad steps, O moon, thou climb'st the skies!
> How silently, and with how wan a face!
> What! may it be that even in heavenly place
> That busy archer his sharp arrows tries?
> Sure, if that long-with-love-acquainted eyes
> Can judge of love, thou feel'st a lover's case:
> I read it in thy looks; thy languished grace
> To me, that feel the like, thy state descries.
> Then, even of fellowship, O Moon, tell me,

Is constant love deemed there but want of wit?
Are beauties there as proud as here they be?
Do they above love to be loved, and yet
Those lovers scorn whom that love doth possess?
Do they call 'virtue' there—ungratefulness?

Addressing an inanimate object, part of nature (the moon), developing an idea at length (that the moon is a forlorn lover) – these are common Renaissance poetic characteristics. Take a moment to understand what the poet is saying, not worrying if there are details of meaning that escape you. The *busy archer* in line 4 is Cupid, the god of desire, and *if that* in line 5 simply means 'if'. Notice also the lengthy compound in line 5: *long-with-love-acquainted*. Unusual compounds like this were mentioned in 15.4.3. Line 12 is a little tricky. The words *above* and *love* do not go together; it is not 'above love', but 'they above' (i.e. in the sky), 'love to be loved'.

Once you have a general understanding of the poem, think about its form. How many lines are there? In 11.1 we saw a way of indicating rhyme by using the letters of the alphabet. The rhyme scheme of the first four lines is 'abba'. Use letters to show the rhyme scheme for the rest of Sidney's poem.

It will also be useful to work out where the strong stresses fall in the lines, something you will be asked to do several times in this chapter. You might use the 'DUMdiDUM' method. Read the lines to yourself, aloud, exaggerating where the stressed syllables come. Then replace the words with DUM (for a strongly stressed syllable) and 'di' for a weakly stressed one. This makes the first line 'diDUMdiDUMdiDUMdiDUMdiDUM'. A way of representing this in writing is to use 'S' for strong syllables, 'W' for weak ones, so the first line would be 'WSWSWSWSWS'. How many strong stresses are there in each line of Sidney's poem? Try working this out for several lines.

The poem has fourteen lines. Lyrical poems of exactly this length, and with the formal characteristics we shall now look at, are called **sonnets**. They were extremely popular in Elizabethan literature, and indeed in later times. The exact format which sonnets took varied from poet to poet, and indeed part of the genre's attraction was that it lent itself to variations. The rhyme scheme in Sidney's poem is 'abba abba cdcd ee', a common sequence in many Italian sonnets. A more common sequence in English poetry, including Shakespeare, is 'abab cdcd efef gg'. Sometimes (though not always), the fourteen lines fall into three groups of four lines, and these are called **quatrains** (related to the French word *quatre* meaning four). The final two rhyming lines are a couplet (a term we came across in 11.1). Sometimes these rhyme groupings could be used, as in Sidney's sonnet, to reflect 'sense groupings'. The poem's argument, focus, or topic may change with each new quatrain, and the concluding couplet often carries some final, pithy, statement. Sometimes (again as here), there is a particularly noticeable 'change of direction' in the argument at the beginning of the third quatrain, in line 9. This was called the *volta* in Italian (meaning 'turning point'). Look through Sidney's sonnet and take note of these formal characteristics.

Sonnets originated in Italy, and the poet Petrarch (Francesco Petrarca, 1304–74) was an early exponent. He wrote a collection of sonnets to one Laura, whom he loved, but who was unattainable (she was already married; the theme of unrequited love is very strong in many sonnets). Petrarch's work swept Europe. As the scholar Gabriel Harvey wrote: 'All the noblest Italian, French, and Spanish Poets, haue in their seuerall Veines Petrarchised.' The person who 'Petrarchized' in English was the poet Thomas Wyatt (1503–42). He translated many Petrarchan sonnets, and wrote a number of imitations of his own. He also altered the sonnet form, adding the final couplet we see in Sidney's version.

Philip Sidney, the writer of our sonnet, was regarded as one of the best Elizabethan poets. His 'unattainable lover' was probably one Penelope Devereux. She was represented in the sonnet cycle by Stella (the Latin for 'star'), and he was Astrophel (Greek *astro* = star, and *phel*= lover). Sidney also wrote a prose pastoral romance called *Arcadia*, and an influential *Defence of Poetry*, which was partly also a 'defence of English', since he argues in it that English was a language sufficiently elegant to carry poetic expression.

Sidney has been chosen here to represent a large body of lyrical poetry of the Elizabethan age, far too large to consider in any detail. Another important name is Edmund Spenser (1552–59). His most famous work is a very long poem called *The Faerie Queene*, published in 1590. It is an allegory which praises Queen Elizabeth and deals indirectly with religious conflicts. As far as sonnets are concerned, it is a form in which (as in so many others) Shakespeare excelled. His sonnets are without equal. Why not take a look at some of his better-known ones? Some first lines are: 'When to the sessions of sweet silent thought', 'My mistress' eyes are nothing like the sun', and 'That time of year thou mayst in me behold'. You will find the poems online or in poetry anthologies.

Earlier you were asked to count strong stresses in the lines of Sidney's sonnet. Since we will be asking similar questions about other passages in this chapter, we will leave the answer till later.

18.2 Drama

We are going to continue to find Shakespeare's name everywhere. It is certainly dominant in the field of drama, a flourishing genre in Elizabethan times. Here is a 'Rough Guide' to a play written by a dramatist other than Shakespeare.

Dr Faustus

- **Background:** A play with its first known performance in 1594. It is based on a German legend about a sixteenth-century conjurer and necromancer (a communicator with the dead). The story was later used by the German writer Goethe, whose poetic drama *Faust* was completed in 1832.

- **Authorship**: The dramatist Christopher Marlowe (1564–93). He was a man of violent disposition, who led a stormy life which ended in a brawl in a tavern. Other well-known plays by him are *The Jew of Malta* and *Edward II*.
- **Content**: Faustus, who is a scholar, becomes dissatisfied with traditional types of knowledge and takes to magic. He makes contact with Mephastophilis, a demon in the service of Lucifer, the Devil. Faust agrees to sell his soul to the Devil in return for twenty-four years in which Mephastophilis will serve him and grant his every wish. A number of scenes follow in which Faustus travels around in space and time (like an early version of Dr Who), having all his desires met. This includes a meeting with Helen of Troy – 'Was this the face that launched a thousand ships?', he asks when he sees her. But Faustus suffers huge anguish as the twenty-four years draw to a close. He is finally carried off to hell.
- **Value**: Jonson spoke of 'Marlowe's mighty line' and his poetry can be memorable. As the quotation below shows, it could also be passionate (as well as a little bombastic – a characteristic Renaissance trait). In dramatic terms, the play can be seen as an attempt to portray on the stage actions spanning a length of time. In philosophical terms, the play can be interpreted as being about Renaissance man trying to break away from the bonds of a medieval universe ruled by God.
- **Quotation**: The twenty-four years are up, and Faustus' time on earth is soon to end. He is getting agitated:

> The stars move still, time runs, the clock will strike,
> The devil will come, and Faustus must be damn'd.
> O, I'll leap up to my God!—Who pulls me down?—
> See, see, where Christ's blood streams in the firmament!
> One drop would save my soul, half a drop: ah, my Christ!—
> Ah, rend not my heart for naming of my Christ!
> Yet will I call on him: O, spare me, Lucifer!—
> Where is it now? 'tis gone: and see, where God
> Stretcheth out his arm, and bends his ireful brows!
> Mountains and hills, come, come, and fall on me,
> And hide me from the heavy wrath of God!
> No, no!

Activity 18A (*Faustus questions*) draws attention to some linguistic aspects of this quotation. You may want to look at it now.

The full title of Marlowe's play is *The Tragical History of Doctor Faustus*. Though the play has its comic moments (Faustus sees fit to spend some of his twenty-four years playing practical jokes), it is easy to see from the summary given above why the play was regarded as a tragedy. As it happens, the next section's 'Rough Guide' is also for a tragedy. But the Elizabethans wrote comedies too. We have seen a short example of comedy in Shakespeare's 'rogues in buckrom' passage (in 13.4). One of the earliest examples of a comic play was the anonymous *A Ryght Pithy, Pleasaunt and merie Comedie: Intytuled Gammer Gurtons Nedle*, known as *Gammer Gurton's Needle* for short. It was written in about 1553. In the story, Grandma Gurton loses her sewing needle, which finally reappears inside the breeches of her servant Hodge. The comic potential is clear.

Ben Jonson (1572–1637) was chief among the comic satirists of the period, and his plays include *Volpone*, a satire on miserliness. In *The Alchemist* he attacks alchemy and those who are duped by it. The nineteenth-century critic Coleridge said the play had one of the most perfect plots in literature.

18.3   William Shakespeare

William Shakespeare was born in Stratford-upon-Avon in 1564, and became a member of a London acting troupe called the 'Lord Chamberlain's Men' in 1594 (they changed their name to the 'King's Men' in 1603 when James I became king). From 1599, they acted at London's Globe Theatre – a theatre that has been rebuilt and revived in recent times. At the end of his life, Shakespeare retired to Stratford, where he died in 1616.

Shakespeare's plays can be roughly divided into Comedies, Histories, Tragedies, and Romances. Well known among the Comedies are *A Midsummer Night's Dream*, *As You Like It* and *Twelfth Night*. Plays like *Richard III*, *Henry IV (Parts 1 and 2)*, and *Henry V* cover English history, while the topic is classical history in *Julius Caesar* and *Coriolanus*, among others. The four major tragedies are *Othello*, *Macbeth*, *King Lear*, and *Hamlet* (there is a 'Rough Guide' about this play below). The Romances were written in Shakespeare's later years. They are plays, often with tragic as well as comic elements, but which have pastoral or magical conclusions. The best known are *The Winter's Tale* and *The Tempest*.

Though these divisions are useful, it is a characteristic of Shakespeare's plays to mix genres. Some of the comedies contain elements very close to tragedy, and the tragedies sometimes have moments of comedy. Indeed, some of his plays (like *Measure for Measure* and *Troilus and Cressida*) are called 'problem plays', partly because of their extreme mixture of tragic and comic elements. Notice, too, that the amusing 'rogues in buckrom' interlude (involving Shakespeare's comic masterpiece, the character of Falstaff) comes from the history play, *Henry IV, Part 1*, which is otherwise full of serious and sometimes tragic events.

Here is a 'Rough Guide' to one of Shakespeare's best-known plays:

Hamlet

- **Background**: Perhaps Shakespeare's most celebrated tragedy. The 'revenge tragedy' was a popular Renaissance genre of which Thomas Kyd's *Spanish*

Tragedy was an example. Like many of Shakespeare's plays, *Hamlet* appeared in various forms. The full version most used today lasts almost four hours on the stage, one of Shakespeare's longest. It was probably completed in 1601, two years before Queen Elizabeth died.

- **Authorship:** Information about Shakespeare is given in the text.
- **Content:** Old Hamlet, King of Denmark, has died. His brother Claudius has married his widow Gertrude and taken over the throne. The dead Hamlet appears as a ghost, and reveals that he was killed by Claudius. He commands Hamlet, his son, to avenge his murder by killing Claudius. But young Hamlet is of a reflective, scholarly disposition, and not a man of action at all. He procrastinates, feigning madness for a while to gain time. Disillusioned with women because of his mother's remarriage, he forsakes his beloved Ophelia, and she dies of grief. Hamlet also murders her father, impetuously mistaking him for Claudius. As a result of a number of failed attempts by Hamlet to act decisively, many of the characters in the play, including Hamlet himself, end up dead.
- **Value:** The character of Hamlet is complex and well-drawn; he is one of English literature's best-known figures. He is a thinker – Baugh (1948) calls him 'the perfect tabernacle for the questioning modern brain'. The tragedy is that he is required to do something he is mentally ill-equipped to do. As in others of Shakespeare's plays, the theme of 'appearance versus reality' looms large in *Hamlet*, as the hero struggles to make sense of the situation he is in. His struggles are expressed in a number of celebrated soliloquies (speeches expressing thoughts aloud), the most famous of all being the one below.
- **Quotation:** Hamlet's famous soliloquy finds him thinking about life and death. Here is the beginning of the speech:

> To be, or not to be – that is the question;
> Whether 'tis nobler in the mind to suffer
> The slings and arrows of outrageous fortune
> Or to take arms against a sea of troubles
> And by opposing end them. To die, to sleep –
> No more – and by a sleep to say we end
> The heartache and the thousand natural shocks
> That flesh is heir to. 'Tis a consummation
> Devoutly to be wished. To die, to sleep –
> To sleep – perchance to dream. Ay, there's the rub.
> For in that sleep of death what dreams may come
> When we have shuffled off this mortal coil
> Must give us pause.

Activity 18B (*Hamlet questions*) looks at some linguistic elements of the quotation.

If you go back to our 'rogues in buckrom' passage in 13.4, you will find that it is written in prose. Shakespeare's sonnets – mentioned earlier in 18.1 – were written in rhymed verse, of course. But much of his dramatic writing uses a kind of verse that is unrhymed. The *Hamlet* quotation is an example, as indeed is Marlowe's Dr Faustus speech. This type of unrhymed verse is called **blank verse**.

Much blank verse, and indeed much Elizabethan rhymed verse (including the sonnets) use a rhythmical scheme (or **metre**), called the iambic pentameter, which we will now take a look at.

18.4 The iambic pentameter

To understand metre, you have to be able to recognize and count syllables and stresses. Syllables are relatively easy to recognize, though the concept of the syllable (like many linguistic concepts) is difficult to define in a rigorous way. According to the *Shorter Oxford English Dictionary*, a syllable is 'a unit of pronunciation having one vowel sound, with or without surrounding consonants, forming the whole or a part of a word'. The word *cat* has one syllable, *cattle* has two, and *catastrophe* has four.

Stress relates to how much prominence is given to a syllable. It plays an important role in English pronunciation, where we like to give strong stress to some syllables, weak stress to others (which is not the case in all languages). Though it may be a useful shorthand in some contexts to talk about syllables being **stressed** or **unstressed**, there are in fact many recognizable degrees of stress in English; you can, for example, have **primary stress, secondary stress** and so on.

On most occasions, counting syllables and stresses in poetry is easier than the description above makes it sound. Yes, there will be complications and cases of uncertainty. But as long as you are prepared to avoid agonizing and do not expect absolute certainly, you can get quite far.

In the quotations we have looked at in this chapter – Sidney's sonnet, Marlowe's *Dr Faustus* and Shakespeare's *Hamlet* – you were asked to count stressed syllables. Complications and uncertainties apart, you will probably have arrived at the figure of five. The lines usually have five strong stresses. They are what are called **pentameters** (*penta* is the Greek for 'five').

If you run the DUMdiDUM test on the lines of all three passages, you will find that in general (again, with exceptions) the sequence is diDUMdiDUMdiDUM-diDUMdiDUM. So for the first line of Sidney's sonnet:

With	how	sad	steps	O	moon	thou	climb'st	the	skies
di	DUM	di	DUM	di	DUM	di	DUM	di	DUM

There are, in other words, five sequences of 'diDUM'. Or, using the symbols 'W' and 'S', we have five sets of 'WS'. Sequences like these, which make up lines of poetry, are called **feet**, and this particular foot (a weak stress followed by a strong one) is called an **iamb**. Another common metrical foot has the opposite configuration – strong + weak – and is called the **trochee**. Here are some **trochaic** lines from Shakespeare's *Macbeth*, though there is a final weak syllable missing from each line:

> Liver of blaspheming Jew,
> Gall of goat, and slips of yew
> Silver'd in the moon's eclipse.

You can now see what an iambic pentameter (IP) is. It is a sequence of five iambic feet – five 'diDUMs' strung together. It was an extremely common metre in Elizabethan times as well as later. It is certainly the overall pattern found in the pieces of verse we have looked at here.

But we have to say 'overall pattern' because there are lines which do not conform entirely to the IP sequence. Indeed, if all lines were to conform, the effect would be tedious – relentless waves of diDUMdiDUM. Maybe you found examples of non-conforming lines in our quotations. Before reading on, look at the lines below. Try and specify what is irregular about them:

Sure, if that long-with-love-acquainted eyes	*Sidney*, line 5
The devil will come, and Faustus must be damn'd	*Faustus*, line 2
Or to take arms against a sea of troubles	*Hamlet*, line 4

To conform rigidly to the IP pattern, Sidney's line would involve the first word (*sure*) being unstressed and the second word (*if*) stressed. To read the line in that way would be quite unnatural. Instead of the first four syllables being WSWS, what we have here is SWWS. This is sometimes called a **trochaic inversion**, because the first foot is 'inverted' from a WS iamb into a SW trochee.[1] You have a similar irregularity in the *Faustus* line. If you try to read it as a regular IP, many of the stresses fall in unnatural places. The first two stresses are fine (WS), but then you have two syllables (*-vil will*) which are unstressed. So the line's first five stresses are WSWWS. At the beginning of the *Hamlet* line, we seem to have the same irregular sequence (SWWS) that we found in the Sidney's example. Then there is another irregularity at the end. IPs are supposed to end with a strong stress, on a 'DUM'. But this line ends with a 'di' – the last word is *troubles*: SW. This is called a **feminine ending**. All these irregularities are common in predominantly IP verse, and skilful writers like Shakespeare will use irregularities for artistic effect. If you want practice at identifying IPs with and without irregularities, take a look at Activity 18C (*IP or not IP – that is the question*).

18.5 The turning tide

This has been a very short survey of a very long period of rich literature. You could fill in the picture a little more by writing some 'Rough Guides' of your own. Activity 18D (*More EModE 'Rough Guides'*) invites you to do this.

Queen Elizabeth – the last Tudor monarch – died in 1603, and James I – the first Stuart – became the new ruler. His arrival heralded a new age. We may still regard this as the EModE period, but during the seventeenth century – the last century this book covers – attitudes towards language changed dramatically. So too did views about good writing and literature. Even Shakespeare, so much praised for his genius, starts to come in for linguistic criticism. Thus the seventeenth-century poet John Dryden, although he loved Shakespeare, says that 'his whole style is ... pestered with figurative expressions', and complains of 'his serious swelling into bombast'. And even Jonson – the very one who praised Shakespeare's 'well turned, and true filed lines' – also accuses him of, on occasions, using 'monstrous syntax'. Some tide or another has clearly turned. This tidal movement is the topic of the next chapter.

Activity section

18A   Faustus questions   AS

(a) Some things to find in the passage:
  (i) a word which (because of its suffix) looks as if it might be of Romance origin (hint: look in the first five lines; the suffix is discussed in 15.4.1);
  (ii) an example of a negative sentence not using do-support (this was described in 16.3);
  (iii) variation between the -eth and -s suffixes (as described in 16.2);
  (iv) the use of a suffix to change a noun into an adjective;
  (v) inversion of subject and verb following an adverb (see 10.2.4).
(b) Count the number of stresses in the lines. In some lines you will find this difficult, but you may be able to come up with a figure that is generally true. Work through a few lines.
(c) Our Marlowe quotation was taken from an edition done by the Rev. Alexander Dyce (1798–1868). Notice how elaborate the punctuation is. Count how many punctuation marks there are (count [!–] as two).

18B   Hamlet questions   AS

(a) Three words which are still used in PDE are *outrageous*, *shuffle* and *rub*. But their modern meanings do not seem to quite fit here. What do you think they meant?
(b) *Consummation*. What language do you think this word might come from? Does it sound Germanic or Romance? Another interesting word is *coil*. If you have access to *OED*, look it up. What is the date of its first citation? Find out something about the word's etymology.

(c) A question about the rhetorical structure of the speech: the phrase 'To die, to sleep' is repeated (in lines 5 and 9). Look at what is said after the phrase each time; how does it differ?

(d) How many stressed syllables are there in most lines?

18C   IP or not IP – that is the question   AS

Here are five Shakespeare quotations. Some lines are regular IPs, some are irregular IPs, and there is one which is not an IP at all. Identify stresses in the lines using the 'WS' method. For each example, decide whether it is a regular or irregular IP, or not an IP at all. What IP irregularities are shown? What can you say about the one non-IP example?

(i) The more my wrong, the more his spite appears (*The Taming of the Shrew*)
(ii) And beg thy pardon ere he do accuse thee (*Richard II*)
(iii) That thou no more wilt weigh my eyelids down (*Henry IV, Part 2*)
(iv) Earth hath swallowed all my hopes but she (*Romeo and Juliet*)
(v) Thrice the brinded cat hath mew'd
Thrice, and once the hedge-pig whin'd. (*Macbeth*)

18D   More EModE 'Rough Guides'

Use the internet or other sources to write your own 'Rough Guides' to some or all of the works below, all but one of which have been mentioned in the text. Use the same headings as in the text: background/authorship/content/value/quotations – though for some entries you may not find something to say under every heading. If you can work together with others, you might share the load, doing one 'Rough Guide' each, and ending up with several which together give a more detailed picture of the period's literature. The works are:

Sidney's *Defence of Poetry*
Gammer Gurton's Needle
Spenser's *The Faerie Queene*
Shakespeare's *Romeo and Juliet*
Jonson's *The Alchemist*
Shakespeare's sonnets

Answer section

Activity 18A

(a) (i) *firmament*. An ME word from Latin *firmamentum*; (ii) *rend not my heart*; (iii) line 9 has *stretcheth* and *bends*; (iv) *ireful*; (v) *yet will I call*.

(b) This issue will be considered in 18.4.
(c) 37.

Activity 18B

(a) *outrageous* could mean 'cruel'; In both EModE and PDE, *shuffle* could mean 'to move without lifting the feet'. Shakespeare may have been responsible for *shuffle off*, meaning 'discard', 'do away with'. *Rub* could mean 'impediment'.
(b) *Consummation* is related to the Latin *consummatio*, and comes into English from the Anglo-Norman *consumatiun*. It is certainly a Romance word. *Coil* means 'bustle'. The first *OED* citation for this sense is 1567. The etymology is uncertain. Perhaps it comes from the Gaelic word *coleid* meaning 'stir'.
(c) Hamlet is thinking about what happens when you *die, sleep*. After the phrase he considers two possibilities. The first is oblivion, the second is a state where we may have bad dreams.
(d) This issue will be considered in 18.4.

Activity 18C

Examples (i) and (iii) are regular IPs, (ii) has a feminine ending, and (iv) shows an irregularity we have not come across. One way of analysing it is to say it is a regular IP, except that there is a weak syllable missing at the beginning of the line. Example (v) is not an IP at all. Instead of 'WS' you have 'SW' through the lines. These are not iambs, but **trochees**. The lines are **trochaic**. Notice also that there are four rather than five strong stresses. The lines are not pentameters, but **tetrameters** (Greek *tetra* means four).

Further reading

Hadfield (2000) focuses on literature and has short chapters on important authors as well as examples of their work. It also has useful background chapters.

Evans (1994) is a collection of Elizabethan sonnets, with a useful introduction.

Trussler (2006) provides essential information on some major plays. Each chapter is like a longer version of our 'Rough Guides'.

For a very readable introduction to Shakespeare, take a look at B. Crystal (2008).

There are plenty of biographies of Shakespeare available. Though Shapiro (2005) focuses on just one year (1599), it provides a vivid account of the writer at an important moment in his life.

Note

1 Wright (1988) uses the term 'trochaic inversion', while Attridge (1995) has 'inversion'.

'A settled, certain and corrected language'

The seventeenth century

This chapter is about the seventeenth century – the closing part of the EModE period. We will take a quick look at the century's history, which was dominated by the English Civil War. We also consider its 'language history'. The relatively unbridled linguistic developments of the Renaissance gave way to a desire for a more controlled, settled language, and one able to handle the century's interest in scientific development. The chapter considers some language points, along with the literature of the period. In a final section, we look forward to what happened to English in the eighteenth century and thereafter.

Some areas to think about before you read:

- The seventeenth century wanted English to become a language capable of handling scientific thought. Think about the 'language of science' today. What characteristics make it different from everyday English? More generally, what makes a language able to express scientific concepts and arguments?
- It was in the seventeenth century that the need for a comprehensive dictionary of the language came to be realized. What kinds of information should a dictionary contain? Take a look at a dictionary you use a lot and see exactly what information it provides. But think also about the ideal as well as the reality: what would the ideal dictionary be like?
- Languages go through periods of unbridled creative development and periods of consolidation. What period are we going through today (with English, or with your L1 if different)? Why? – what makes people want 'creative development' or 'consolidation' at a particular historical moment?
- Some topics to find out about before you read: Oliver Cromwell, the *Mayflower* and its journey to America, Francis Bacon, the French Academy, attempts to set up an English Academy, Samuel Johnson's *Dictionary of the English Language*.

19.1 From 'stony couch to feather bed': some general history

Queen Elizabeth I died on 24th March 1603. On the same day, James VI of Scotland was proclaimed her successor. His claim to the throne of England came about because Elizabeth died childless and his great-grandmother was Margaret Tudor, Henry VIII's oldest sister. James had been king of Scotland almost from birth. Within two weeks of Elizabeth's death, he was on the road down to London. He was impressed by the wealth of the country he was about to rule. He was, he felt, 'swapping a stony couch for a deep feather bed'. A lavish reception was laid on for him at a house called Theobalds in Hertfordshire, owned by one Sir Robert Cecil. James loved the house, and eventually came to own it. In fact, he died there in 1625.

James, the sixth of Scotland and the first of England, started the Stuart dynasty. He did many good things, including supporting cultural life. A great lover of theatrical masques, he was also responsible for the most influential translation of the Bible into English – the so-called 'King James Bible'. On the negative side, he was slovenly, drank too much, and had several characteristics which helped to spark the event which dominated seventeenth-century English history: the Civil War. One of these characteristics (according to some historians at least) was that, though married, he had homosexual tendencies which led him to choose male favourites in court notable for their looks rather than their efficiency. Especially inept was George Villiers, First Duke of Buckingham, possibly James I's lover. Much ill-feeling was created by the king's advancement of him. In addition, James was a firm believer in the 'divine right of kings', the belief that a sovereign derived authority from God and was not accountable to humans. This led him to treat Parliament badly at a time when that institution was growing in strength. With his good and bad sides, James really did seem to deserve what the French King Henry IV said of him: he was 'the wisest fool in Christendom'.

James died at the age of 58, and was succeeded by his son, Charles I. Though very unlike his father, Charles shared similar unfortunate characteristics. He kept the unpopular Buckingham as a favourite. He too supported culture, but this led to a huge expenditure of money on a lavish banqueting hall in the centre of London, with paintings supplied by Rubens. Van Dyck was appointed the court painter. To make financial matters worse, Charles wanted money to support various military campaigns against Spain, France and Scotland. Such financial demands were very unpopular and put the king in conflict with Parliament. They refused him the funds.

There were also religious conflicts. The Catholic/Protestant split continued to divide the country, and indeed the whole of Europe. Much of England was Protestant, with the Puritans – a group particularly concerned to rid the Church of Catholic influences – in ascendancy. But there were still many Catholics in the land and their possible return to influence was cause for concern. Charles was a Protestant, but it was feared that he had Catholic leanings. His wife (Henrietta Maria of France) was a Catholic, and she had been given permission to practise her religion at court. Charles' brand of Protestantism was also rather conservative. He believed, for example, in the hierarchy of bishops and priests, which was far from Puritan taste.

Money and religion brought the king into conflict with Parliament. The situation was made worse because, like his father, Charles firmly believed in the divine right of kings. He consequently held Parliament in low regard, and when (as happened on a number of occasions) it refused to bow to his will, he dissolved it. Civil war was on the way. The first military clash was in 1642. In the early battles, the advantage went backwards and forwards, from 'Cavaliers' (supporters of the king) to 'Roundheads' (Parliament supporters). Then the Scots joined in (against the king), and a Roundhead leader of military talent, Oliver Cromwell, established a 'New Model Army' – a group of professional soldiers who could be moved around the country as required. The king was eventually defeated and was convicted of treason (interestingly enough, against the people – normally treason is regarded as against the sovereign). He was beheaded. One of the last thoughts he passed on to the world was that 'a subject and a sovereign are clean different things'. Ironically perhaps, given how 'conservatively minded' the English are, they had managed a rebellion 133 years before the American War of Independence and 147 years before the French Revolution. Charles's son, also named Charles, fled to France, and England became a 'commonwealth' – a republic.

But things did not go well for the new republic. Parliament turned out to be ineffective. Cromwell ended up doing what Charles I had done as king – disbanding Parliament when it was not working well. In 1653, Cromwell lost patience, went to Parliament, and told them: 'You have sat too long for any good you have been doing lately … Depart, I say; and let us have done with you. In the name of God, go!' The country desperately needed a strong leader, and by 1657, Parliament was ready to make Cromwell king. He declined the offer, but did become the country's 'Lord Protectorate' – to many eyes, king in all but name. Then, in 1658, Cromwell fell ill and died. By this time, the country had had enough and wanted a king back. Charles was summoned from abroad, and there was rejoicing in the streets as he was crowned Charles II. The Restoration, as it was called, occurred in 1660.

Two events in the 1660s were interpreted by some as God's punishment for killing the king. There was the Great Plague in London (1665–66), in which some 100,000 people died. This was followed in 1666 by the Great Fire of London, with over 13,000 houses being destroyed. A succession of Stuart kings and queens followed Charles II: James II, William III, Mary II and Queen Anne, who ruled until 1714. On her death, Parliament avoided the possibility of a future Catholic monarch by inviting George of Hanover to become king. He was German, a foreigner, and could not speak English. But he was at least a Protestant. George I was the first of the Hanoverian dynasty.

Throughout the seventeenth century, another very important development was taking place: the beginnings of British colonialization in various parts of the world. Britain had in fact made a slow start, and in the sixteenth century it was the Spanish and Portuguese who led the way in exploring, and colonizing, parts of the world outside Europe. A few Elizabethan adventurers, like

Sir Walter Raleigh, explored westwards, and, in his case, attempted to set up a colony in Virginia. But it was in James I's reign that colonial efforts really started in earnest. In 1606, he signed a charter allowing companies to explore the eastern seaboard of what is now the United States, and in 1607, three ships carrying settlers arrived in Virginia and founded Jamestown, named after the king. Incidentally, today's Charleston in South Carolina takes its name from Charles II.

James was anxious to keep the non-conformist religious beliefs of the Puritans under control. They refused to accept the religious authority of either king or Church, and at a religious conference in 1604 (just after James was crowned), he made his feelings towards the Puritans very clear: 'I shall make them conform or I will harry them out of the land or else do worse'. Being harried out of the land was exactly what happened to some of them, and in 1620, a hundred and one Puritans set sail from Plymouth in the *Mayflower*, fleeing religious persecution. They landed at what is now Cape Cod in Massachusetts and established the town of 'New Plymouth' (now called just Plymouth). In 1621, they gave thanks to God for their good harvest. This was the first American Thanksgiving.

Britain was looking to other parts of the world as well. In 1617, the British East India Company was given permission by the Mughal Emperor to trade in India, and a trading post was set up on the Indian west coast in 1619. These were the beginnings of an empire that, by 1922, controlled about a fifth of the world's population.

19.2   The Royal Society: scientific and linguistic aspirations

19.2.1   Science, and a 'corrected' language

In 1626, Francis Bacon – a politician, statesman and scholar – was travelling in the London area with a colleague. As was often the case, Bacon's thoughts were on scientific experimentation, and on this occasion he was considering whether snow, being cold, might be used to preserve meat. To find out, he bought a chicken and stuffed it with snow. It ended badly. In the words of Aubrey, whose collection of short biographies – *Brief Lives* – includes one on Bacon: 'the snow so chilled him, that he immediately fell ... extremely ill', and after a few days died. He really did, one might say, sacrifice his life for science. Bacon's influence on seventeenth-century scientific thinking was great. Take a look at CW19.1 (*Francis Bacon: a 'nerve of genius'*), which tells you more about him.

Bacon's approach to scientific enquiry (his so-called 'New Method') was an important stimulus to the growth of interest in science in seventeenth-century England. When the dust of the Civil War had settled, and England once more had a king, it was proposed that a Royal Society should be established – an idea which Charles II supported. In 1667, the English scholar and theologian

Thomas Sprat wrote a history of the early years of the Society. Its aim was 'to render our country, a land of experimental knowledge'. Language came into the picture because it was recognized that if science was to be managed properly, it was important that the language in which it was expressed (Sprat called it 'the manner of discourse') should be appropriate.

Did not English already possess an appropriate 'manner of discourse'? To many concerned with language matters in the first half of the seventeenth century, the answer was 'most certainly not'. There was much unhappiness with the state of English both at that time and in the recent past. The run-up to Civil War, and the War itself, was a time when freedom in almost everything, including language use, was tolerated. The air was filled with controversy and lively public disputations, and censorship of expression was almost non-existent. Numerous religious groups with exotic names had sprung up. There were the Levellers, the Ranters, the Diggers – all expressing different versions of religious non-conformity. There were also all manner of exotic beliefs followed: in witchcraft, alchemy, astrology. A word sometimes used to characterize many of these groups was 'Enthusiasts'. Today the word refers to someone with an interest in a particular area, but in EModE it had a much stronger meaning – it was someone 'possessed by prophetic frenzy'. Being 'enthusiastic' was something highly antipathetic to the emerging scientific ethos. The Enthusiasts' linguistic habits were as excessive as their beliefs. During the Civil War period, Thomas Sprat noted, English 'received many fantastical terms, which were introduced by our religious sects, and many outlandish phrases which ... writers and translators brought in'. He was disparaging about the 'enchantments of enthusiasm'.

The language of the previous century was no better. Many of what the Renaissance regarded as linguistic virtues – copious, rich, figurative, often outlandish language – came in for attack. Sprat is full of dismissive phrases to describe it: 'vicious abundance of phrase', 'tricks of metaphors', volubility of tongue'. Figurative speech comes in for particular attack. In his *Essay Concerning Human Understanding*, the philosopher John Locke joined in. He has a chapter entitled 'Abuse of words'. 'If we would speak of things as they are', he says, 'we must allow that all the art of rhetoric ... [is] for nothing else but to insinuate wrong ideas ... and mislead the judgment'. Renaissance linguistic virtues really were becoming Restoration linguistic vices. As we saw at the end of Chapter 18 (18.5), even the language of Shakespeare came in for criticism; look back there to remind yourself what Dryden and Jonson said.

If English was to become a fit vehicle for scientific development, it needed to be 'corrected', or 'cleaned-up'. Linguistic 'clean-up operations' were already taking place in other parts of Europe. The earliest attempt was in Florence in the 1580s, where the Accademia della Crusca was set up. *Crusca* is the Italian for 'bran', the husks remaining in the flour-making process. The idea was that the new academy would 'sift through' the language, 'separating the wheat from the chaff'. In France, a French Academy was proposed in 1635. Its aim was 'to labor with all the care and diligence possible, to give exact rules to our language, to render it capable of treating the arts and sciences'.

Though the English eventually baulked at the idea of an English Academy, the Royal Society acted a little like one. In 1664, it set up a committee to look at ways of 'improving' the English language. It was headed by one of the Society's founding members, John Wilkins, and had twenty-two members, including John Dryden, Thomas Sprat, and the writer and diarist John Evelyn. The committee never presented a final report, but the direction in which it was moving was clear. Rhetoric and all the 'devices of fancy' would have to go. Indeed, to Sprat's way of thinking, 'eloquence ought to be banished out of all civil societies'; 'we generally love to have reason set out in plain, undeceiving expressions'. Incidentally, avoidance of 'coarseness' was also important, and much store was put on politeness. It is no wonder that Shakespeare came in for linguistic criticism; if you need reminding of how coarse he could be, look back to the final paragraph of 13.4, where Falstaff lets loose a string of insults at Price Hal.

19.2.2   A 'settled' and 'certain' language

In 1649, a businessman turned scholar, George Snell, published a book entitled *The Right Teaching of Useful Knowledge*. In it he talks about the necessity for English to become a 'settled, certain and corrected language'. The section above deals with the 'corrected' part. 'Settled' and 'certain' were also important. Although, as we saw in 13.2, English had made huge strides in taking over the role of Latin as a language suitable for learned communication, the classical language had by no means entirely lost that role. It is significant that Bacon, who had been educated largely in Latin, used that language extensively. Indeed, *The Advancement of Learning* was the only work of his to be published in English. That was in 1605. Not that much changed during the seventeenth century. Eighty years later, in 1687, Isaac Newton was to write his *Philosophiæ Naturalis Principia Mathematica* also in Latin. The choice of language partly reflects uncertainty about the 'durability' of English (and, incidentally, the other European vernaculars). Here is what Bacon says about the problem: 'It is true, my labours are now most set to have those works, which I had formerly published ... well translated into Latin. For these modern languages will, at one time or other, play the bankrupt with books': 'play the bankrupt' meant 'prove untrustworthy'. The same thought was put more poetically by another person involved in the Royal Society, Edmund Waller. His poem *Of English Verse* contains the following stanza:

> Poets that lasting marble seek
> Must carve in Latin or in Greek;
> We write in sand, our language grows,
> And, like the tide, our work o'erflows.

Notice the reason Waller gives for the lack of durability of English; it is that the language is changing. For it to be useful as a communication tool, it must become stable, unchanging – more 'settled, certain'. The sixteenth century had been concerned with making the language 'copious' – go back and take a look at passage (ii) in CW15.1; that was the word used there to express what that century wanted the language to become. The rallying cry of the seventeenth and eighteenth centuries was certainly not 'more copious'. It was 'more settled'.

In 1665, John Evelyn – a member of the group that founded the Royal Society – wrote a letter to Peter Wyche, a diplomat and translator who was chairman of the language committee. It outlines an ambitious programme for the committee's work. 'I would humbly propose', he wrote, 'that there might first be compiled a Grammar ... To this might follow a Lexicon, or collection of all the pure English words'. The academies set up in Italy and France had expressed similar aims. The Italian Accademia della Crusca published an Italian dictionary, and the French Academy a grammar in 1660 (the *Grammaire de Port-Royal*), and a dictionary in 1694.

Evelyn's ambitious programme was never really fulfilled by the Royal Society. But dictionaries and grammars were in the air. In 15.3 we mentioned an English dictionary that was produced at the beginning of the seventeenth century. It was Cawdrey's 1604 *Table Alphabeticall of Hard Usual English Words*. Several others followed. There was John Bullokar's *An English Expositour* (1616), Edward Phillips's *New World of English Words* (1658), and Elisha Coles' *An English Dictionary* (1676). As time went on, these dictionaries increased in length. What kind of words did they contain? Today we expect most dictionaries to include most of the language's words. But these early dictionaries were essentially lists of 'hard words', intended to help readers come to terms with the flood of new words that had entered the language in the last hundred years. Cawdrey has a quaint way of putting this. In the introduction to his dictionary, he says it was compiled 'for the benefit & helpe of Ladies, Gentlewomen, or any other vnskilfull persons'. A certain gender bias is detectable! There were some dictionaries, like Phillips's, that did contain 'normal' (i.e. not just hard) words, and did also have the purpose of contributing to refining and fixing the language. But it was not until the beginning of the eighteenth century that dictionaries gave proper attention to normal words.

A number of grammars also appeared in the period. These included Paul Greaves's *Grammatica Anglicana*, dated 1594. Notice that the title is in Latin, the language in which the book was written. It really does say something about the status of Latin when a book about English grammar, written at least partly for English people, was written in Latin. Then there was Alexander Gill's *Logonomia Anglica* (1619), and George Snell's *The Right Teaching of Useful Knowledge* (1649). The Bacon-inspired scientific methods that became practised in the seventeenth century were also beginning to be applied to the study of language too, and this led to the production of scientific accounts of the language. In 1653, John Wallis produced two good examples. His *De Loquela, Tractatus*

Grammatico-Physicus was a thoroughly linguistic account of phonetics and speech production, and his *Grammatica Linguae Anglicanae* has a similarly linguistic approach.

19.3 A seventeenth-century text about a cold, wet Christmas

George Fox (1624–91) was a religious dissenter and one of the founders of the Quaker movement. He travelled round the country preaching his dissenting views, and was often met by opposition and violent persecution. To give an example of seventeenth-century English writing, here is a passage taken from his *Journal*, describing what happened to him one December day. You may have to read the passage more than once to understand exactly what is going on. When you have done this, concentrate on the language, noting any aspects of it that capture your attention. When you have thought about this yourself, look at Activity 19A (*A cold, wet Christmas: some language details*), which asks some specific questions:[1]

A cold, wet Christmas

And afterwards I paſſed away through ye Country & att night came to an Inn & there was a rude Company of people & I aſkt ye woman if ſhee had any Meate to bringe mee ſome: & ſhee was ſomethinge ſtrange becauſe I ſaide thee & thou to her; foe I askt her if ſhee had any milke but ſhee denyed it: & I aſkt her if ſhee had any creame & ſhee denyed yᵗ also though I did not greatly like ſuch meate but onely to try her.

   And there ſtoode a churne in her houſe: & a little boy put his hande Into ye churne & pulled it doune: & threw all ye creame In ye floore before my eyes: & soe Itt manifeſted ye woman to be a lyar: & ye woman was amaſed: & tooke ye childe & whipt it ſorely: & bleſſet her ſelfe: but I re-prooved her for her lyinge & deceite & foe I walkt out of her houſe after ye Lord God had manifeſted her deceite & perverſeneſſe: & came to a ſtacke of hay: & lay in ye hay ſtacke all night: beinge but 3 days before ye time called Chriſtmas in ſnowe & raine.

Though the 'style' of the passage is a little odd to modern ears, the language is really not so different from PDE. To look at the points raised in Activity 19A: you can see that the 'long s' (ſ) is still in use, with the 'short s' (s) reserved for the ends of words; these forms were discussed in 14.2.1. The use of capital letters is rather idiosyncratic (a characteristic noted in 14.2.3). There are a few nouns with capitals (like *Country*), and one (*Meate*) which has a capital on one occasion but not another. But there are also capitals for prepositions (like *Into*), and a pronoun (*Itt*). As regards punctuation, there are full stops at the end of paragraphs, but colons dominate, apparently functioning like present-day full stops, or sometimes commas perhaps. Several of the characteristics of EModE spelling discussed in 14.2 are found here. Among these are final 'e's (Mulcaster called them 'superfluities', you will recall from 14.2.2), and there is also consonant doubling (as in *att*).

The text uses a few abbreviated forms. The ampersand (&) features (that was discussed back in 4.1). And *yᵗ* is used as an abbreviation for 'that'. The passage uses *ye*, but not as the personal pronoun. It is here standing for 'the', a usage mentioned in passing in 16.5.

You will not have found too many vocabulary problems in this passage. *Rude* means 'unsophisticated' – a usage that is uncommon but certainly not unknown today. *Try* here means 'test', and *meate* means food (Activity 9C contains an example of that usage).

We will return to the 'cold, wet Christmas passage' in 19.4.3, where we shall pick up a pragmatic point.

19.4   Some language points

By the beginning of the seventeenth century, Early Modern English was close to Late Modern English. But here are three language points – two grammatical and one pragmatic – worthy of attention.

19.4.1   Continuous aspect

In 10.2.6 we discussed the perfect aspect, one use of which is to express actions which have some 'relevance' to the present. There is another aspect which, though it made an appearance in earlier periods of the language, came into general use in the seventeenth century. It is the **continuous** (or **progressive**) aspect. CW19.2 (*The continuous aspect in PDE*) looks at how this aspect is formed and used in PDE. It contains an activity and an explanation. If you have any doubts about the continuous in PDE, you really do need to take a look at this now. What follows concentrates on EModE usage.

In Shakespeare's time, the usage was unsettled, with both continuous and non-continuous forms being found where we would today use the continuous. In *Hamlet*, a character sees the hero reading a book: 'What do you read, my Lord?' he asks. We would today say 'what are you reading?' On the other hand, in *The Two Gentleman of Verona* we have the line: 'How now? What letter are you reading there?' What about the use of continuous aspect to express future time, common in PDE? You could use the 'Shakespeare's Words' website to find out (16.4 gives you site details). Do a search for the word *tomorrow*, and notice what verb forms are used in the sentences you are given. You will find some non-continuous forms, and many uses of *shall/will*. But the continuous aspect is rare, though in *The Two Gentleman of Verona* again, you do find 'To-morrow … Don Alfonso / With other gentlemen … / Are journeying to salute the Emperor'. Sometimes continuous aspect is used in EModE, as in PDE, to express an action which is going on when another, shorter action, takes place. CW19.2 contains a PDE example, and Rissanen (1999) gives an EModE one: 'as ['while'] you are fishing, chaw ['chew'] a little bread … in your mouth'. EModE also uses continuous aspect – again as today – to express irritation at repeated actions. In Webster's play *The Duchess of Malfi* (1612) we find 'For better fall once than be ever falling' (an example also from Rissanen). This play will be mentioned again in 19.5, when we look at literature.

The house is being built at the moment, we say in PDE, using the passive with continuous aspect. In ME and EModE an active continuous was used here. So *The house is building* could be used to mean 'the house is being built'. This 'active for passive' use continued until the beginning of the eighteenth century. Strange to modern ears? Well, some people today say *the parcel is shipping tomorrow,* meaning 'the parcel is being shipped tomorrow'.

Though the continuous aspect was found in OE and ME, Rissanen (1999) cites statistics that show how its use increased in the later seventeenth century. The information comes from the Helsinki Corpus, which was mentioned in CW16.2. The number of instances occurring in the period 1640–1710 is three times the number for 1570–1640.

Where did the continuous forms come from historically? According to one explanation, the construction started out using the preposition *on.* Ælfic (a monk and author, *c.*955–*c.*1010), for example, has the sentence *ac gyrstandæg ic wæs on huntunge* (literally 'but yesterday I was on hunting'). An ME example, using the same verb, is found in Malory, dated around 1470: *and there mette with a knight that had been an-hontynge.* With time the preposition became weakened to our phonetic friend schwa [ə], and written *a-* (go back to 10.2.2 to remind yourself about schwa). Indeed, you might translate Malory's *an-hontynge* with 'a-hunting'. This form is very archaic today, but you do find it in the song which begins: *A-hunting we will go, a-hunting we will go/ Heigh-ho, the derry-o, a-hunting we will go.*[2]

This *a-* prefix is found in Shakespeare. Hamlet, for example, gets close to killing his uncle while the man *is a-praying.* You could again use the 'Shakespeare's Words' website to find some more Shakespeare examples. Click on 'Advanced Search', and choose the 'Part of the word' option. Type *a-* in the box. You will get 157 hits. Many of these will not be what you are looking for – the first will be *sea-maids,* for example (*a-* plus *maids*). But you will find some good examples too, including *a-making, a-cursing,* and *a-ducking* ('immersed in water').

With time, even the unstressed *a-* disappeared, leaving no prefix at all. So the sequence was (in this theory at least, and using a modern 'sentence' to illustrate):

He was on hunting → *He was a-hunting* → *He was hunting*

19.4.2 *Its*

At various points during this book (in 6.1.1 for OE, and 10.2.1 for ME), we have discussed how possession is expressed, often signalled in PDE by use of the suffix -'s in the singular (*the girl's book*), and -s' in the plural (*the girls' book*). But we have not really discussed the genitive pronoun forms of these, called the **possessive pronouns**. Remind yourself of what these are in PDE by filling in the blanks in this 'table'. The associated subject personal pronouns are given on the left:

I	my name	You	your name
He	_____ name	She	_____ name
It	_____ name	We	_____ name
They	_____ name		

The missing forms are *his*, *her*, *its*, *our*, and *their*. These PDE forms were largely fixed during the EModE period, but there is one that lagged behind the others. It is the neuter possessive pronoun, *its*. Before reading on, take a look at Activity 19B (*How its was said*). This shows you the forms used in EModE, and gives a suggestion of their chronology. If you would like to look at more examples, there are another six at CW19.3 (*Some more of it*).

At the beginning of the EModE period, the most common neuter possessive was *his*. We can see where this came from by going back to OE, where the pronoun forms were *hit*, *him*, *his*, *hit* (nominative, accusative, genitive and dative). As you will recall from 10.1 and 10.2, ME was a period when much syncretism took place, and these accusative and dative forms merged, leaving *hit* and *his* as the only two remaining. The initial 'h' of *hit* then got dropped, first just when it was unstressed and then in all cases. Hence our PDE *it*. But the neuter possessive form remained as *his*. This is common in Shakespeare, as shown in Activity 19B, example (i) – *his beams*.

His is of course now the masculine possessive pronoun too, and so it was in EModE. This meant that EModE had the same possessive pronoun for masculine and neuter. Such overlap went against the movement of English towards marking natural gender (take a look at CW6.1 to remind yourself of that). To eliminate the overlap, various ways of avoiding the neuter *his* were developed. One illustrated in the activity was to use *of it*, shown in example (v) – *the fall of it*. Another used *thereof*. So instead of *in Bethlehem, and in all its coasts*, the Bible has *in Bethlehem, and in all the coasts thereof*. The other forms illustrated in the activity all show some version of the root word *it*. The root form itself came into use for a while. Example (ii) has *it head* and *it young* from Shakespeare. But this usage died out early in the seventeenth century, and thereafter two forms became dominant. One was *it's*, as in example (iv) – *between it's lips*. Where did this come from? Without doubt there is analogy with the noun genitive form -'s which we saw at the beginning of this section in the phrase *the girl's book*. If you say *girl's* meaning 'of the girl', then why not say *it's* meaning 'of it'? It took until the beginning of the nineteenth century for the apostrophe version to disappear off the scene. The other form was *its* without the apostrophe, as in example (iii): *makes its sally out*. Though found occasionally in the sixteenth century, it was the early decades of the seventeenth century when this really took off. The change happened relatively quickly. In a paper which looks in detail at this possessive pronoun, Nevalainen and Raumolin-Brunberg (1998) talk about 'the breakthrough of *its*', and the 'extraordinary rapidity of [the] change'. Presumably the need to eliminate the use of *his* for both masculine and neuter was the reason for such speed.

19.4.3   A pragmatic crime and punishment: more on *thou*

We spent quite some time in 17.1 looking at the complex pragmatics associated with the use of *thou* and *you*. We came across one case where inappropriate use of *thou* was being proposed as a way of irritating someone. To remind you: in Shakespeare's *Twelfth Night*, one character is given advice on how to get into an argument: *If thou thou'st him some thrice, it shall not be amiss*. Similar feelings towards *thou* were present in the seventeenth century. John Wallis, whose *Grammar* was mentioned 19.2.2, had this to say: 'Notice also that it is customary in English (and also in contemporary French and other languages) to use the plural number [*you*] when addressing only one person … To use the singular [*thou*] in addressing someone usually implies disrespect or close familiarity'.[3] If it was used inferior to superior, then even more so. The historian Thomas Fuller, writing in 1655, has this to say: 'if proceeding from ignorance [it] hath a smack of clownishness; if from affection, a tang of contempt'.

But people like Fox saw it differently. Much of the momentum behind various Puritan groups was to abolish hierarchies between people – both inside and outside the Church. Indeed, it was a spirit of egalitarianism that drove on the Civil War and the removal of the monarchy. In linguistic terms, the abolition of hierarchies and the spirit of egalitarianism suggested that *thou* should be the normal form of address to *all* individuals, making no distinction between inferiors and superiors. *You* was regarded as a plural form, used only when addressing more than one person.

Fox believed this deeply, so when he 'said thee and thou' to the woman in the 'Cold, wet Christmas' story, he was not being contemptuous, or trying to start an argument. He was acting out of principle. The result was hunger, and a night in a cold, wet haystack.

Incidentally, Fox and others of similar religious persuasion had other linguistic curiosities which from time to time caused trouble. The word *professor* could be used to refer to someone who appeared ('professed') to be religious but was not really so. And the word *steeplehouse* was used for 'church', the argument being that the latter word should not be used for a building. CW19.4 (*Fox in trouble again*) contains another example of Fox using *thou* and ending up in trouble.

19.5   Seventeenth-century literature: a full stop, or just a comma?

The death of Queen Elizabeth in 1603 might be regarded as an abrupt full stop at the end of the Elizabethan Age. But history does not contain many full stops; there are often just commas that lead on to the next part of history's sentence. Jacobean (the adjective associated with King James I) drama followed on from Elizabethan drama. There were clear changes of emphasis, but many writers – including Shakespeare – straddled the two eras. Jacobean drama was more morbid, pessimistic, melancholic. There were many revenge tragedies, including John Webster's *The Duchess of Malfi* (1613), Middleton and Rowley's *The Changeling*, and Tourneur's *The Atheist's Tragedy*. The age's morbidness is well captured by the twentieth-century poet, T. S. Eliot, who has a verse about the dramatist Webster (1580–1634) in a poem called *Whispers of Immortality*. It begins: *Webster was much possessed by death / And saw the skull beneath the skin*. That says it all.

Also straddling the age were the so-called metaphysical poets, chief among whom was John Donne (1572–1631). Others in the group include George Herbert (1593–1633), Andrew Marvell (1621–78), and Abraham Cowley (1618–67). The term 'metaphysical' was used by Samuel Johnson. It does not mean that the poets discussed abstract philosophy (the meaning of 'metaphysical' today) but that they used bizarre images to link ideas together in a somewhat intricate and abstract way. As Johnson put it: 'The most heterogeneous ideas are yoked by violence together; nature and art are ransacked for illustrations, comparisons, and allusions.' As an example, one of Donne's most celebrated poems is called *The Flea*. In it, the poet draws attention to a flea which has just bitten both him and the lady to whom the poem is addressed. He uses this image to persuade the lady to become his lover. 'Our blood is combined together in this flea', he is saying, 'so why shouldn't we become joined in some more amorous way?' A bizarre image linking together heterogeneous ideas.

Drama fared badly under Puritan influence, but after the Restoration in 1660, it flourished again, with fun-loving Charles II as king. Restoration comedy is known for its sexually explicit nature. A good example of the genre is William Wycherley's *The Country Wife*, dated 1675. A central character is Mr Horner, who seduces other people's wives by spreading round the story that he is impotent. This makes husbands think he is a safe person for their wives to know. His ruse is highly successful and works against Margery, a simple country girl not used to wicked London ways. The play contains scenes so sexually explicit that they can shock even today's apparently unshockable audiences.

Another writer of dramas, as well as poems, was Aphra Behn (1640–89), one of the first women to have earned her living by the pen. Virginia Woolf – a celebrated writer of a later age – said of her that 'all women together ought to let flowers fall upon the tomb of Aphra Behn'. She wrote fifteen plays in all, the most popular being *The Rover*. The poet John Dryden (1631–1700) also wrote dramas, including *Marriage à la Mode* (1672). But perhaps his greatest achievements were in satiric verse. He wrote a satire on the playwright Thomas Shadwell, entitled *Mac Flecknoe*. The genre of this poem was mock-heroic, which treats an object of derision (in this case Shadwell) in an epic, heroic style in order to make fun of it. Here is what the Prince *Mac Flecknoe* (a character based on the minor poet Flecknoe) says when trying to find his successor as ruler of the 'kingdom of poetic dullness':

> Shadwell alone, of all my sons, is he
> Who stands confirm'd in full stupidity.
> The rest to some faint meaning make pretence,
> But Shadwell never deviates into sense.

Very funny, and very nasty. The genre became popular in the eighteenth century, particularly in the work of Alexander Pope – who also, incidentally, satirizes the unfortunate Shadwell.

One literary figure, John Milton (1608–74), stands out above all others in the seventeenth century, a true man of his age. A republican and a Puritan, he was a master of polemical prose, writing many pamphlets on religious and civil topics. His tract called *Areopagitica* is a passionate defence of freedom of speech and the liberty of the press, and arguably influenced the form of the First Amendment to the United States Constitution (dealing with freedom of worship and speech). His shorter poetical works include an elegy on the death of a friend, called *Lycidas*, and a sonnet. 'On his blindness' – Milton went totally blind by the age of 43. How can a sightless person properly serve God?, Milton asks in his sonnet. The poem's last line is *They also serve who only stand and wait*. His poetic drama *Samson Agonistes* also deals with the theme of blindness. It tells the Biblical story of how the Israelite Samson – a man of supernatural strength – was captured by the Philistines, had his hair (the source of his strength) cut off and his eyes plucked out, so that he was 'blind among enemies', 'eyeless in Gaza'. Milton's most famous poems are also on Biblical themes. They are *Paradise Lost* and *Paradise Regained*. Milton's influence on later writers has been great, reaching into modern popular culture – Philip Pullman's popular trilogy entitled *His Dark Materials* (completed in 2000) takes its title from Book 2 of *Paradise Lost*. Here is a 'Rough Guide' to Milton's poem:

Paradise Lost

• **background**: The poem, written in blank verse, appeared in its final twelve-book form in 1674. It is an epic poem, on a topic entirely appropriate for a seventeenth-century English epic – the fall of man, as told in the Bible.

Milton describes the theme as 'not less but more Heroic' than those of Homer or Virgil; 'heroic' means 'grand and epic'. The poet's aim was to 'justifie the ways of God to men', no less.

- **authorship**: Information about John Milton is given in the text.
- **content**: The poem begins with Satan being thrown from heaven, together with his lieutenant Beelzebub and the other 'fallen angels'. Satan sets up a palace, called Pandemonium (a word of Milton's invention). They consider how to take revenge on God. Knowing that God has created 'another World, the happy seat / Of som new race call'd Man', Satan decides that revenge may lie in an attack on this new race. He travels to the Garden of Eden, with the aim of tempting Man (in the form of Adam and Eve) away from God. Satan takes the shape of a serpent, and persuades Eve to eat the fruit of the Tree of Knowledge. Adam does so too, in solidarity with Eve. As a punishment, God orders them to leave the Garden, and Sin and Death come into the world. In the last lines of the poem, Adam and Eve leave Paradise, repentant: 'They, hand in hand, with wandering steps and slow, / Through Eden took their solitary way'. In a following poem, *Paradise Regained*, Milton tells how Christ came to earth and defeated Satan by overcoming the Devil's temptations.
- **value**: Though containing plenty of religious discussion, the poem is richly dramatic, especially the first two books. Similarly rich is the character of Milton's Satan, and a number of critics see him as the poem's 'hero'. The nineteenth-century poet William Blake said Milton was 'of the devil's party without knowing it'. Partly because he was writing an epic in the classical style (after the *Odyssey* and the *Iliad*), Milton injects elements of Latin into his English. Some are critical of this. T. S. Eliot, for example, said Milton wrote English 'like a dead language'. But Milton was a master of the sublime. Dryden describes the poem as 'one of the greatest, most noble and sublime poems which either this age or nation has produced'.
- **quotation**: In this passage, from Book 1, Milton describes how Satan and his 'crew' are thrown out of heaven. The 'him' of the first line is Satan; the Almighty Power is, of course, God:

> Him the Almighty Power
> Hurld headlong flaming from th' Ethereal Skie
> With hideous ruine and combustion down
> To bottomless perdition, there to dwell
> In Adamantine Chains and penal Fire,
> Who durst defie th' Omnipotent to Arms.
> Nine times the Space that measures Day and Night
> To mortal men, he with his horrid crew
> Lay vanquisht, rowling in the fiery Gulfe
> Confounded though immortal: But his doom
> Reserv'd him to more wrath; for now the thought
> Both of lost happiness and lasting pain
> Torments him; round he throws his baleful eyes

That witness'd huge affliction and dismay
Mixt with obdurate pride and stedfast hate:
At once as far as Angels kenn he views
The dismal Situation waste and wilde,
A Dungeon horrible, Perhaps end hereon all sides round
As one great Furnace flam'd, yet from those flames
No light, but rather darkness visible
Serv'd only to discover sights of woe,
...

Activity 19C (*Paradise Lost questions*) has questions drawing your attention to some language aspects of this quotation. If you are going to look at this activity, do so before reading on.

Questions (a) and (b) in the activity draw attention to Milton's syntax which sometimes sounds more like Latin than English. Take the first few words, for example – *Him the Almighty Power / Hurld headlong*. The word order here is OSV. Perhaps this unusual order reflects the practice of a synthetic language, like Latin, which permitted more variation in word order. Then there is the *who* in line 6. It refers to Satan, the *him* of the first line. PDE would not normally allow a relative clause to be so distant from mention of the person being referred to – another example of the style of a synthetic language where concerns to do with sentence position are not so important. A further celebrated example of 'unEnglish' syntax occurs in Book 5 of *Paradise Lost*. God is speaking, and tells the angels that they must obey his son Christ as much as they obey him. The words are: *Him who disobeys / Me disobeys*. How would this be said in PDE?

The words and phrases that Milton uses are similarly steeped in the classics. The vivid phrase *darkness visible* in the quotation is based on one in Seneca. Milton also frequently uses words with their Latin meanings. He talks about Satan's *horrid hair* (*horridus* in Latin meant 'bristling'). Then, in another part of *Paradise Lost*, he talks about a *corny reed* (Latin *cornus* meant 'horn'), and a bush which is *implicit* with other vegetation – the Latin verb *implicare* meant 'entangle'. Milton may not have been the first to use these words in these senses, though he does seem to have invented *horrent*, with the same meaning as *horrid*.

Activity 19D (*Seventeenth-century 'Rough Guides'*) suggests that you might write some other 'Rough Guides' for seventeenth-century literature.

19.6   1700: another comma, or a real full stop?

Right at the beginning of this book, in 1.3, we made the point that there have been various dates given as the end of the EModE period. We have chosen 1700 because it is the point at which the language is well into the process of settling down, and is also the beginning of a new century which had its own new directions. But 1700 really was more of a comma than a full stop, and many of the eighteenth century's new directions started life in the seventeenth. Here, to conclude, are two of these – developments which have been mentioned in this chapter, and which are important to the future of English.

One is the language's 'settling' and 'correcting'. The eighteenth century is sometimes called the 'Age of Authority'. It is the time when interest in fixing the language reached a peak. This is best symbolized by arguably the century's prime linguistic achievement, Samuel Johnson's massive, ground-breaking *Dictionary of the English Language*, which appeared in 1755. Though truly ground-breaking, we have seen that the desirability for such a dictionary was a seventeenth-century perception. 19.2.2 talks about the aspiration of the Royal Society in this direction, and mention was made there of various dictionaries, including Cawdrey's. The 'Age of Authority' really did begin in the seventeenth century.

The second development relates to Britain's colonial movements, which gained momentum in the seventeenth century. We discussed these beginnings in 19.1. This really is where the future lies, and where this book would need to go if it were to continue beyond 1700. Exploration and colonization begun in the Stuart dynasty led to the spread not just of the British people, but of the English language too. English really has now become a world language, not because of any importance which our small island in north Europe now has, but because the British moved out to the four corners of the earth, and gave their language to countries which today have made it their own. English has moved on from the era which this book has largely been about, the time when the British 'owned' the English language. Its ownership is now far, far wider. How that came about is another story…

Activity section

19A   A cold, wet Christmas: some language details

Here are some specific language points to consider in the 'cold, wet Christmas passage':

(a) Fox uses the 'long s' form. Check what was said about this in 14.2.1. Does Fox follow the 'rules' given there about the use of long and short 's'?

(b) Notice the use of capital letters. When are they found? What parts of speech have capitals in the passage?

(c) Look at the punctuation. One punctuation mark is predominant. What is it? When are full stops used?

(d) Notice points at which words are spelt differently from in PDE. What are the common differences?

(e) The passage contains some abbreviations, presumably to save writing time and space. What are these?

(f) We have come across *ye* at various points in this book. But it has usually meant something different from here. What does it mean here?

(g) What do you think these words may mean: *rude, meate, try*?

Finally, you may wish to produce a 'PDE translation' of the passage; not quite so easy as it looks, perhaps, but not too difficult either…

19B How *its* was said

Here are six EModE sentences showing different forms of the neuter possessive pronoun (*its* in PDE). Identify these forms. Look at the dates of the examples. The forms and the dates together may lead you towards some speculations about the pathway which led to PDE *its*. For more examples, look at CW19.3.

  (i) *How far that little candle throws his beams*
     1596 Shakespeare (*The Merchant of Venice*)

 (ii) *The hedge-sparrow fed the cuckoo so long,*
     That it had it head bit off by it young
     1605 Shakespeare (*King Lear*)

(iii) *The infant … makes its sally out of the womb*
     c.1666 Harvey (*Morbus anglicus*)

(iv) *As mild and gentle as the cradle babe*
     Dying with mothers dug between it's lips
     1590 Shakespeare (*Henry VI, Part 2*)
     dug = nipple

 (v) *Great was the fall of it*
     1612 King James Bible

(vi) *in Bethlehem, and in all the coasts thereof*
     1612 King James Bible

19C *Paradise Lost* questions AS

The answers to (a) and (b) are discussed in the text. The others are given in the *Answer section*.

(a) The first few lines of the quotation contain some odd word orders (involving the word *him*). What is deviant about this word order for us today? Look back to what was said about word order in 10.2.4 (and 10.2.5 is relevant also).

(b) Line 6 begins with the word *who*. Who is being referred to? This too is a curious piece of syntax. What is curious about it?

(c) Notice the use of capitals. What parts of speech have them? Can you identify when capitals are used?

(d) There are a few examples of alliteration in the passage. Find these. You may like to remind yourself what was said about alliteration in 7.3 and 11.2.

(e) What is the verse form of this passage (and the whole of *Paradise Lost*)? It is one you have met before. The second line could be said to deviate slightly from this metre. How?

(f) *Durst*. This is a word that has briefly been mentioned in an earlier chapter. Do you recall what was said about it? Find this mention.

(g) There are a number of words in the passage which have Romance (often Latin) origins – 2.3 will remind you about Romance languages. Identify some where you suspect this may be the case. If you have access to a dictionary which gives etymologies, look these words up to check your suspicions.

19D Seventeenth-century 'Rough Guides'

Use the internet or other sources to write your own 'Rough Guides' to some or all of the works below, most of which have been mentioned in the text. Use the same headings as in the text: background/authorship/content/value/quotations – though for some entries you may not find something to say under every heading. If you can work together with others, you might share the load, doing one 'Rough Guide' each, and ending up with several which together give a more detailed picture of the period's literature. The works are:

> Webster's *The Duchess of Malfi*
> A short selection of John Donne's poems. A good choice might be: *The Flea, The Good Morrow, A Valediction: forbidding Mourning*, and the holy sonnet *Death*
> Dryden's *Mac Flecknoe*
> Congreve's *The Way of the World*
> Aphra Behn's *The Rover*
> Milton's *Lycidas*

Answer section

Activity 19C

Questions (a) and (b) are discussed in the text.

(c) In general, it is nouns that have capitals – but certainly not all nouns. There are some adjectives with capitals too. Notice that these are only ones coming before a noun with a capital (*Almighty Powr, Ethereal Sky* and so on). Is there any rhyme or reason to the use of capitals? Perhaps adjectives and nouns considered particularly important are given capitals.

(d) There is alliteration in *hurld headlong, durst defie, mortal men, lost happiness and lasting pain, waste and wilde, Furnace flam'd, serv'd … sights of woe*. Milton is not here engaged in any kind of Alliterative Revival (11.2

talks about this). Alliteration was a figure of classical rhetoric, and it is classical poets that he is following.

(e) The poem is written in iambic pentameters (discussed in 18.4). It would be possible to read the beginning of the second line – *Hurld headlong* – as WSW, making the first foot an iamb. But you may feel that the first word requires a stress, so that you have two stressed syllables next to each other (SSW).

(f) *Durst* is mentioned in 16.4 as a modal verb. It was the simple past of *dare*.

(g) Among the Romance words in the quotation are *obdurate, omnipotent, combustion, perdition,* and *ethereal.*

Further reading

Schama (2001) provides a vivid history of this period. There is also a set of DVDs available for Schama's complete history series.

Jones (1953) was also recommended for Chapter 13. It gives an excellent overall account of the rise of English. The final chapters deal with the seventeenth century.

Rissanen (1999) covers the syntactic points discussed in this chapter.

Grossman (2011) includes some key text, plus coverage of individual authors.

Crystal (2003) continues the story of English, tracking its development into a world language.

Notes

1 The passage is taken from Penney (1911), available online at https://archive.org/stream/ agv9012.0001.001.umich.edu/agv9012.0001.001.umich.edu_djvu.txt. 'Long s' forms have been added.

2 You can hear a version of this on YouTube (https://www.youtube.com/watch?v= MliUSZhRWHg). Some of the examples in the paragraph have been taken from Denison (1993).

3 The quotation from Wallis is translated from Latin by J. A. Kemp, and is taken from his edition of the grammar (Kemp, 1972).

References

Ackroyd, P. 2010 *The Canterbury Tales: A Retelling*. Harmondsworth: Penguin

Alexander, M. 1970 *The Earliest English Poems*. Berkeley: University of California Press

Armitage, S. 2009 *Sir Gawain and the Green Knight*. London: Faber and Faber

Attridge, D. 1995 *Poetic Rhythm: An Introduction*. Cambridge University Press

Bailey, C.-J. N., and Marold, K. 1977 'The French lineage of English'. In Meisel (1977), 21–53

Bailey, R. W. 1991 *Images of English: A Cultural History of the Language*. Cambridge University Press

Barber, C. 1981 '"You" and "thou" in Shakespeare's *Richard III*'. In Meredith (1981), 273–89

—— 1997 *Early Modern English* (revised edition). Edinburgh University Press

Barber, C., Beal, J. C., and Shaw, P. A.2009 *The English Language* (second edition). Cambridge University Press

Baugh, A. C. 1948 *A Literary History of England*. London: Routledge & Kegan Paul

Baugh, A. C., and Cable, T. 2013 *A History of the English Language* (sixth edition). London: Pearson Education

Bennett, J. A. W., and Smithers, G. V. 1982 *Early Middle English Verse and Prose*. Oxford University Press

Bergs, A., and Brinton, L. J. (eds) 2012 *English Historical Linguistics*, Vol. I. Berlin: Mouton de Gruyter

Bishop, I. 1968 *Pearl in Its Setting: A Critical Study of the Structure and Meaning of the Middle English Poem*. New York: Barnes & Noble

Blake, N. (ed.) 1992 *The Cambridge History of the English Language. Volume II, 1066–1476*. Cambridge University Press

Bright, J. W. (ed.) 1904 *The Gospel of Saint John in West-Saxon*. Boston: D. C. Heath & Co

Brown, P., and Levinson, S. C. 1987 *Politeness: Some Universals in Language Usage*. Cambridge University Press

Brown, R., and Gilman, A. 1989 'Politeness theory and Shakespeare's four major tragedies'. *Language in Society* 18: 159–212

Bryson, B. 2007 *Shakespeare*. London: Harper Press

Burgess, A. 1992 *A Mouthful of Air*. London: Hutchinson

Burnley, D. 1992 'Lexis and semantics'. In Blake (1992), 409–499

Burrow, J. A. 2008 *Medieval Writers and their Work: Middle English Literature* (second edition). Oxford University Press

Burrow, J. A., and Turville-Petre, T. 2004 *A Book of Middle English* (third edition). Oxford: Wiley-Blackwell

Calvo, C. 1990 *Power Relations and Fool-Master Discourse in Shakespeare: A Discourse Stylistic Approach to Dramatic Dialogue*. PhD thesis, Nottingham University. Available online at http://core.ac.uk/download/pdf/99293.pdf

Clark, C. 1970 *The Peterborough Chronicle, 1070–1154* (second edition). Oxford University Press

Crystal, B. 2008 *Shakespeare on Toast: Getting a Taste for the Bard*. Cambridge: Icon Books

Crystal, D. 2003 *English as a Global Language* (second edition). Cambridge University Press

—— 2004 *The Stories of English*. London: Penguin

—— 2005 *Pronouncing Shakespeare*. Cambridge University Press

—— 2008 *Think on My Words*. Cambridge University Press

—— 2013 *Spell It Out: The Singular Story of English Spelling*. London: Profile Books

Culpeper, J. 2015 *History of English* (third edition). London: Routledge

Culpeper, J., and Kytö, M. 2010 *Early Modern English Dialogues: Spoken Interaction as Writing*. Cambridge University Press

Davis, N. 2004 *Paston Letters and Papers of the Fifteenth Century, Part I*. Oxford University Press

Davis, P. 2007 'The Shakespeared brain'. *The Reader*, 23. In collaboration with N. Roberts, V. Gonzalez-Diaz, and G. Thierry. (http://dev.amblesideschools.com/sites/default/files/THE%20SHAKESPEARED%20BRAIN.pdf)

Denison, D. 1993 *English Historical Syntax*. London: Longman

Denison D., and Hogg, R. 2006 'Overview'. In Hogg and Denison (2006), 1–42

Dobson, E. J. 1957 *English Pronunciation: 1500–1700*. Oxford University Press

Donoghue, D. 2004 *Old English Literature: A Short Introduction*. Oxford: John Wiley and Sons

Drabble, M. 1985 *The Oxford Companion to English Literature*. Oxford University Press

Durkin, P. 2014 *Borrowed Words*. Oxford University Press

Ellegård, A. 1953 *The Auxiliary Do: The Establishment and Regulation of Its Use in English*. Stockholm: Almqvist and Wiksell

Ellis, H. (ed.) 1965 *Holinshed's Chronicles of England, Scotland, and Ireland*. New York: Ams Press Inc

Evans, M. (ed.) 1994 *Elizabethan Sonnets*. London: Phoenix

Fennell, B. A. 2001 *A History of English: A Sociolinguistic Approach*. Oxford: Blackwell

Fischer, O. 1992 'Syntax'. In Blake (1992), 207–408

Fraser, A. 1992 *The Six Wives of Henry VIII*. London: Weidenfeld & Nicolson

Freeborn, D. 2006 *From Old English to Standard English*. Basingstoke: Palgrave Macmillan

Fry, S. 2007 *The Ode Less Travelled: Unlocking the Poet Within*. London: Arrow

Görlach, M. 1991 *Introduction to Early Modern English*. Cambridge University Press

Graddol, D., Leith, D., and Swann, J. (eds) 1996 *English: History, Diversity and Change*. London: Routledge

Grégoire, S. 2006 'Gender and language change: The case of early modern women'. Paper available online at http://homes.chass.utoronto.ca/~cpercy/courses/6362-gregoire.htm

Grossman, M. 2011 *The Seventeenth-Century Literature Handbook*. Oxford: Wiley-Blackwell

Hadfield, A. 2000 *The English Renaissance*. London: Wiley & Sons

Hazlitt, W. C. 1864 *Shakespeare Jest Books*. New York: Burt Franklin

Heaney, S. 2000 *Beowulf: A New Translation*. London: Faber & Faber

Higham, N., and Ryan, M. 2013 *The Anglo-Saxon World*. New Haven: Yale University Press

Hinman, C. 1996 *The First Folio of Shakespeare*. New York: W. W. Norton

Hogg, R. 1992 'Phonology and morphology'. In Hogg, Blake and Lass (1992), 67–167

—— 2002 *An Introduction to Old English*. Oxford University Press

Hogg, R., and Denison, D. (eds) 2006 *A History of the English Language*. Cambridge University Press

Hogg, R., Blake, N. F., and Lass, R. (eds) 1992 *The Cambridge History of the English Language, Volume 1. The Beginnings to 1066*. Cambridge University Press

Holmes, J. 2013 *An Introduction to Sociolinguistics* (fourth edition). London: Routledge

Hope, J. 1994 'The use of *thou* and *you* in Early Modern spoken English: Evidence from depositions in the Durham ecclesiastical court records'. In Kastovsky (1994), 141–51

Horobin, S. 2013 *Chaucer's Language* (second edition). Basingstoke: Palgrave Macmillan

Horobin, S., and Smith, J. 2002 *An Introduction to Middle English*. Edinburgh University Press

Hughes, G. 1991 *Swearing: A Social History of Foul Language, Oaths and Profanity in English*. Oxford: Blackwell

Jespersen, O. 1905 *Growth and Structure of the English Language*. Leipzig: Teubner

—— 1909 *A Modern English Grammar on Historical Principles*, Vol. 1. Heidelberg: Carl Winter

Johnson, K. 2013 *Shakespeare's English*. London: Routledge

Jones, R. F. 1953 *The Triumph of the English Language*. Stanford University Press

Jucker, A. H. (ed.) 1995 *Historical Pragmatics: Pragmatic Developments in the History of English*. Amsterdam and Philadelphia: John Benjamins

—— 2011 'Greetings and farewells in Chaucer's Canterbury Tales'. In Pahta and Jucker (2011), 229–40

Jucker, A. H., and Taavitsainen, I. 2013 *English Historical Pragmatics*. Edinburgh University Press

Kastovsky, D. 1992 'Semantics and vocabulary'. In Hogg, Blake and Lass (1992), 290–408

—— (ed.) 1994 *Studies in Early Modern English*. Berlin: Mouton de Gruyter

—— 2006 'Vocabulary'. In Hogg and Denison (2006), 199–270

Kemp, J. A. 1972 *John Wallis: Grammar of the English Language*, a new edition. London: Longman

Kökeritz, H. 1953 *Shakespeare's Pronunciation*. New Haven: Yale University Press

König, E., and Van der Auwera, J. 2002 *The Germanic Languages*. London: Routledge

Kopytko, R. 1995 'Linguistic politeness strategies in Shakespeare's plays'. In Jucker (1995), 515–40

Lass, R. 1992 'Phonology and morphology'. In Blake (1992), 23–155

—— (ed.) 1999 *The Cambridge History of the English Language – Volume III: 1476 to 1776*. Cambridge University Press

—— 1999a 'Phonology and morphology'. In Lass (1999), 56–186

Lutzky, U. 2012 *Discourse Markers in Early Modern English*. Amsterdam: John Benjamins

Lynn, J., and Jay, A. 1989 *The Complete Yes Prime Minister*. London: BBC

MacCarthy, P. 1950 *English Pronunciation* (fourth edition). Cambridge: Heffer & Sons

McCrum, R., Cran, W., and MacNeil, R. 1986 *The Story of English*. London: Faber and Faber

McDonald, R. 2001 *Shakespeare and the Arts of Language*. Oxford University Press

McEnery, T. 2009 *Swearing in English*. London: Routledge

McIntosh, A. 1963 '*As You Like It*: A grammatical clue to character'. *A Review of English Literature* 4(4): 68–81

Machan, T. W. 2003 *English in the Middle Ages*. Oxford University Press

Mantel, H. 2010 *Wolf Hall*. London: Fourth Estate

—— 2013 *Bring up the Bodies*. London: Fourth Estate

—— forthcoming *The Mirror and the Light*. London: Fourth Estate

Marsden, R. 2004 *The Cambridge Old English Reader*. Cambridge University Press

Meisel, J. M. (ed.) 1977 *Langues en Contact*. Tübingen: TBL Verlag Narr

Meredith, P. (ed.) 1981 *Leeds Studies in English*, 12

Mitchell, B. 1964 'Syntax and word order in the *Peterborough Chronicle* 1122–1154'. *Neuphilologische Mitteilungen* 65: 113–44

—— 1994 *An Invitation to Old English and Anglo-Saxon England*. Oxford: John Wiley and Sons

Mitchell, B., and Robinson, F. C. 2011 *A Guide to Old English* (eighth edition). Chichester: Wiley-Blackwell

Mugglestone, L. (ed.) 2006 *The Oxford History of English*. Oxford University Press

Mulholland, J. 1967 '"Thou" and "you" in Shakespeare: A study in the second person pronoun'. *English Studies* 48: 1–9

Nevalainen, T. 1999 'Early Modern English lexis and semantics'. In Lass (1999), 332–458

—— 2006 *An Introduction to Early Modern English*. Edinburgh University Press

Nevalainen, T., and Raumolin-Brunberg, H. 1998 '*Its* strength and the beauty of *it*: The standardisation of the third person neuter possessive in Early Modern English'. In Rydén, van Ostade and Kytö (1998), 73–117

Nevalainen, T., and Raumolin-Brunberg, H. 2003 *Historical Sociolinguistics: Language Change in Tudor and Stuart England*. London: Pearson Education

Page, R. I. 1987 *Runes: Reading the Past*. London: British Museum Press

Pahta, P., and Jucker, A. H. (eds) 2011 *Communicating Early English Manuscripts*. Cambridge University Press

Penney, N. (ed.) 1911 *The Journal of George Fox*. Cambridge University Press

Platzer, H. 2001 'Grammatical gender in Old English: A case of "No sex, please, we're Anglo-Saxon"?' *Vienna English Working Papers* 10/1: 34–48

Pyles, T., and Algeo, J. 1993 *The Origins and Development of the English Language* (fourth edition). New York: Harcourt Brace & Co

Quirk, R. 1959 'English language and the structural approach'. In Quirk and Smith (1959), 13–46

—— 1962 *The Uses of English*. London: Longman

Quirk, R., and Smith, A. H. (eds) 1959 *The Teaching of English*. London: Secker & Warburg

Rissanen, M. 1999 'Syntax'. In Lass (1999), 187–331

Roach, P. (2004) 'British English: Received Pronunciation'. *Journal of the International Phonetic Association* 34(2): 239–45

Rothwell, W. 1998 'Arrivals and departures: The adoption of French terminology into Middle English'. *The Anglo-Norman Online Hub* 1–18 (www.anglonorman.net)

Rydén, M., Tieken-Boon van Ostade I., and Kytö, M. (eds) 1998 *A Reader in Early Modern English*. Frankfurt: Peter Lang

Salmon, V. 1986 'The spelling and punctuation of Shakespeare's time'. In Wells and Taylor (1986), xlii–lvi

Salmon, V., and Burness, E. (eds) 1987 *Reader in the Language of Shakespearean Drama*. Amsterdam: Benjamins

Sampson, G. 1980 *Schools of Linguistics*. Stanford University Press

Schama, S. A. 2000 *A History of Britain: At the Edge of the World? 3000 BC–AD 1603*. London: BBC Worldwide Ltd

—— 2001 *History of Britain – Volume 2: The British Wars 1603–1776*. London: BBC Books

Schendl, H. 2001 *Historical Linguistics*. Oxford University Press

—— 2015 'Code-switching in early English literature'. *Language and Literature*, 24(3): 233–48

Schlauch, M. 1965 'The social background of Shakespeare's malapropisms'. In Salmon and Burness (1987), 71–99

Schleicher, A. 1868 *Fabel in indogermanischer Ursprache*. Beiträge zur vergleichenden Sprachforschung auf dem Gebiete der arischen, celtischen und slawischen Sprachen. 5/1868. Dümmler, Berlin, S. 206–208

Shapiro, J. 2005 *1599: A Year in the Life of William Shakespeare*. London: Faber and Faber

Short, M. (unpublished) 'Stylistics and "He Wishes for the Cloths of Heaven" by W. B. Yeats'

Sisam, K., and Tolkien, J. R. R. 2009 *A Middle English Reader and a Middle English Vocabulary*. New York: Dover

Strang, B. M. H. 1970 *A History of English*. London: Methuen

Swann, J. 1996 'Style shifting, codeswitching'. In Graddol, Leith and Swann (1996), 301–24

Thomas, J. 1983 'Cross-cultural pragmatic failure'. *Applied Linguistics* 4/2: 91–111

Thomason, S. G., and Kaufman, T. 1988 *Language Contact, Creolization and Genetic Linguistics*. Berkeley: University of California Press

Tolkien, J. R. R. 1936 'Beowulf: The monsters and the critics'. *Proceedings of the British Academy* 22: 245–95

Tout, T. F. 1922 *France and England: Their Relations in the Middle Ages and Now*. Historical Series No. XL. Manchester University Press

Townend, M. 2006 'Contacts and conflicts: Latin, Norse, and French'. In Mugglestone (2006), 61–85

Traugott, E. C. 2012 'Middle English pragmatics and discourse'. In Bergs and Brinton (2012), 466–79

Treharne, E. (ed.) 2000 *Old and Middle English: An Anthology*. Oxford: Blackwell

Trotter, D. A. 2000 *Multilingualism in Later Medieval Britain*. Martlesham: Boydell & Brewer

Trussler, S. 2006 *The Faber Pocket Guide to Elizabethan and Jacobean Drama*. London: Faber and Faber

Turville-Petre, T. 2006 *Reading Middle English Literature: An Introduction*. Oxford: Wiley-Blackwell

Wales, K. M. 1983 '*Thou* and *You* in Early Modern English: Brown and Gilman re-appraised'. *Studia Linguistica* 37: 107–25

Warburg, J. 1962 'Notions of correctness'. Supplement to Quirk (1962)

Weir, A. S. 2009 *Elizabeth the Queen*. London: Vintage

Wellman, F. L. 1903 *The Art of Cross-Examination*. New York: Macmillan

Wells, S., and Taylor, G. (eds) 1986 *William Shakespeare: The Complete Works, Original-Spelling Edition*. Oxford: Clarendon Press

Windeatt, B. 2008 *Troilus and Criseyde: A New Translation*. Oxford: Oxford Paperbacks

Wolfe, P. M. (1972) *Linguistic Change and the Great Vowel Shift in English*. Berkeley: University of California Press

Wright, G. T. 1988 *Shakespeare's Metrical Art*. Berkeley: University of California Press

Wright, L. (ed.) 2006 *The Development of Standard English, 1300–1800: Theories, Descriptions*. Cambridge University Press

Wright, T. (ed.) 1996 *Political Songs of England*. Cambridge University Press

Index

References to figures are shown in *italics*. References to tables are shown in **bold**. References to maps are shown in ***bold italics***. References to endnotes consist of the page number followed by the letter 'n' followed by the number of the note, e.g. 123n1 refers to note no. 1 on page 123.